IMAGES
of America

1947 Woodward Tornado

On the Cover: This photograph was taken looking north at 1722 Main Street, the site of the Farrand-Wood Apartments. The remains of the West Ward School (present-day Woodward Christian Academy) can be seen in the background. Five people search through the rubble for belongings. Francis Valentine faces the camera with his hands on his hips, and his aunt Mable Farrand-Wood stands to his left. She lost her husband, Sam, in the storm. (Courtesy of Plains Indians & Pioneers Museum.)

IMAGES
of America

1947 WOODWARD TORNADO

Robin D. Hohweiler
and Dr. Deena K. Fisher

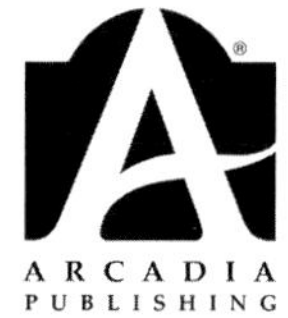

ISBN 978-1-4671-0771-6

Published by Arcadia Publishing
Charleston, South Carolina

Printed in the United States of America

Library of Congress Control Number: 2021950609

For all general information, please contact Arcadia Publishing:
Telephone 843-853-2070
Fax 843-853-0044
E-mail sales@arcadiapublishing.com
For customer service and orders:
Toll-Free 1-888-313-2665

Visit us on the Internet at www.arcadiapublishing.com

This book is dedicated to the memory of Robert P. Roberson (1943–2021), whose love for and promotion of the history of Northwest Oklahoma was infectious.

This book is also dedicated to the memories of the victims and survivors of the 1947 Woodward tornado, as well as the first responders who stepped in to save so many lives.

Contents

Acknowledgments

First and foremost, we wish to thank the museum board and staff of the Plains Indians & Pioneers Museum in Woodward, Oklahoma, for allowing access to their vast collection of photographic images from the horrific 1947 storm. Without that access, there would not be a 1947 Woodward tornado book. Except where otherwise noted, all the images in this publication are from the museum's collection.

Of the museum staff, our thanks to Robert Roberson, former executive director; Tammy Hawbaker, curator; and Nancy McCormick, gift shop manager, for their time and patience in helping us locate images, scanning images, exchanging documents, and offering advice. We especially wish to thank Tammy Hawbaker for doing the deep dig to find original photographs for scanning as necessary and particularly for finding a little-known set of prints that made an important addition to the photographs in chapter four.

We also wish to thank Chad Williams and his staff at the Oklahoma Historical Society for their efforts in obtaining rare images from "Tornado Town."

Finally, we would be remiss not to thank Arcadia Publishing for publishing this book. Also, thanks go to Lindsey Givens and Stacia Bannerman for having faith in the idea and taking a chance on us in publishing a book so quick on the heels of *Woodward* (Past & Present series).

Thanks to everyone else who contributed information, listened to the idea, and encouraged success. Now go buy a book.

Introduction

It would be difficult to discuss those events or people who shaped the history of Northwest Oklahoma and specifically the city of Woodward without including the 1947 Woodward tornado. The storm wrought such damage on the small community following a path that was more than 100 miles long and would today be graded as an F-5 with winds averaging 250 miles per hour in the core. At the height of the storm's destructive force, winds at the core of the storm were calculated to be upward of 450 miles per hour. With a funnel on the ground estimated to be nearly two miles wide at one point, the sheer devastation cannot be overstated. The lives lost (in some cases, entire families) and the destruction left in the wake of the storm had a profound, lasting impression on those who survived.

Those people in 1947 did not have the advantage of advance severe weather warning systems that most probably take for granted today. It was the 1947 Woodward tornado that prompted the US Weather Bureau (later the National Weather Service) to begin the development of advance warning systems, though it would be another 10 years before they were deployed around the country.

Unfortunately, the number of remaining survivors of the storm and its aftermath dwindle with every passing year. Their stories have been told and retold to subsequent generations, and fortunately, much of that history has been recorded in print, video, and audio. Still, it is difficult for those of us today, steeped though we may be in the rich first-person histories that we heard growing up, to fully appreciate the sheer terror and sickening horror those four minutes in 1947 brought to so many 75 years ago.

There are countless stories associated with the 1947 storm. Because of space limitations, we have necessarily left out the bulk of those stories, including only a few. Also, we have done our best to ensure the locations of businesses and homes are correct, but few records (city directories and the like) of Woodward in 1947 exist.

We wanted to create a visual historical record so that people could get a genuine sense of what happened in April 1947. Unless otherwise noted, all photographs appearing in this book came from the archival collection of the Plains Indians & Pioneers Museum in Woodward, Oklahoma, and are published with the museum's express consent.

The one common thread throughout just about all of these photographs is the Fisher Grain elevator, an omnipresent landmark for fixing location in what appears to be an otherwise bleak, barren landscape. The elevator complex, despite taking what would have been the full force of the tornadic winds, remained structurally intact with only the glass in its headhouse (on the west end of the structure) blown out. The reader will find references to the Fisher Grain complex throughout this book. It made for a helpful landmark.

As with any publication, there must be nuggets—those bits of information that a reader has never known and transforms a mere reading into a thoughtful ride through a time that few of us experienced. We have done our utmost to ensure the accuracy of these nuggets, and we certainly hope you will enjoy reading them as much as we enjoyed writing about them.

A quick word about locations. Any publication that deals with structures that no longer exist runs the risk of incorrectly stating the exact location of that structure. We did our very best to avoid those location errors but found that property owners, for reasons that would likely fill another book, rebuilt their businesses or residences in a completely different location.

Robin Hohweiler was raised in Woodward and attended Woodward Public Schools. His love for the area and its people brought him back home following careers in the US Navy and the US Intelligence Community. Robin is a published writer and (very) amateur filmmaker who currently works as the executive director of the Plains Indians & Pioneers Museum. His family has been ranching and farming in Northwest Oklahoma for more than 100 years. He and his wife, Mary Ann, and their three dogs of indeterminate ancestry live on the family farm (a certified Oklahoma Centennial Farm) just east of Fargo, Oklahoma.

Dr. Deena K. Fisher, a native of Elk City, Oklahoma, has lived and worked in Woodward since 1989. In 1996 she became the first director and, in 2002, dean and professor of history of the Woodward Campus of Northwestern Oklahoma State University. She has published extensively throughout her academic career. Deena has a deep passion for history. She is a longtime board member and past president of the Plains Indians & Pioneers Museum. She is the current president of the Board of Directors of the Oklahoma Historical Society. She and her husband, Tom, reside in Woodward with their two dogs, Rowdy and Maverick.

One

April 9, 1947, 8:42 p.m., the Endless Night

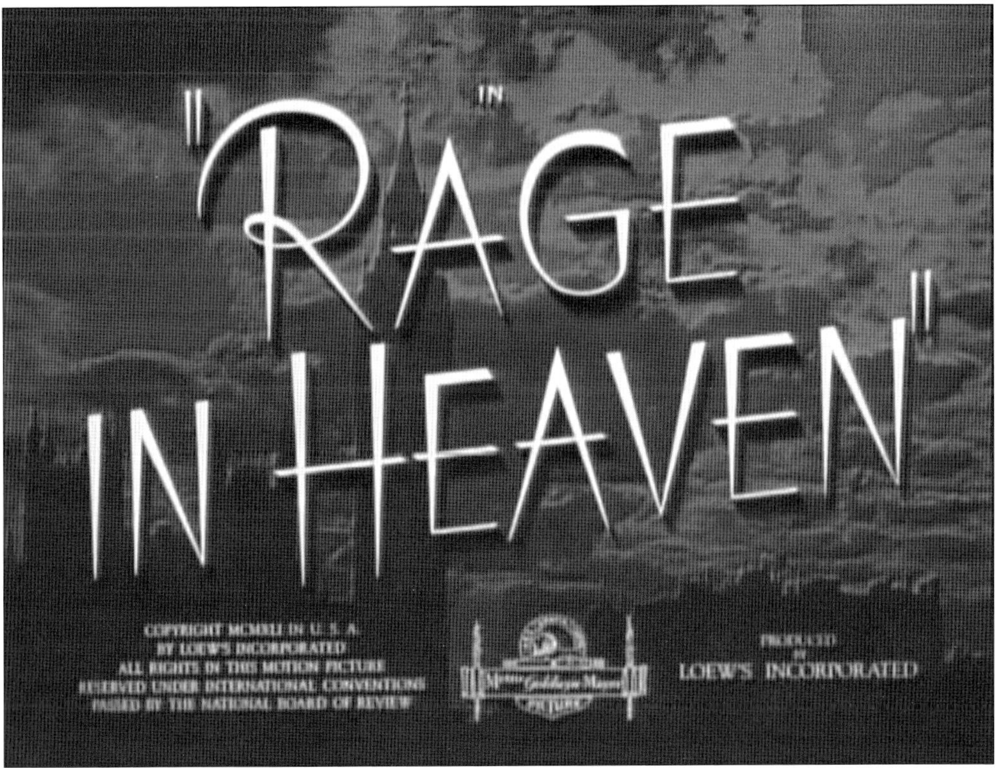

The 1941 film *Rage in Heaven* was playing at the Woodward Theatre on the evening of April 9, 1947, when the tornado struck just to the north of the downtown business district. Quick action by one of the theater's owners likely saved a number of lives that night. He moved quickly to lock the front doors and keep people inside the theater until the storm had passed.

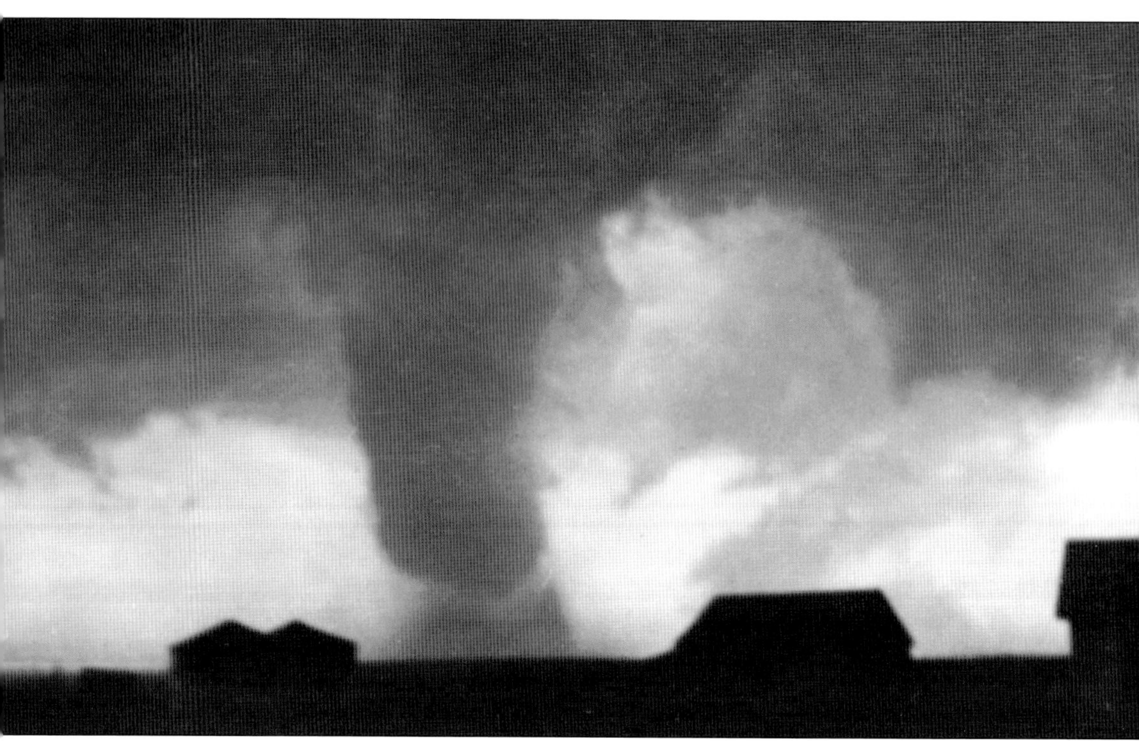

This is the only known photograph of the tornado funnel believed to be the storm that hit Woodward. The image was captured by a man named Jimmy Wright, who worked for a farm implement company in Woodward at the time. The photograph is believed to have been taken somewhere west of Woodward. By the time the storm hit the edge of town, it measured 1.8 miles at the base and was packing winds in excess of 250 miles per hour in the core. The storm struck Woodward with little to no warning. More than 100 city blocks were obliterated in a matter of minutes, leaving thousands homeless. In the end, nearly 100 were dead and close to 1,000 were injured.

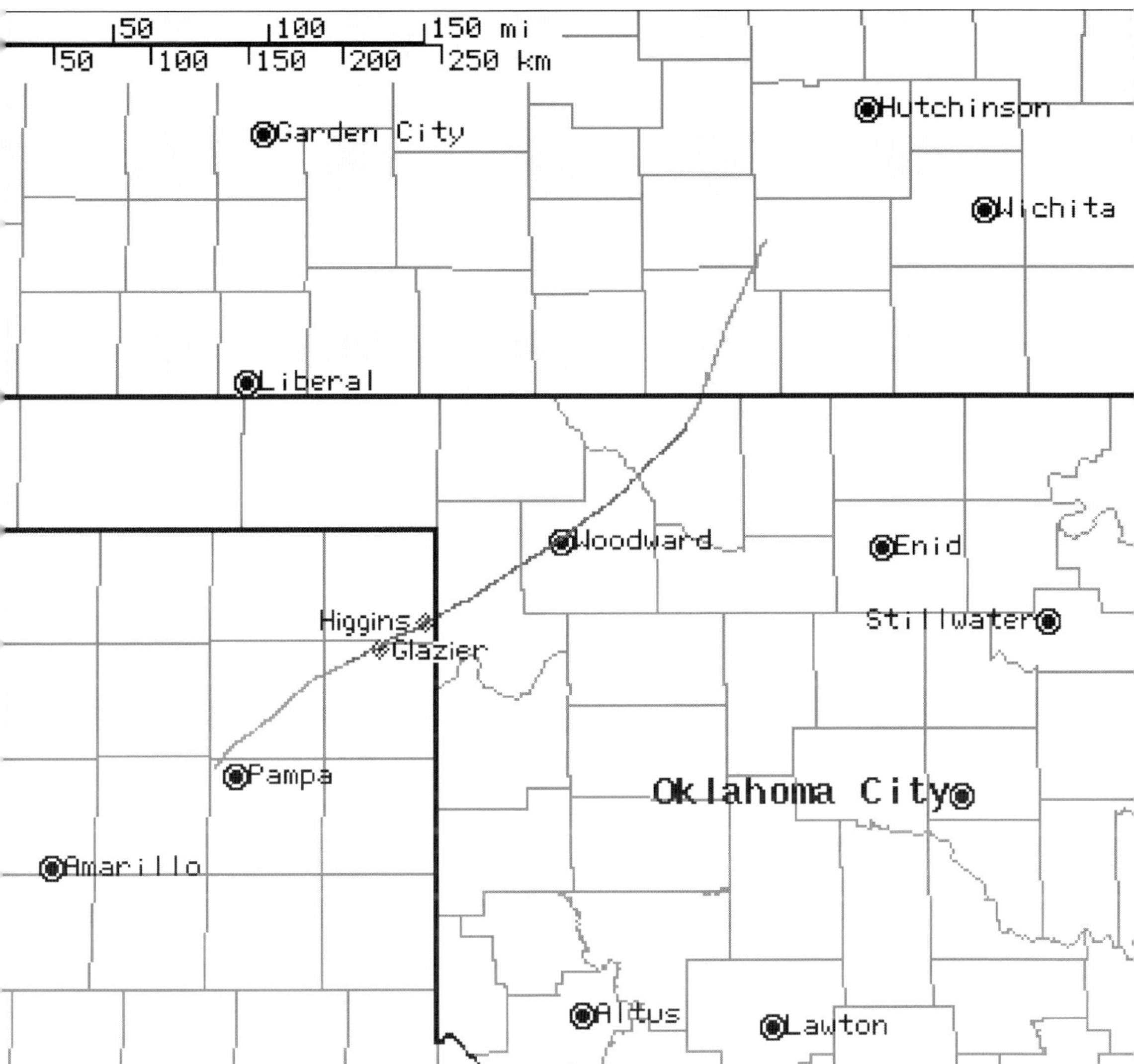

This map from the site weather.gov shows the 1947 Woodward tornado track. The entire line marks the path of the storm from near Pampa, Texas, up into south-central Kansas. The storm that was the Woodward tornado moved from southwest of Glazier, Texas, to just south of the Kansas state line in Woods County, Oklahoma. The remainder of the track (Pampa, Texas, to Glazier, Texas, and Woods County into south-central Kansas) was originally reported to be from the Woodward tornado also but is now thought to be others in a family of five or six tornadoes. The Woodward tornado moved along the ground for 100 miles at a forward speed of 50 miles per hour. (Courtesy of the National Weather Service.)

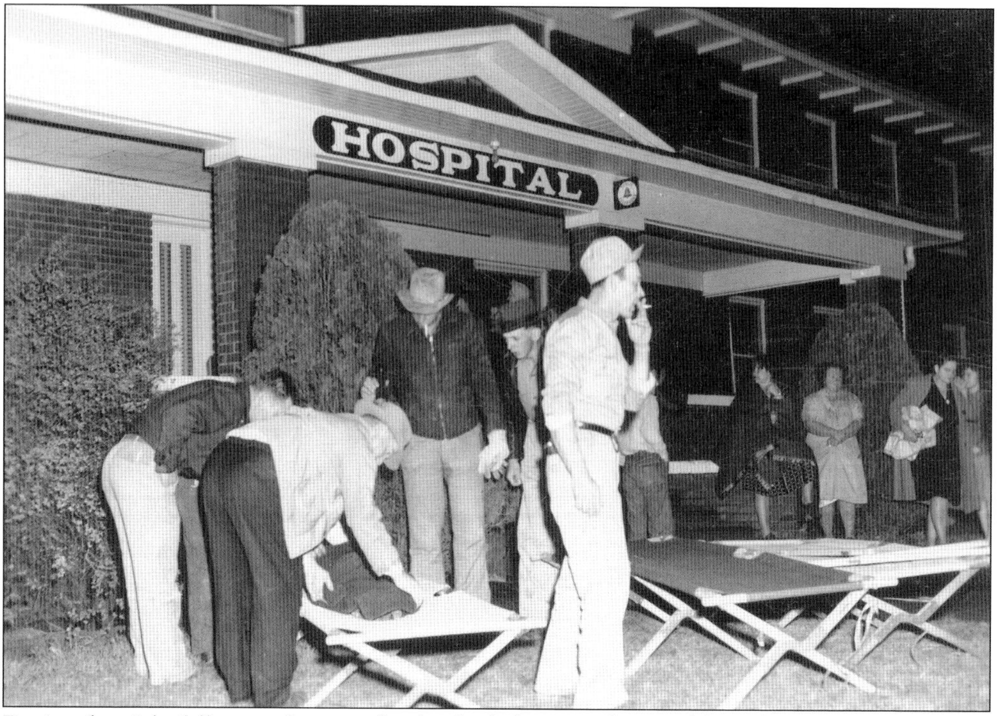

During the night following the tornado, the dead, dying, and injured from the monster storm were brought to the 22-bed Woodward Hospital at Fourth Street and Locust Avenue. The facility was quickly overwhelmed. The dead were laid out on the lawn in front of the building and covered with sheets. Those with minor injuries were lined along the hallways. Note the woman in the light-colored dress on the right who appears to be in shock.

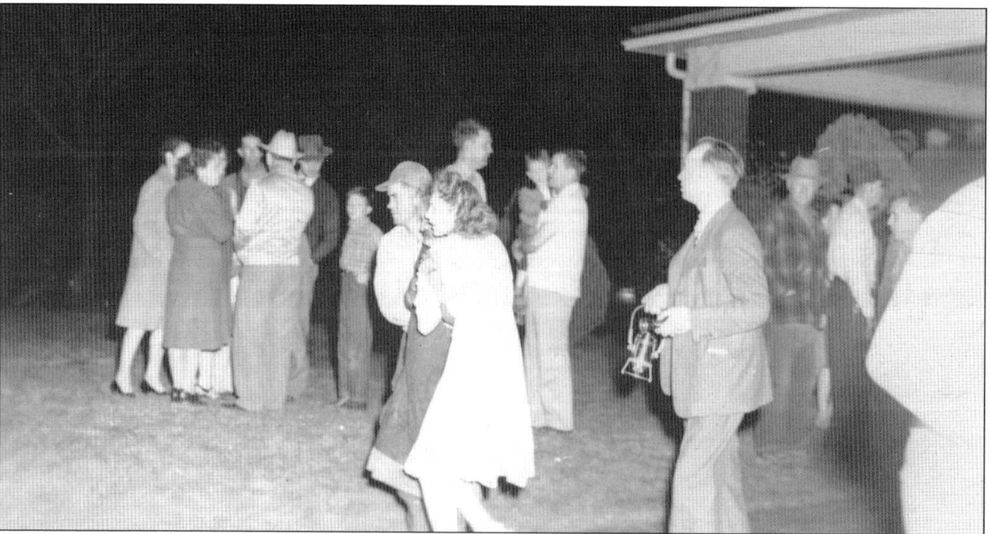

Late in the night of April 9, 1947, people come to the Woodward Hospital looking for friends and relatives. The man in the foreground with a lantern appears to be searching for a loved one. A couple is helping an elderly woman away from the hospital. In the coming days, many of the injured would be moved to the community center in Central Park (now Centennial Park) and the Baker Hotel downtown and further transported to other area hospitals.

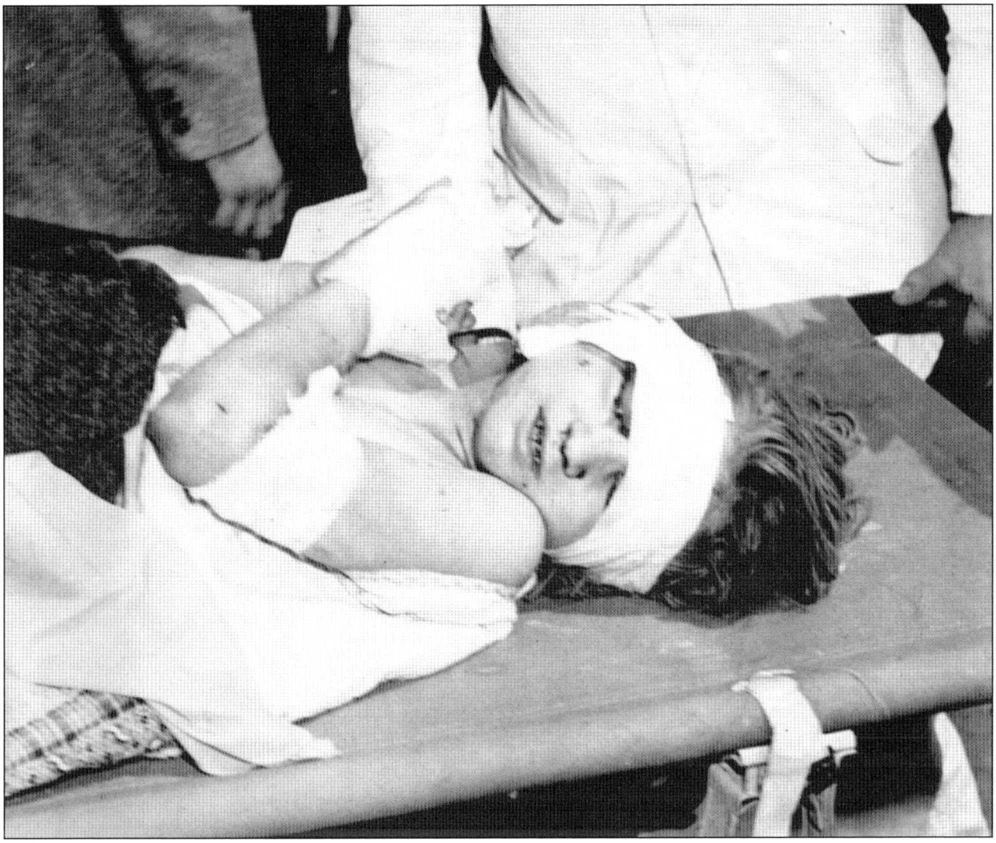

Two young victims of the tornado were brought into the hospital for care the night of the storm. The child in the photograph above was identified as Glenda Shearer. In the photograph to the right, the child is not identified and was later moved to Oklahoma City for treatment. The image ran in a newspaper there with the caption "Hardened war veterans shuddered with disbelief Thursday as rescue planes disgorged their cargo of mutilated children from the Woodward tornado. This small girl, cut and bruised in a score of places, was typical of the survivors." Military medical corps personnel from Tinker Field, as it was known in 1947, arrived in Woodward soon after the tornado and assisted in treating the scores of injured. (Both, courtesy of the Oklahoma Historical Society.)

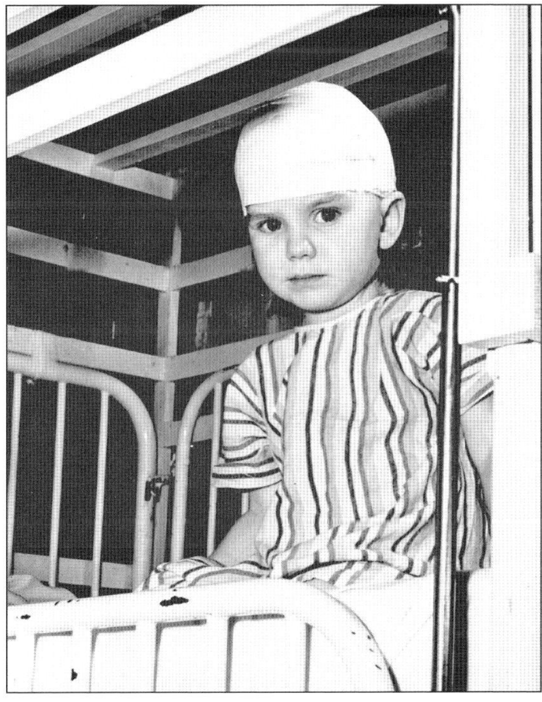

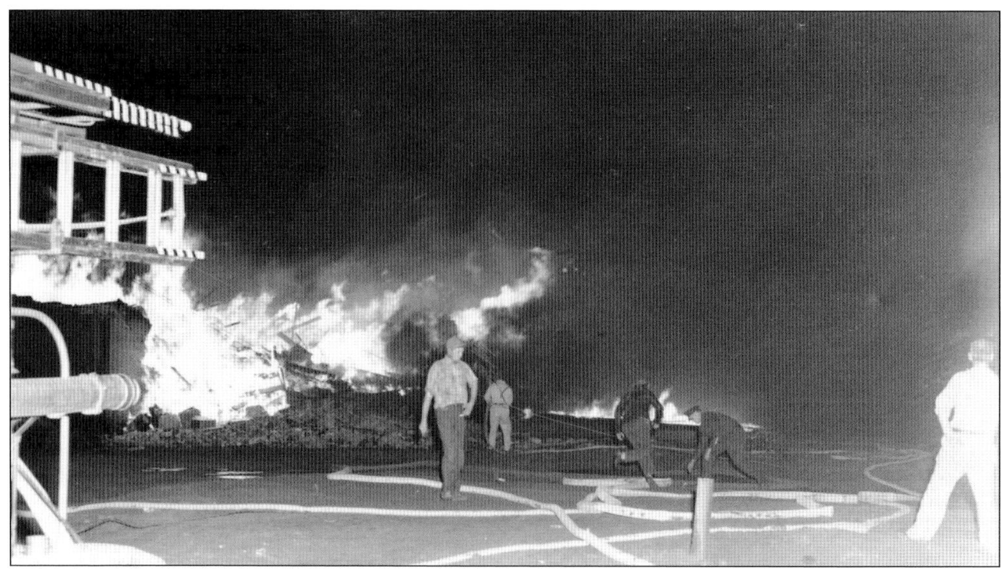

These two photographs show a structure fire along Webster Avenue. The structure is completely engulfed in flames despite firefighters' efforts to quell the inferno. The location was the Big Seven Store and served the residents of the North Ward. When this image was captured by Everett McDonald of the McDonald Studio, the structure was beyond saving. There are firehoses laid across the ground in both photographs. Dangling power lines can be seen in both images, and the air is filled with embers from burning debris. A likely cause of the fire was a broken natural gas line. Area fire crews got most of the fires under control within a few hours, though their efforts were hampered by the lack of pressure in the waterlines due to no electricity. Fortunately, they were aided by the torrential rains that followed the tornado.

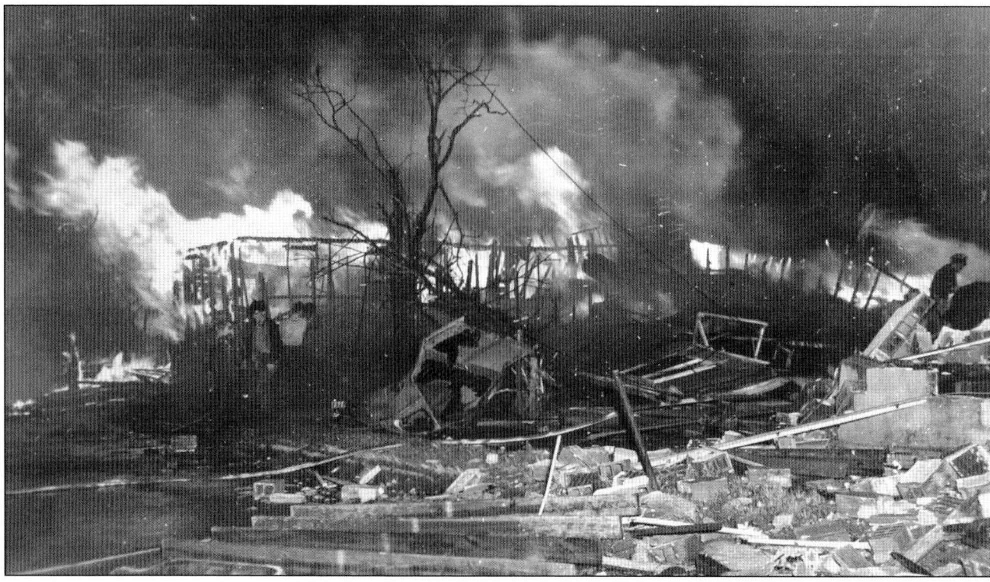

Two

Two Mysteries from the Endless Night

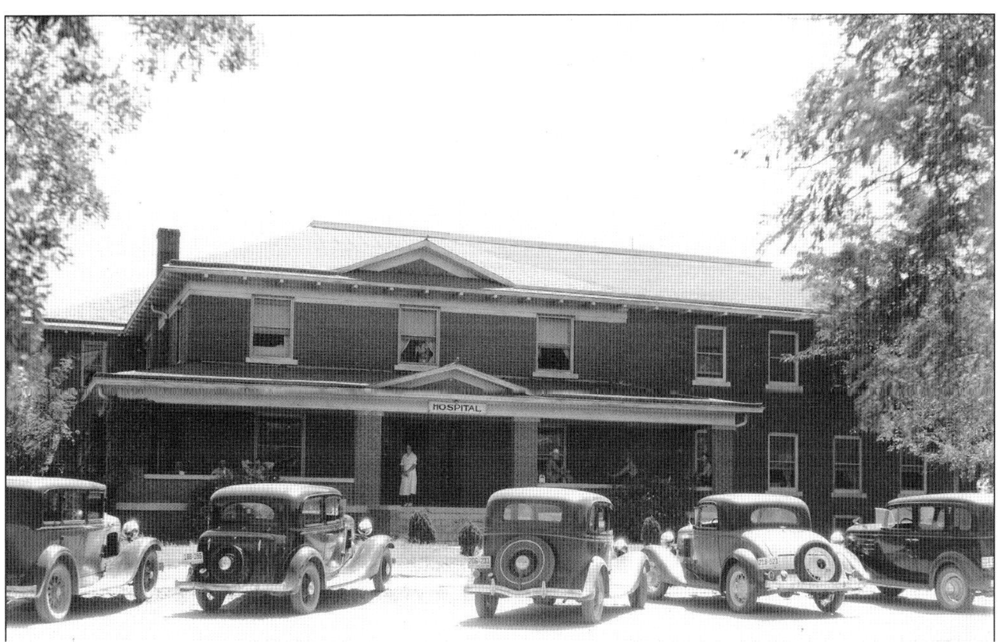

In horrific storms like the 1947 Woodward tornado, there are always tragic stories of lives lost or properties destroyed. There were two mysteries, still unsolved, from the storm that truly made it an endless night for those who survived. One girl, with reportedly minor injuries, disappeared without a trace from Woodward's Memorial Hospital the night of the storm. Three girls, possibly sisters, were found dead and never identified. Whether the two incidents were somehow related will likely never be known.

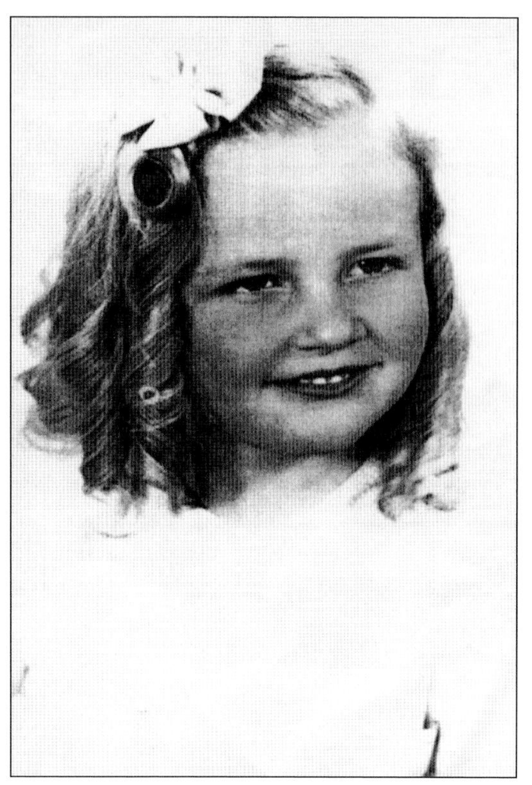

Joan Gay Croft was a four-year-old girl whose home was destroyed in the tornado. Her mother was killed, and her father was severely injured and taken to a hospital in Oklahoma City. Joan Gay had a minor injury: a long sliver of wood embedded in her lower leg. She and her sister, Jean, were taken to the local hospital, where they were placed on a cot in the basement. Sometime during the night, two men came into the basement, said they were relatives of the girls, and carried Joan Gay away.

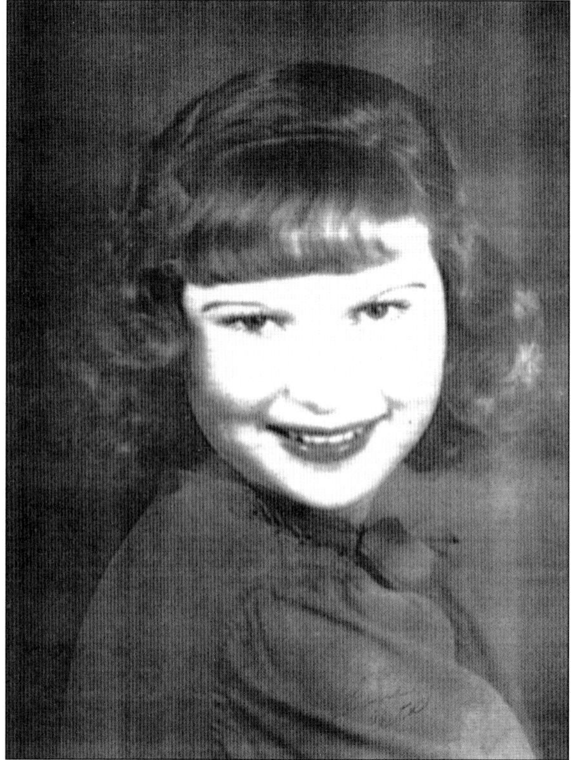

Joan Gay's mother, Cleta Mae Croft, died in her home during the 1947 Woodward tornado at the age of 26. Joan Gay disappeared from Woodward's Memorial Hospital late in the night of the storm and has never been heard from again.

THE DAILY OKLAHOMAN

Joan, 4, Her Mother Dead, Still Missing at Woodward

A LITTLE blue-eyed blonde, last seen in Woodward the morning fter the city was razed by a tor-ado, is still missing.

She is 4-year-old Joan Gay Croft.

Joan's mother was killed in the orm. Her father, Olin Croft, and er sister, Jean, were injured.

Last week Croft was back in Voodward, looking for his youngest aughter.

Joan was last seen in Woodward Memorial hospital, according to the nvestigation made by the state ighway patrol. She and her sis-er Jean were taken there by a eighbor. When she left they were ing side by side, each tagged. It as planned that they would go to e same hospital.

On Saturday, Jean was released from Crippled Children's hospital She doesn't know what became o her little sister.

A SEARCH of all the hospital known to have admitted victim of Woodward's disaster has faile to unearth any clue as to wha happened to the child.

The highway patrol describe Joan as chubby, with shoulder length blonde hair, blue eyes. Sh has three faint scars on her fore head.

When Joan Gay was first report ed missing it was suggested that sh had died of her injuries. The high way patrol and the Red Cross bot maintain her injuries could not hav been fatal. She was described a having had "severe facial abra sions."

The *Daily Oklahoman* newspaper published an article about the mysterious disappearance of Joan Gay Croft from Woodward's Memorial Hospital the night of the storm. The story was made into an episode of *Unsolved Mysteries* in 1994. Following that episode of the popular television series, a number of women came forward claiming that they could be Joan Gay Croft. All have been disproved, some through the use of DNA testing.

ARTMENT OF COMMERCE
Bureau of the Census

STANDARD CERTIFICATE OF LIVE BIRTH
State of Oklahoma 97-37774

State File No. ....
Registrar's No. 215

519 (P)

PLACE OF BIRTH:
County Woodward
City or town Woodward
IF OUTSIDE OF CITY OR TOWN LIMITS PUT RURAL
Name of hospital or institution:
The Memorial Hospital
IF NOT IN HOSP. OR INST. GIVE ST. NO. AND LOCATION.
Mother's stay before delivery:
Hospital or institution .... ,In this community ....
SPECIFY WHETHER YRS., MO., OR DAS.

2. USUAL RESIDENCE OF MOTHER:
(a) State Oklahoma
(b) County Harper
(c) City or town Buffalo
IF OUTSIDE CITY LIMITS, WRITE RURAL
(d) Street No. R.R.
IF RURAL, GIVE LOCATION

Full name of child Joan Gay Croft
4. Date of birth 10-28-42 (MO. DA. YR)
Sex: female
6. Twin or triplet .... If so-born 1st 2nd, or 3rd 613
7. No. months of pregnancy 8
8. Is mother married? yes

FATHER OF CHILD
Full name Hutchinson Olin Croft
Color or race White
Age at time of this birth 37 yrs.
Birthplace Anthony, Kansas
CITY, TOWN, COUNTY ST. OR FOREIGN COUNTRY
Usual occupation Farming
Industry or business ....

MOTHER OF CHILD
15. Full maiden name Cleta Mae Goble
16. Color or race White
17. Age at time of this birth 22 yrs.
18. Birthplace Woodward, Oklahoma
CITY, TOWN, COUNTY ST. OR FOREIGN COUNTRY
19. Usual occupation Housewife
20. Industry or business ....

Children born to this mother:
How many other children of this mother now living? 1
How many other children born alive but now dead? 0
How many children were born dead? 0

22. Mother's mailing address for registration notice:
Mrs Cleta Mae Croft
Buffalo, Oklahoma
R.R.

(a) Was a solution of Silver Nitrate used in eyes? yes
(b) Was Blood test for syphilis made? yes DO NOT GIVE RESULT OF TEST

I hereby certify that I attended the birth of this child who was born alive at the hour of 10 37 p.m. on the date above stated and that the information given was furnished by ~~Stillborn~~ Mrs Croft, related to this child as her mother

Date received by local registrar Oct 31-1942
Registrar's own signature Eva Hopkins
Date given name added .... by .... REGISTRAR

Attendant's own signature Joe L. Duer, M.D.
M. D., midwife or other M.D. Date signed 10/29/42
Address Woodward, Okla.

State Department of Health
State of Oklahoma
OKLAHOMA CITY, OKLAHOMA 73152

ROGER C. PIRRONG
STATE REGISTRAR OF VITAL STATISTICS

CERTIFIED COPY MUST HAVE EMBOSSED SEAL

I hereby certify the foregoing to be a true and correct copy, original of which is on file in this office. In testimony whereof, I have hereunto subscribed my name and caused the official seal to be affixed, at Oklahoma City, Oklahoma, this date.

FEB 03 1994

Pictured is Joan Gay's birth certificate from October 1942. Interestingly, she was born in the same hospital from which she later disappeared. Her father, Olin Croft, after he was released from the hospital in Oklahoma City, began what became for him a lifelong search for his missing daughter. Eventually, he and his remaining daughter, Jean, left Woodward without ever having received any other word of what happened to Joan Gay Croft.

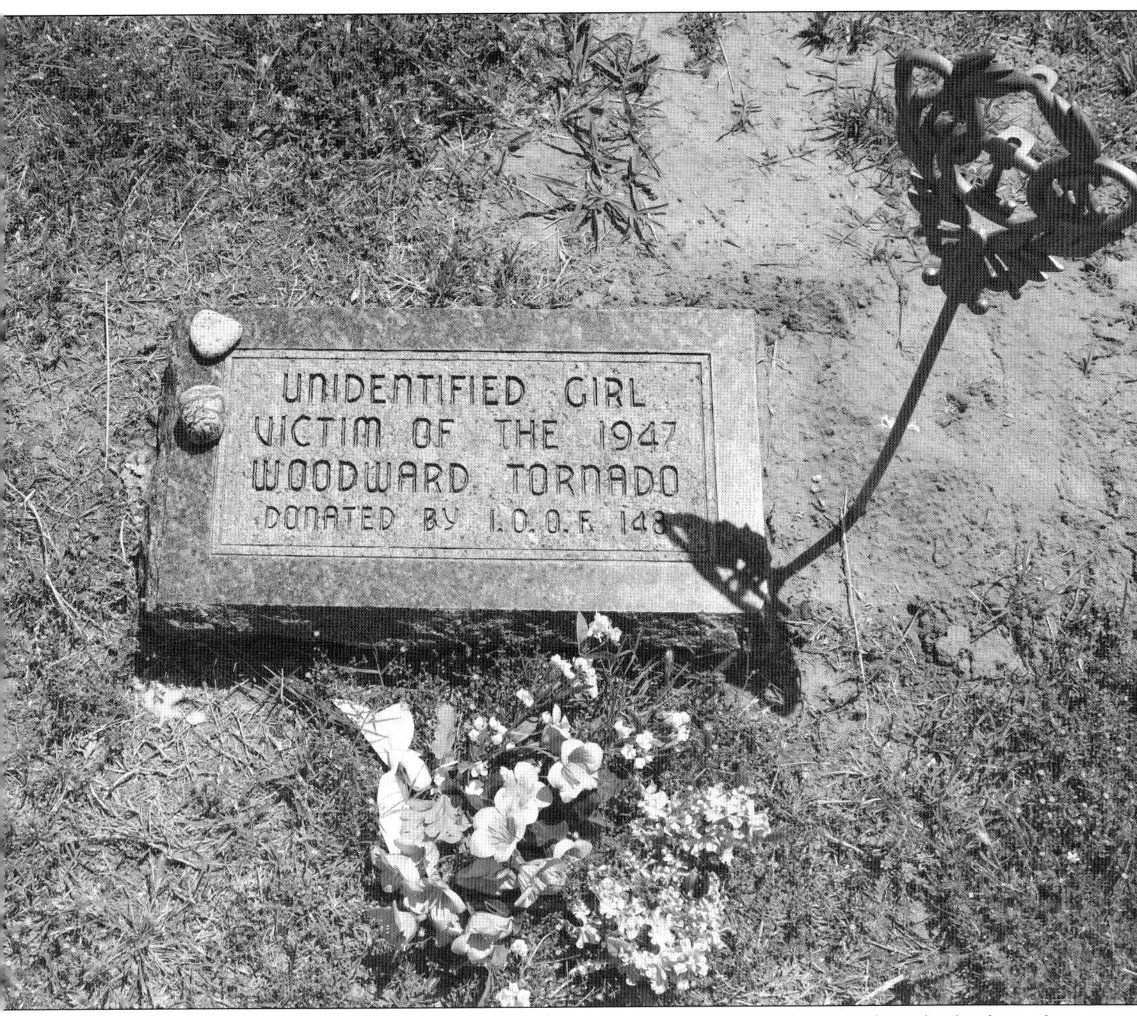

Very soon after the tornado in April 1947, word began to spread around town that the bodies of four unidentified young girls, aged six months to twelve years, had been found among the rubble and debris. Soon, one of the little girls was identified as 18-month-old Treana Dale Holster; her body was claimed by relatives. The remaining three—a blond-haired girl, approximately twelve years old; a reddish-blond girl, approximately three; and, an infant girl, approximately six months old—were never identified. All three were buried in unmarked graves by the Red Cross. At some point in the 1950s, the Independent Order of Odd Fellows (IOOF) Lodge 148 in Woodward placed a marker on the resting place of the six-month-old girl. (Photograph by Robin Hohweiler.)

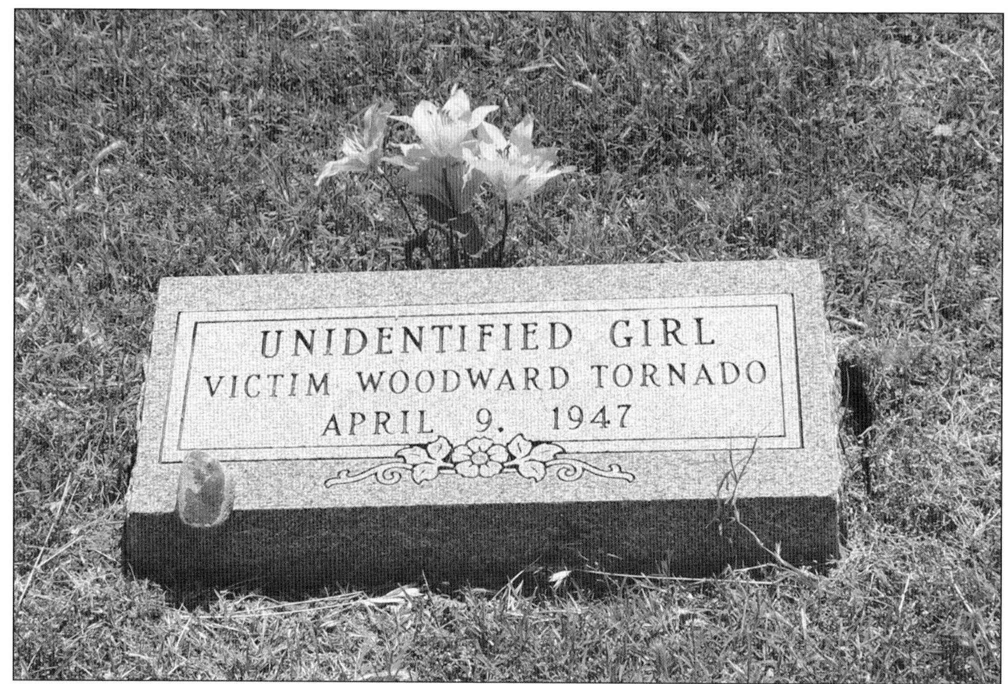

There was an effort to at least identify the 12-year-old. School teachers from across the region were brought to the morgue to view the remains. None recognized the girl. Finally, a list of the names of every girl enrolled in Woodward County schools near the same age was compiled. Volunteers fanned out across the area to locate each girl. All were accounted for. The other two girls remained in unmarked graves about 100 feet east of the infant girl's grave until 1987, when a local citizen donated two markers. (Both photographs by Robin Hohweiler.)

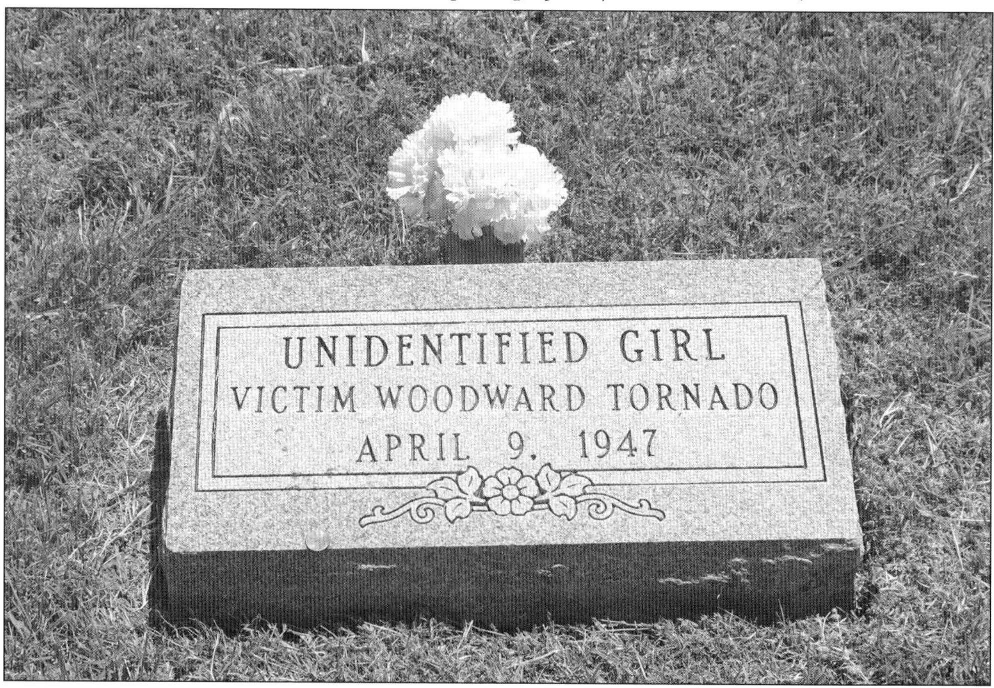

Three

Two Stories of Tragic Loss

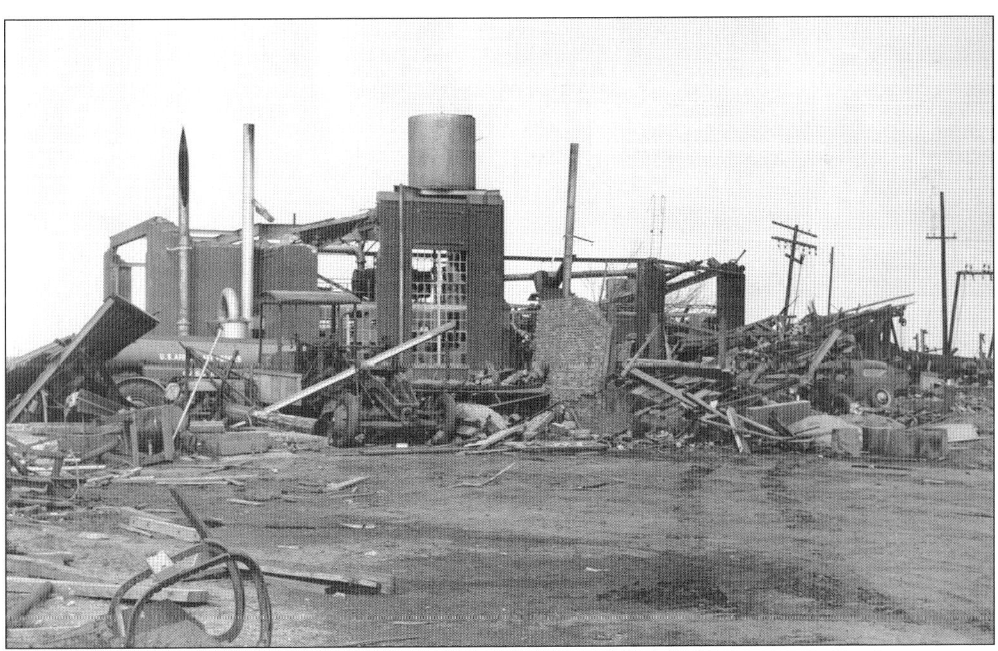

Of all the stories of heartbreak and tragedy that followed the 1947 Woodward tornado, few compare in poignancy to those of E.V. Walker, whose heroic act of self-sacrifice probably saved innumerable lives, and Mary Eliza Kezer (also known as "Miss Dolly"), whose life was one of redemption and perseverance. The photograph shows the remains of the Oklahoma Gas & Electric (OG&E) electric power plant after the tornado.

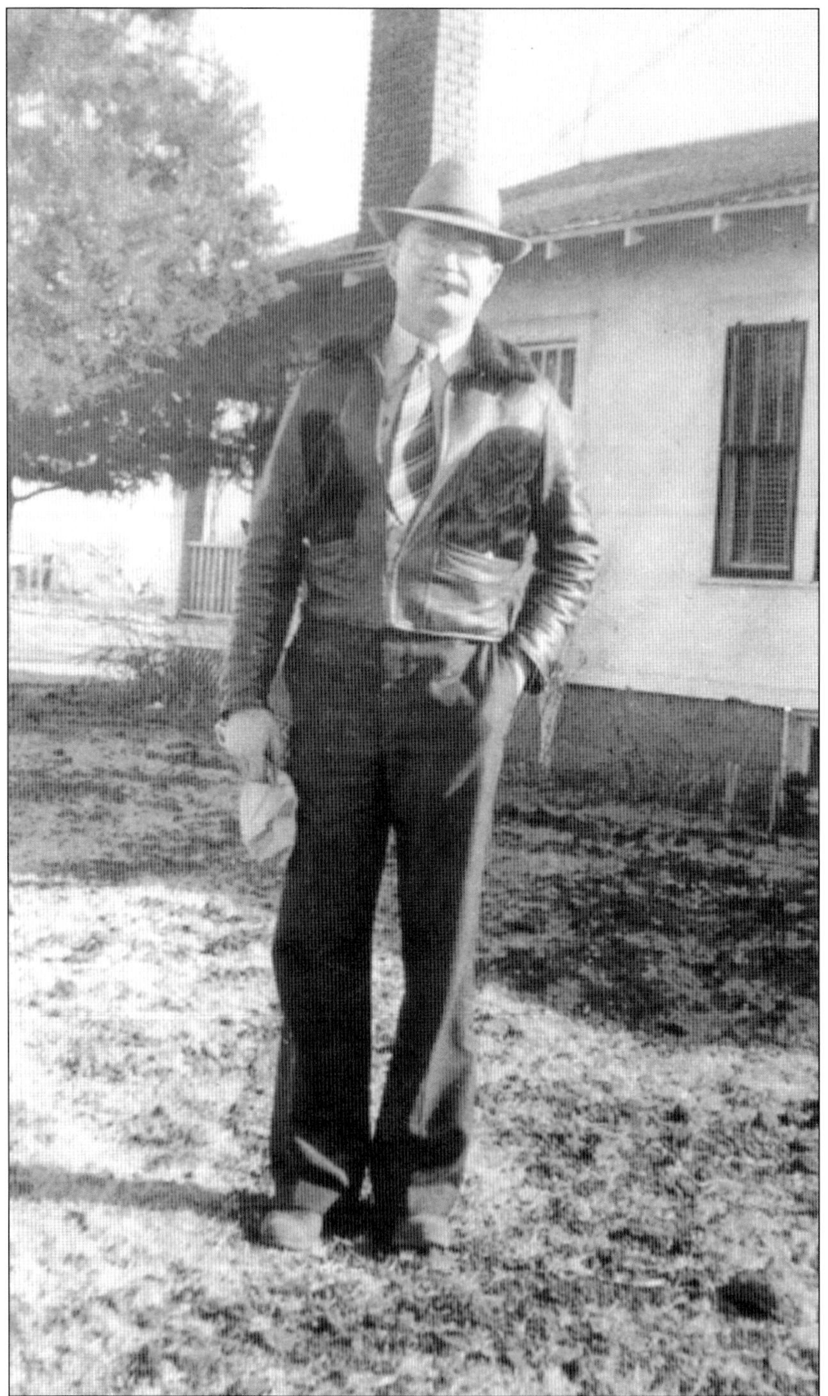

Erwin Vincent "Jack" Walker was an employee of OG&E who did not usually work nights but had agreed to cover the shift of another employee on April 9, 1947. He remained at his post as the storm approached to throw the master switch so that downed power lines would not harm anyone. The power plant took a direct hit by the tornado, and he was killed. He lived for a short time, buried beneath the rubble as other employees tried in vain to dig him out.

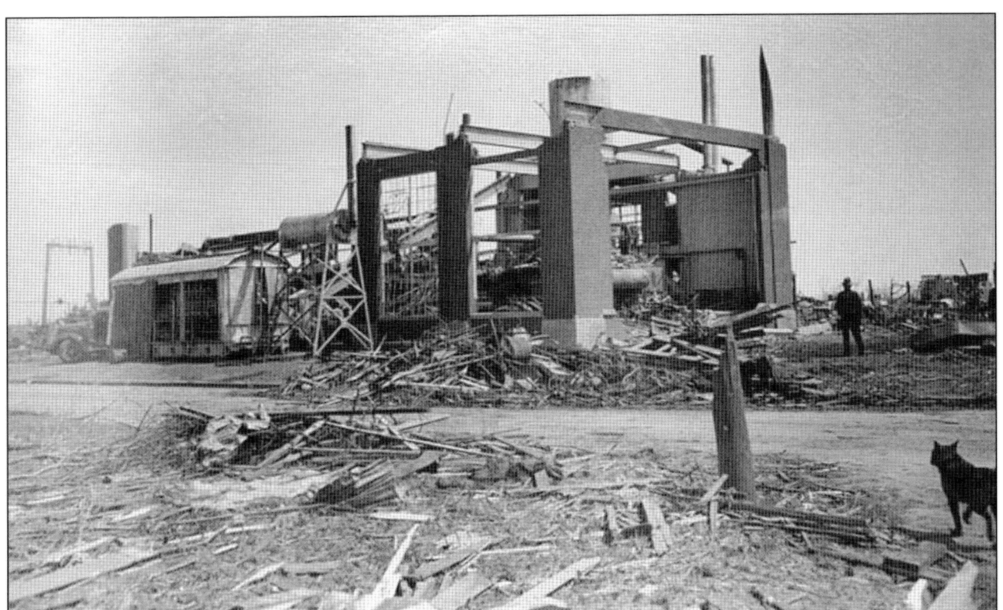

This photograph is another angle of the OG&E power plant on the north edge of town. Following the destruction of the power plant, rescue workers and people trying to get aid or get to a shelter had to use kerosene lanterns or flashlights to find their way around in the darkness.

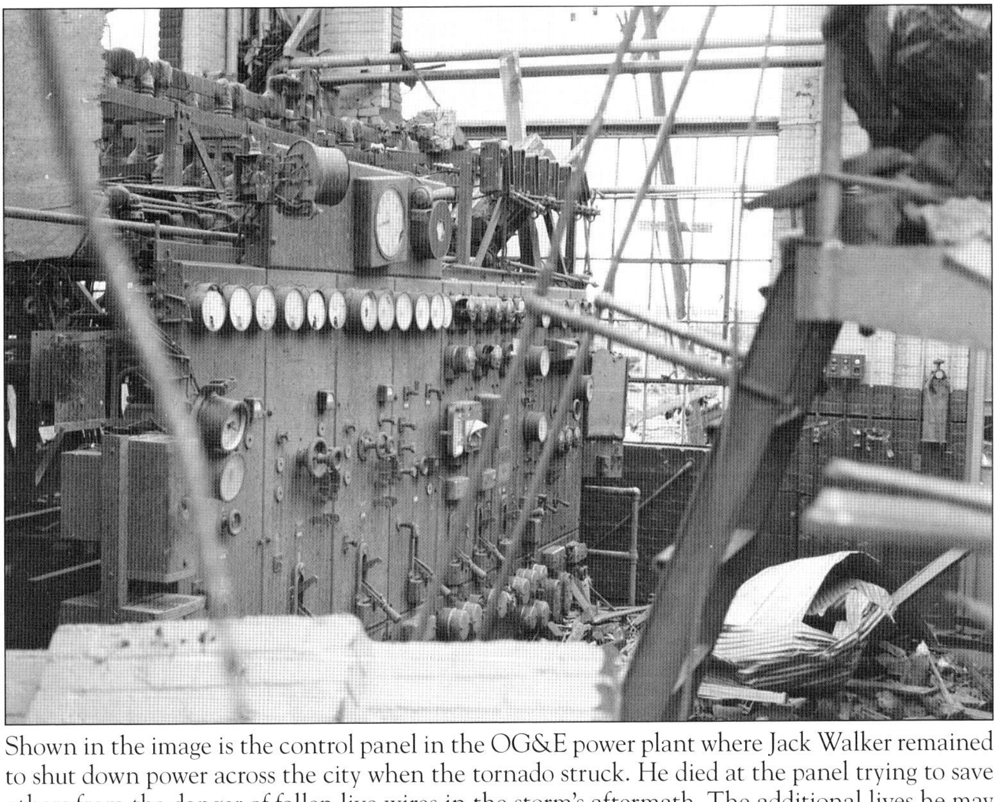

Shown in the image is the control panel in the OG&E power plant where Jack Walker remained to shut down power across the city when the tornado struck. He died at the panel trying to save others from the danger of fallen live wires in the storm's aftermath. The additional lives he may have saved by his heroic efforts are incalculable.

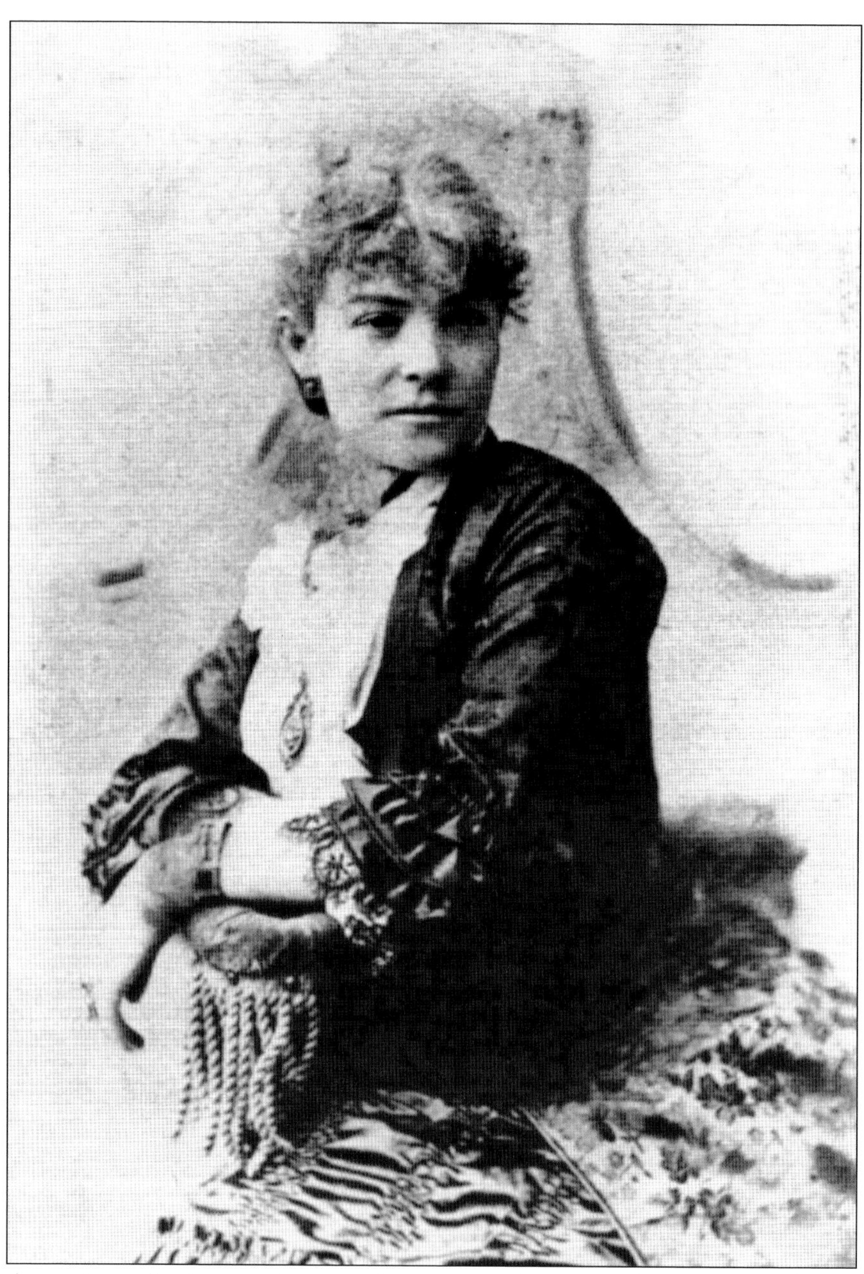

Mary Eliza "Miss Dolly" Kezer arrived in Woodward not long after the opening of the Cherokee Outlet. She took a job as a dance hall madam after moving to Woodward from Denver, Colorado, where she was a high-society escort for men who became rich in the area's silver mines. She was 36 years old when she arrived in dusty, wind-swept Northwest Oklahoma and soon came to the startling realization of just how very different her new surroundings were from what she had experienced in Denver. Still, she would remain in Woodward for 53 years, finally living on a small homestead southwest of the city. The early-day madam walked away from the red-light district in the early 1900s, reportedly following an all-night party when she realized that her life, no matter how much she attempted to put up an elegant front, was cheap and tawdry. She was sickened by her realization and committed to making a personal change.

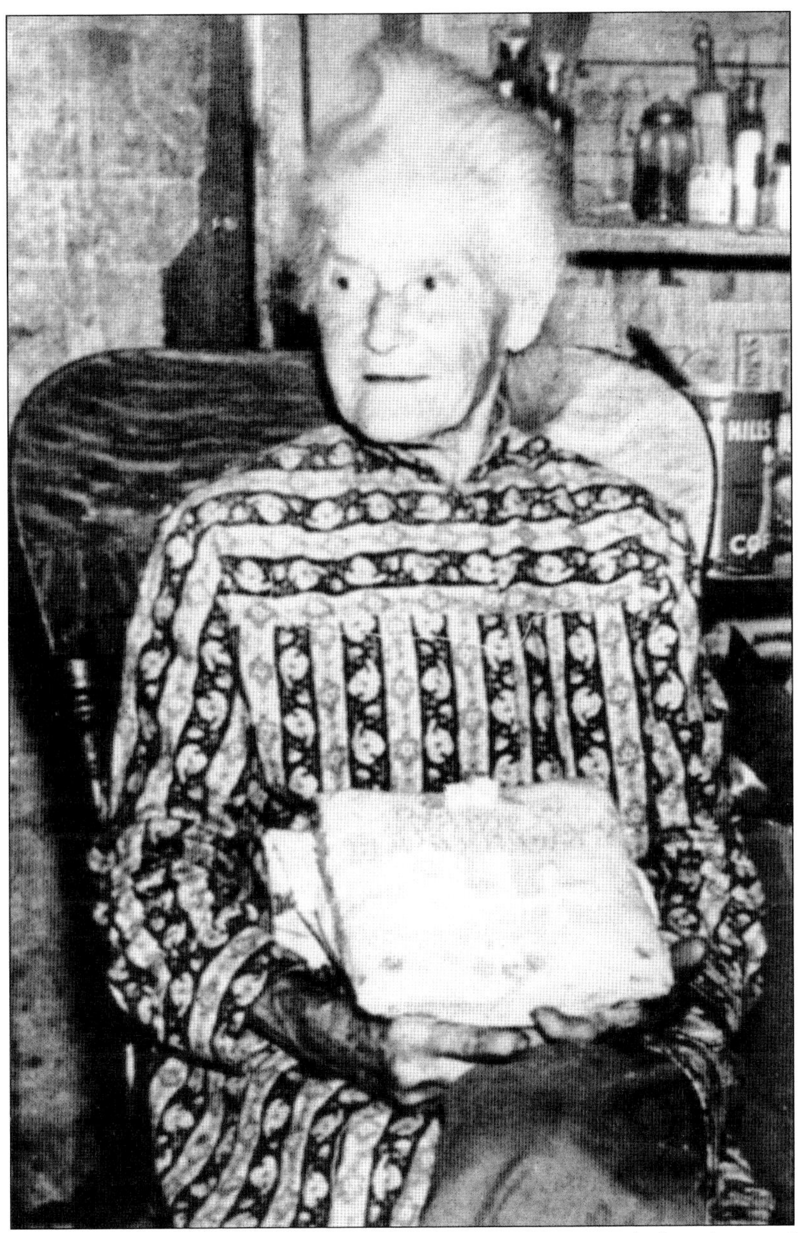

This photograph shows Kezer celebrating her 84th birthday five years before she perished in the 1947 Woodward tornado. After committing to leaving her life as a Woodward madam, she later said she spent the rest of the night in prayer. Miss Dolly then reportedly sold her jewelry and offered to send the girls who worked for her home if they desired to leave. A friend—some stories have it as an attorney, others say it was a stranger—filed on an unclaimed piece of land southwest of town. To make ends meet, she laundered clothes for Woodward townspeople. She walked into town and picked up dirty laundry. She walked back to her farm, cleaned the linens and clothing, and then walked them back into town. The money she made from doing the laundry of others bought her lumber, wire, and food for herself and her dog. Her neighbors frequently cut her fences and allowed their cattle to destroy her few crops. Despite leaving her former life, it would take many years before people began to accept and respect her.

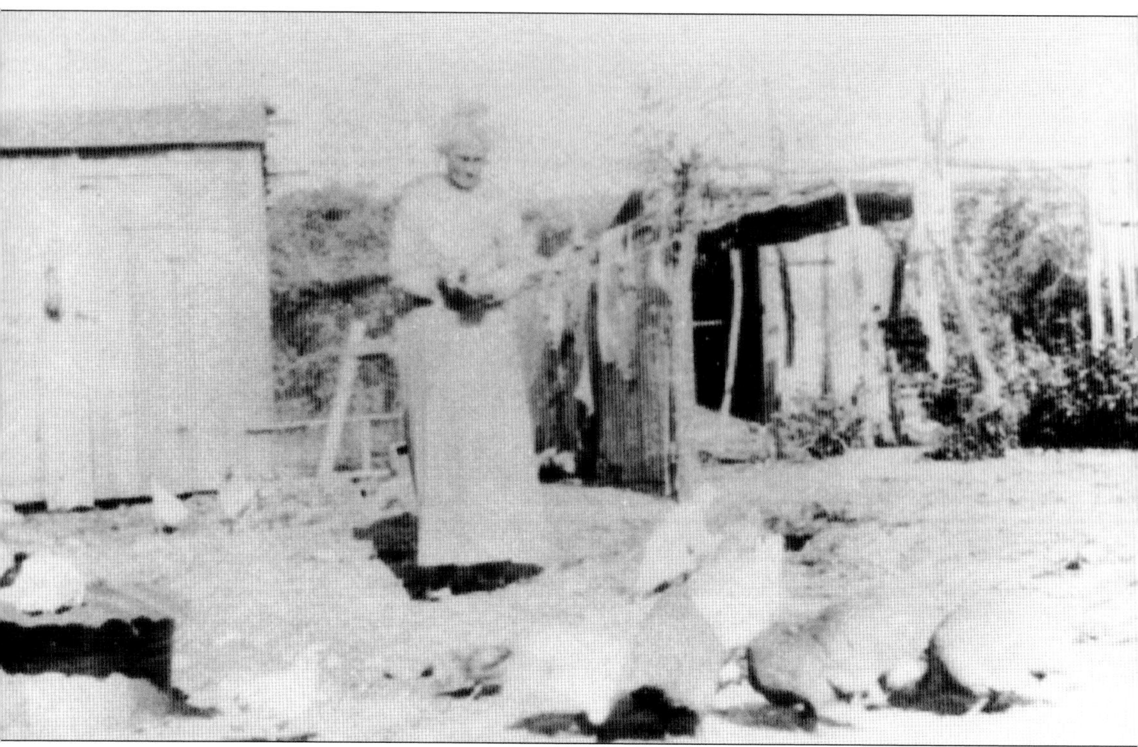

This photograph shows Mary Eliza Kezer feeding her chickens shortly before her death. In early April 1947, she called Grace McDonald (Grace and her husband, Everett, owned McDonald Studio) and asked for a ride into town. She took a bath that night, saying she wanted to meet her Lord clean. Three days later, she was found dead, face down in the mud, clutching the door frame of her splintered cabin. It is believed that Kezer was the first death in Woodward County from the monster storm. From her farm, the tornado continued up present-day Thirty-Fourth Street, scooping up water from the Field Station Lake, which contributed to the copious amounts of mud that covered much of Woodward. After her death, workers cleaning up the wreckage of her farmstead found $1,556 in cash and another $7.58 in silver amid the rubble.

Four

Picking Up the Pieces and Healing the Wounds

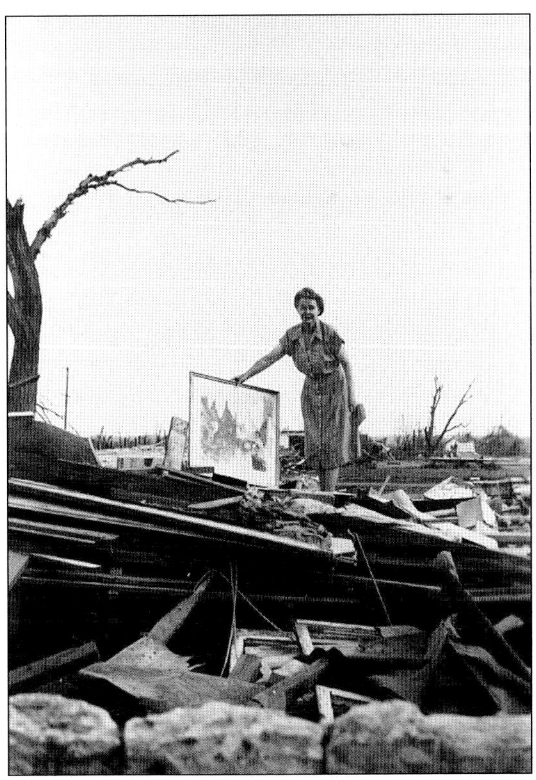

This home was located at 1302 Seventeenth Street (the southeast corner of Seventeenth Street and Oklahoma Avenue). The structure was completely flattened by the tornado. Standing atop the rubble is Mary Sue Sparks holding up a painting she found amid the ruins. The Sparks family rebuilt their home in the same location where it remains today. Communications in the aftermath of the storm were all but nonexistent. Shortwave radio operators spread the news until phone circuits could be restored.

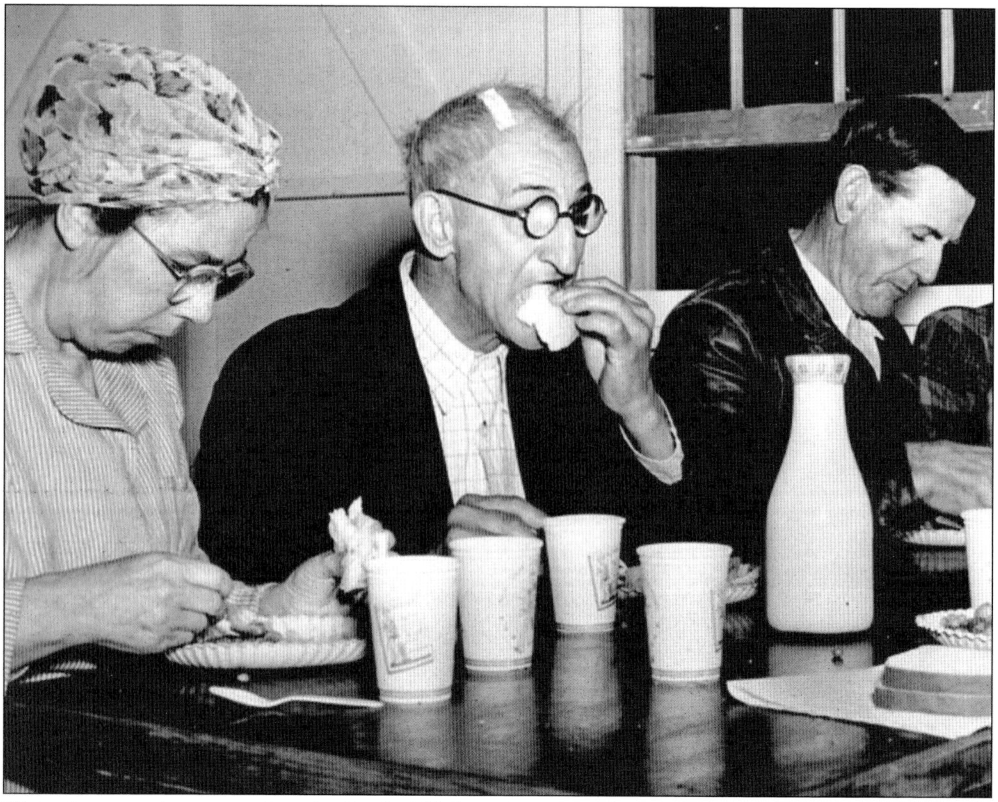

This photograph appeared in the *Daily Oklahoman* on April 22, 1947, with the following caption: "Survivors of the Woodward tornado, including an elderly man who suffered a cut on his head during the storm, enjoy a meal brought in and prepared by volunteers at a shelter." Aid organizations including the Red Cross, Salvation Army, and the US Army arrived in Woodward mere hours following the storm. (Courtesy of the Oklahoma Historical Society.)

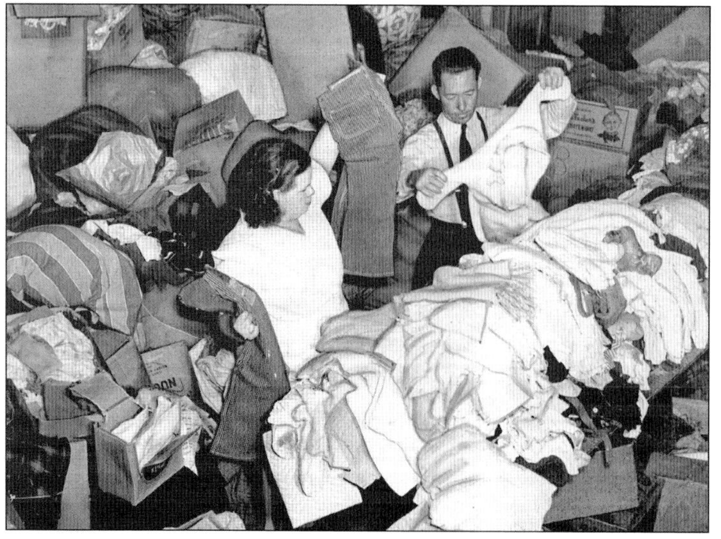

Along with the arrival of relief organizations in Woodward came tons of materials and clothing for the victims of the storm. This photograph ran in the *Oklahoma Times* newspaper on April 11, 1947, with the caption "Clothing for tornado victims poured into Woodward all day Thursday and Friday. Somebody was needed to sort it for size and sex." (Courtesy of the Oklahoma Historical Society.)

This photograph shows Dr. E.H. Arrendall of Ponca City, assisted by Nurse A.C. Cuppy of Enid. Both were among the 50-plus volunteer medical personnel who traveled to Woodward immediately after the tornado to assist with the care of the wounded. Dr. Arrendall is shown applying sutures to a wound on the head of Lucille Crouse. Within 24 hours of the storm's passing, the Red Cross sent in 1,000 cots and 5,000 blankets.

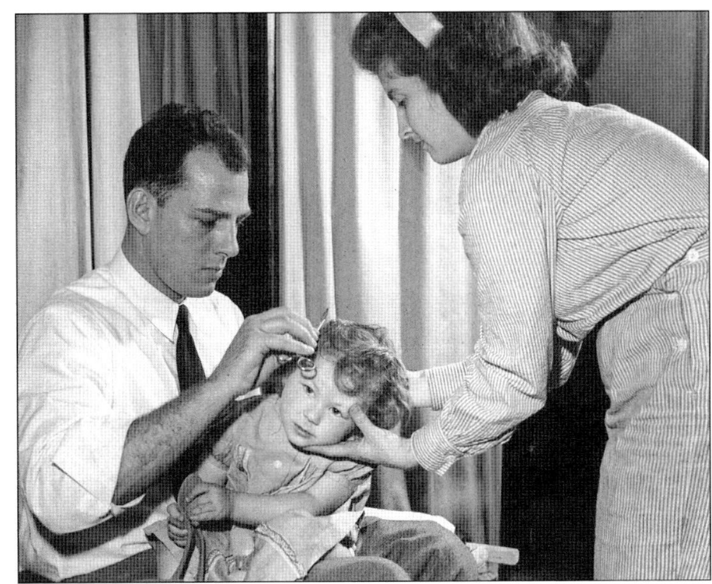

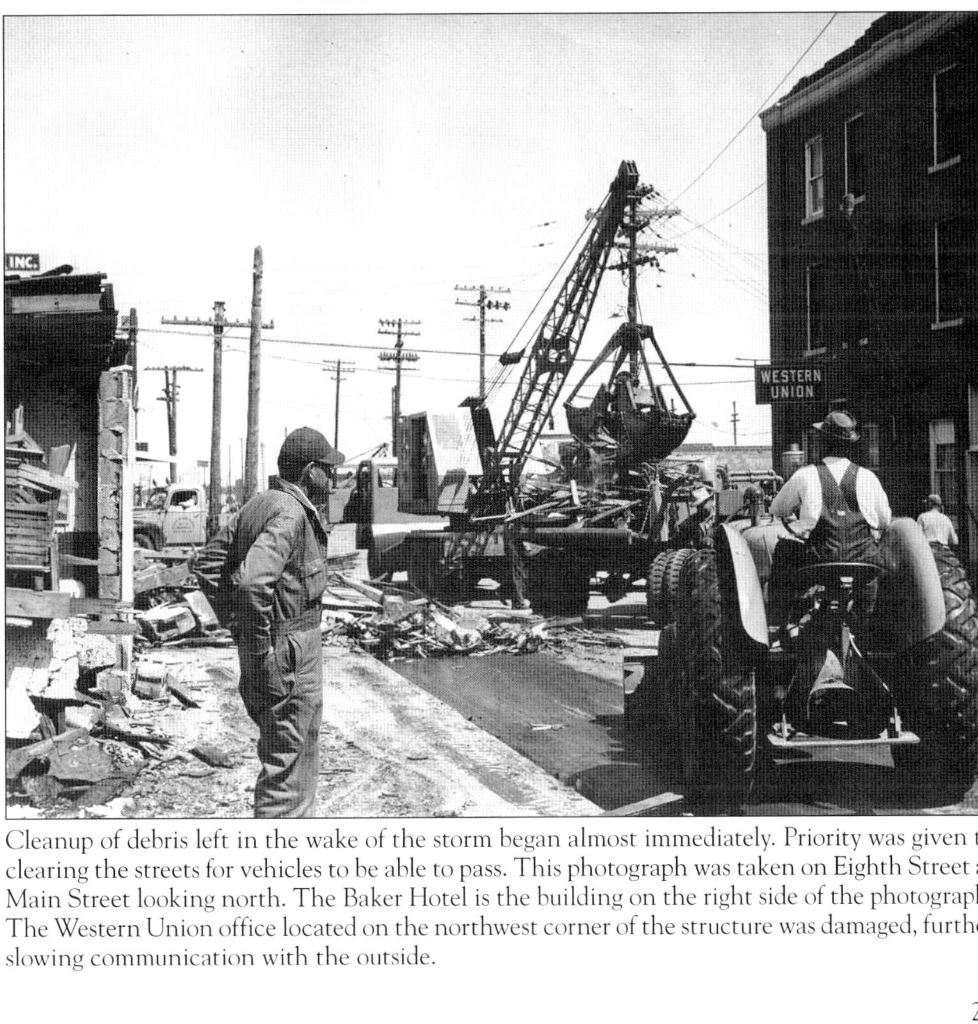

Cleanup of debris left in the wake of the storm began almost immediately. Priority was given to clearing the streets for vehicles to be able to pass. This photograph was taken on Eighth Street at Main Street looking north. The Baker Hotel is the building on the right side of the photograph. The Western Union office located on the northwest corner of the structure was damaged, further slowing communication with the outside.

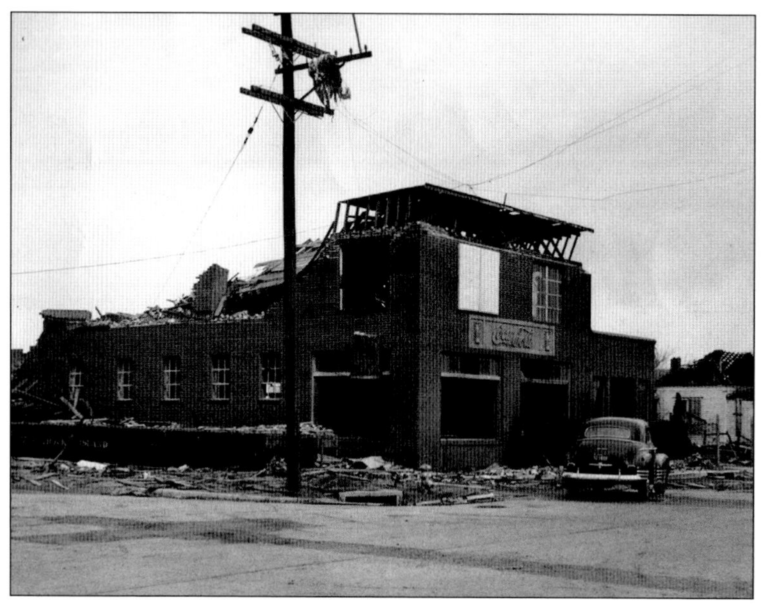

This photograph shows the extensive damage to the Coca-Cola bottling plant on Ninth Street, just north of the Santa Fe Railway tracks. The Coca-Cola plant was a major employer in Woodward at the time having been started by Jeff Warren in the early 1900s. The building was rebuilt following the tornado with the original front facade remaining intact.

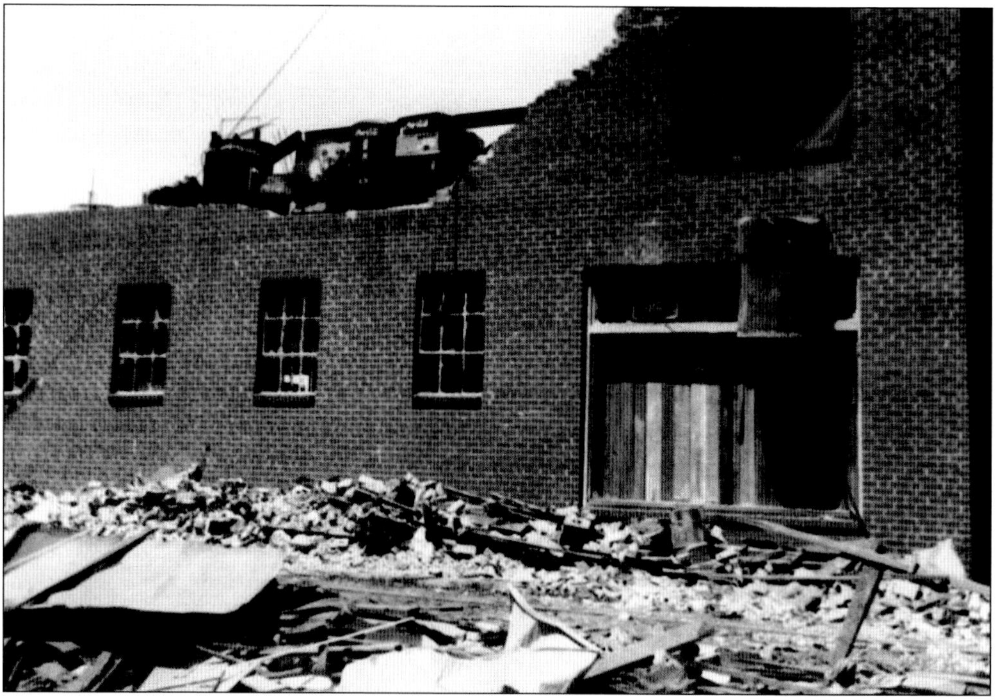

This is another photograph of the Coca-Cola bottling plant taken on April 20, 1947. Note that the dumpster visible in the above photograph is not in place yet. What appear to be Coke vending machines can be seen exposed on the second floor. The reconstructed building continued to serve as a hub for soft drink distribution in the region into the 21st century.

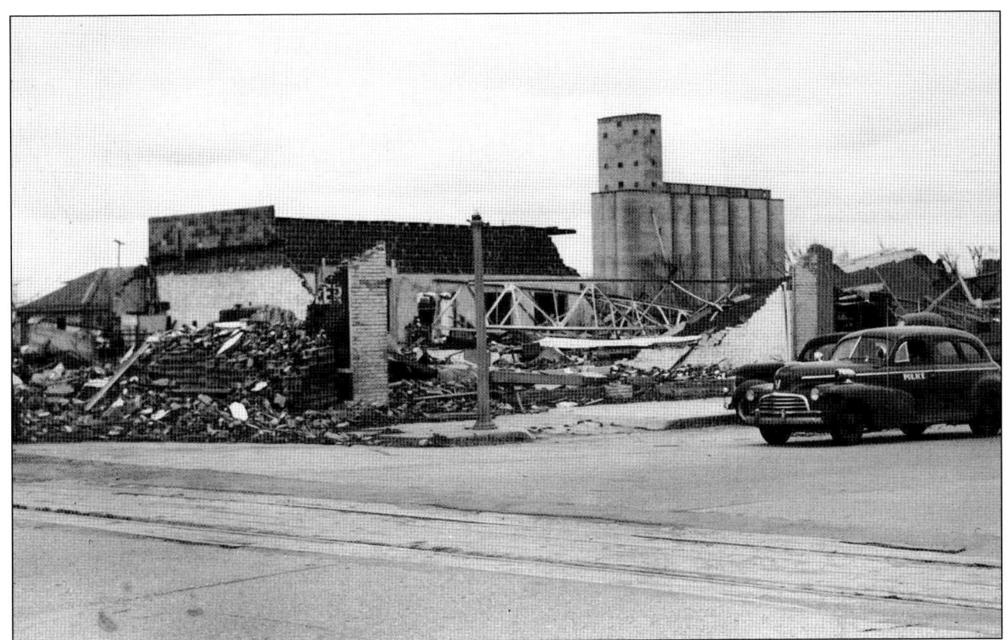

This photograph was taken from the south side of Main Street near the tracks of the Missouri-Kansas-Texas Railroad (MKT or "the Katy") looking northeast. The destroyed building in the foreground is the current location of Peak Fitness. Once again, the Fisher Grain elevator complex serves as a landmark for fixing location.

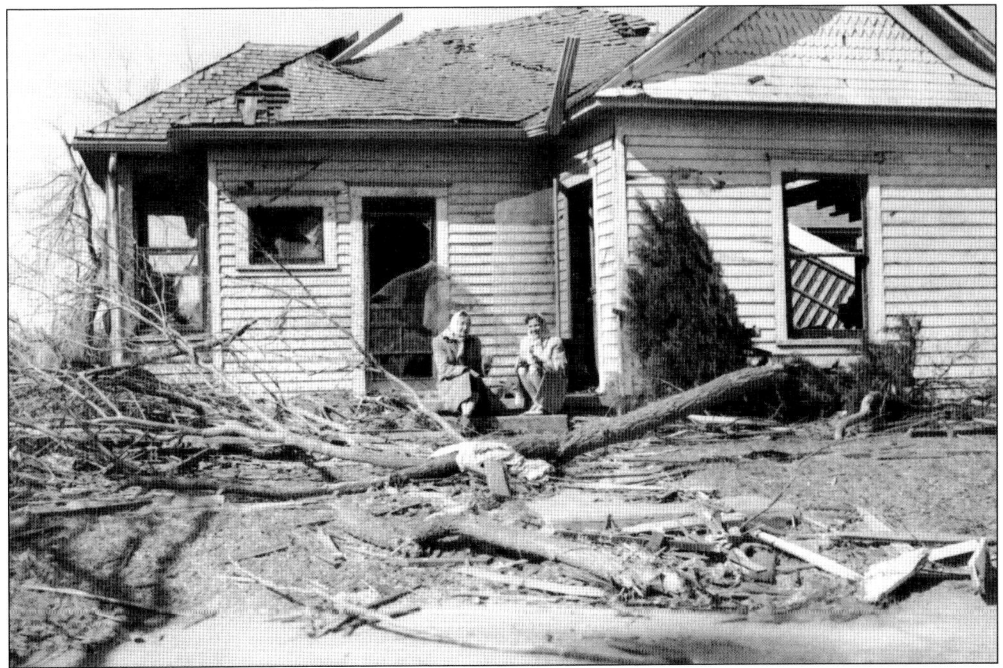

These two women appear to be enjoying a respite from the destruction and shock that surrounds them as they enjoy a snack and one another's company. Following the storm, the survivors were anxious to get things back as they were before, though for most, it would be a year or more before that would happen.

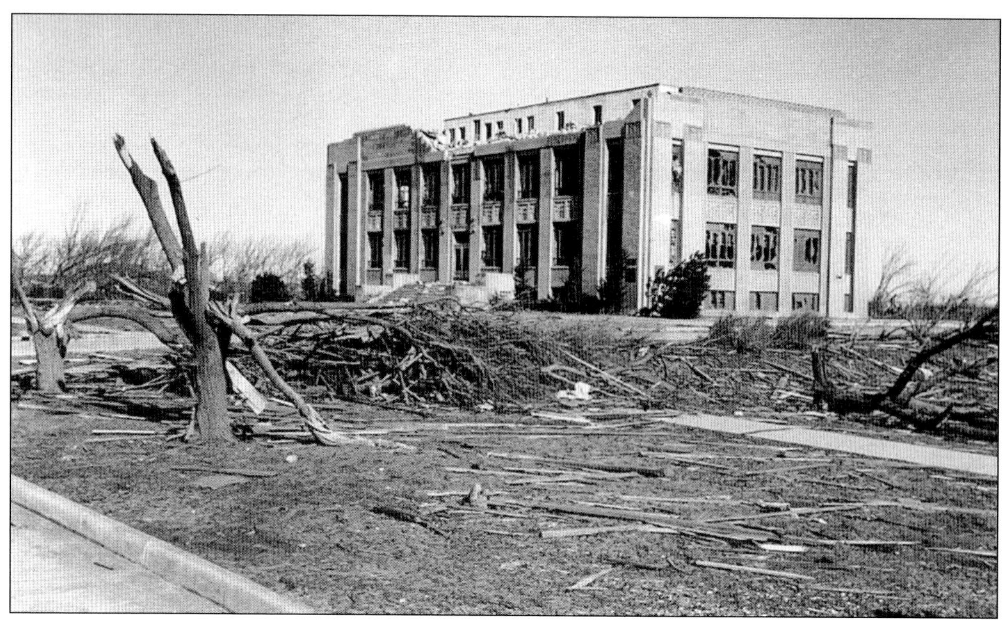

These two photographs show the damage to the Woodward County Courthouse at 1600 Main Street. The structure was built in 1935. It suffered severe structural damage to the upper third of the building. Nearly all windows on the building were blown out. In the photograph below, taken the day after the tornado, pedestrians can be seen walking in front of the courthouse with debris strewn across the lawn.

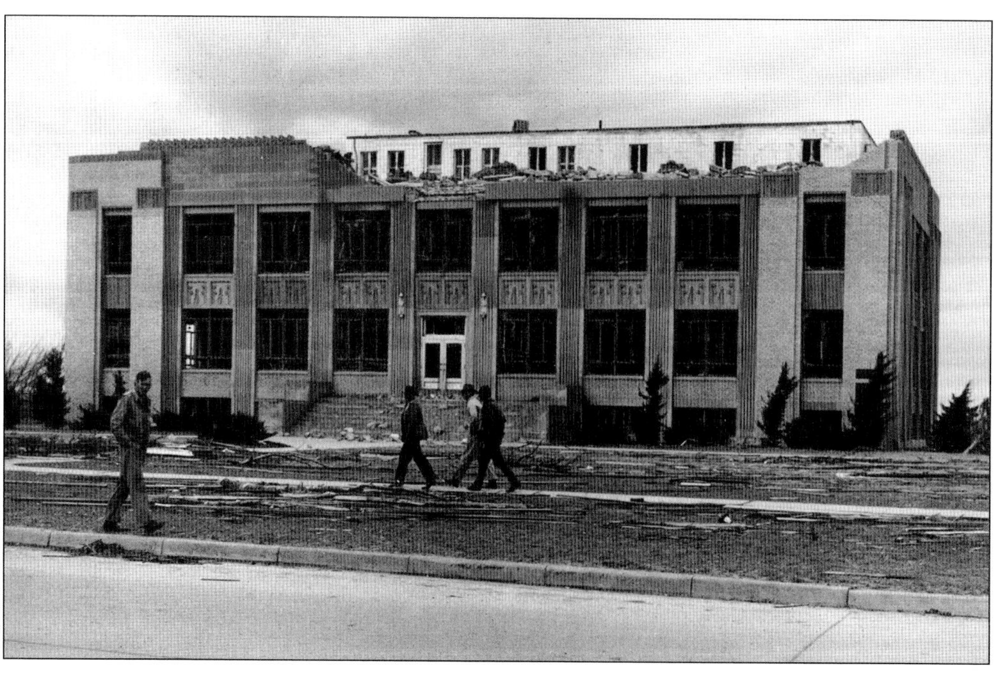

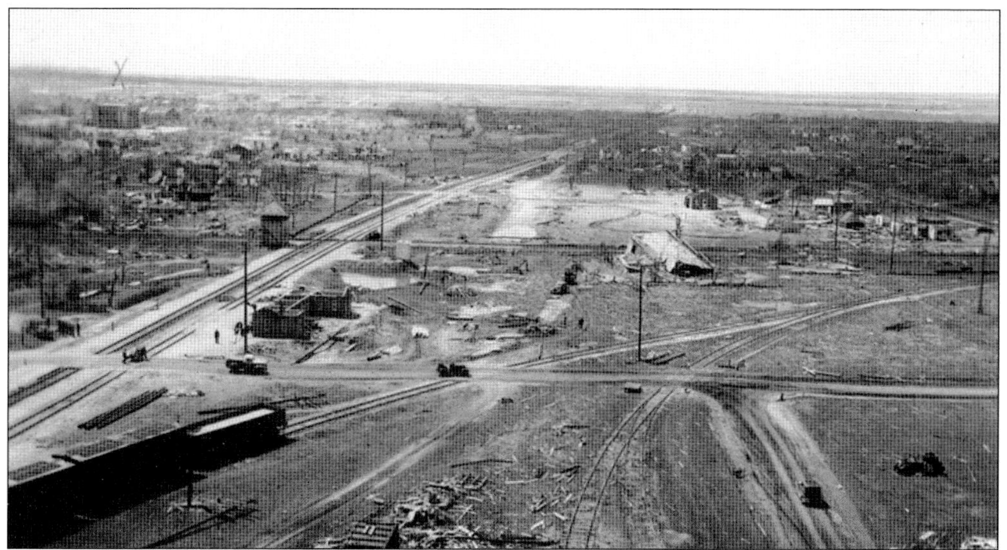

This aerial photograph was possibly taken from atop the Fisher Grain elevator headhouse looking west. Note the switching tower where the Santa Fe and MKT Railways crossed. Railroad cars can be seen on their sides. The Woodward County Courthouse is located in the upper left. This image provides a good perspective of a dense residential area of town left nearly barren in the tornado's wake.

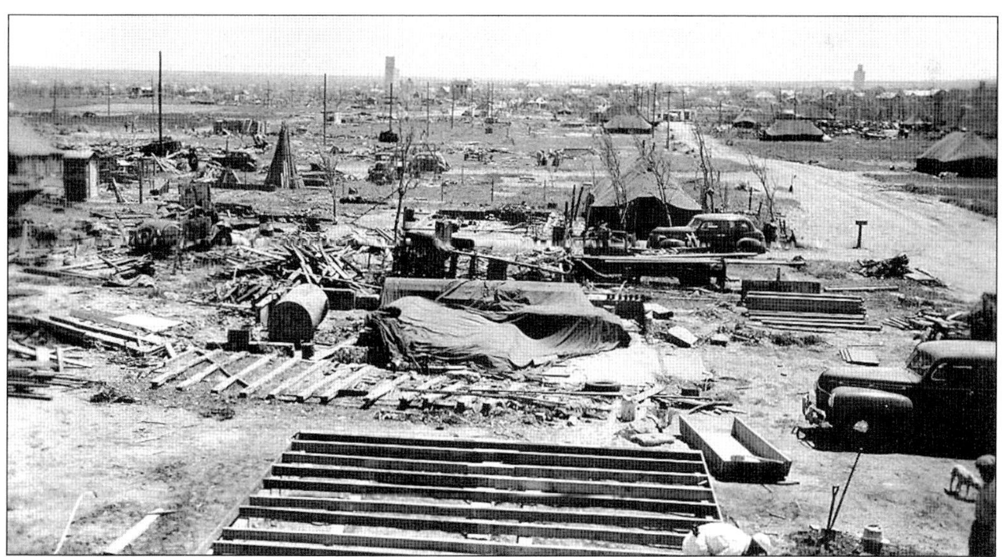

This photograph was taken looking east from the homesite of S.J. Catlett as reconstruction is underway at Twenty-Fifth and East Main Streets. The Fisher Grain elevator can be seen in the upper left. To the right of that is the Woodward County Courthouse. The tents scattered throughout the foreground were provided by the Army as temporary shelters.

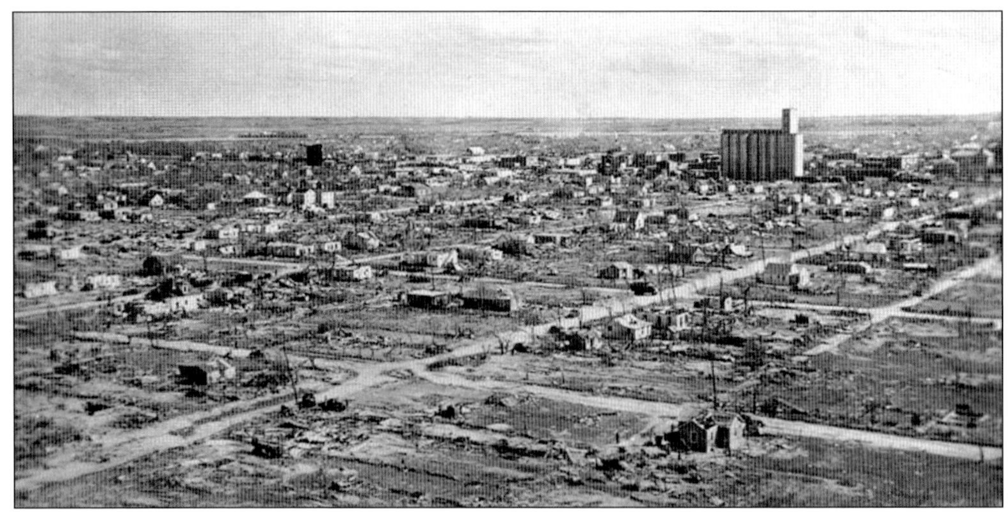

This photograph was taken from an airplane. The point of view is to the southeast and shows the devastation to the north end of Woodward. The north end of town was hit very hard, though the west side of Woodward appears to have sustained the full force of the tornado. Note the seeming randomness of the destruction, where one house may remain standing but the neighboring house is gone.

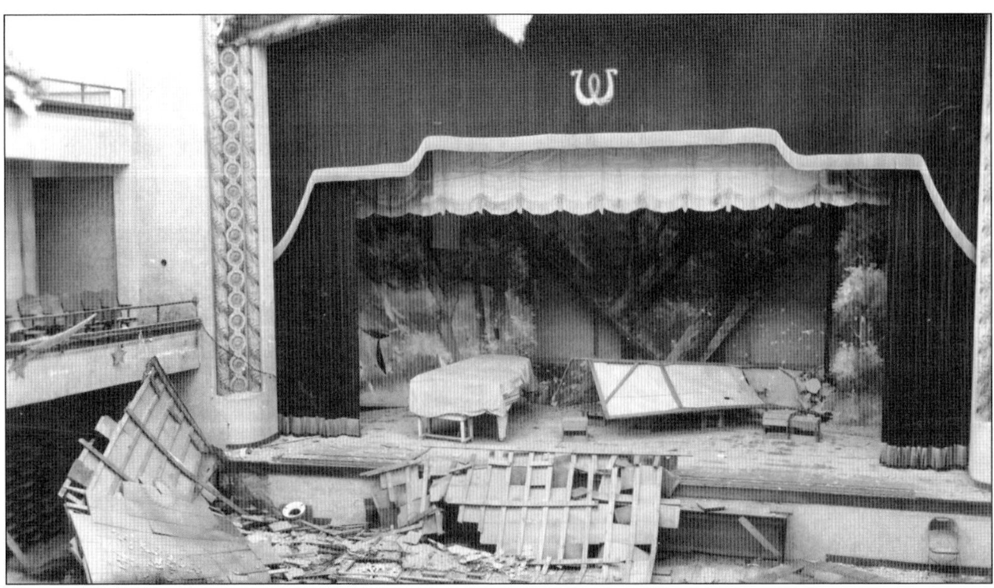

This photograph shows the damage to the interior of the Woodward Convention Hall after the tornado. Pieces of the ceiling tiles and roof structure can be seen on the floor in front of the stage. Although the image does not show it well, one can see what appears to be blue sky above the stage curtains, indicating that the roof was at least partially torn off in the storm.

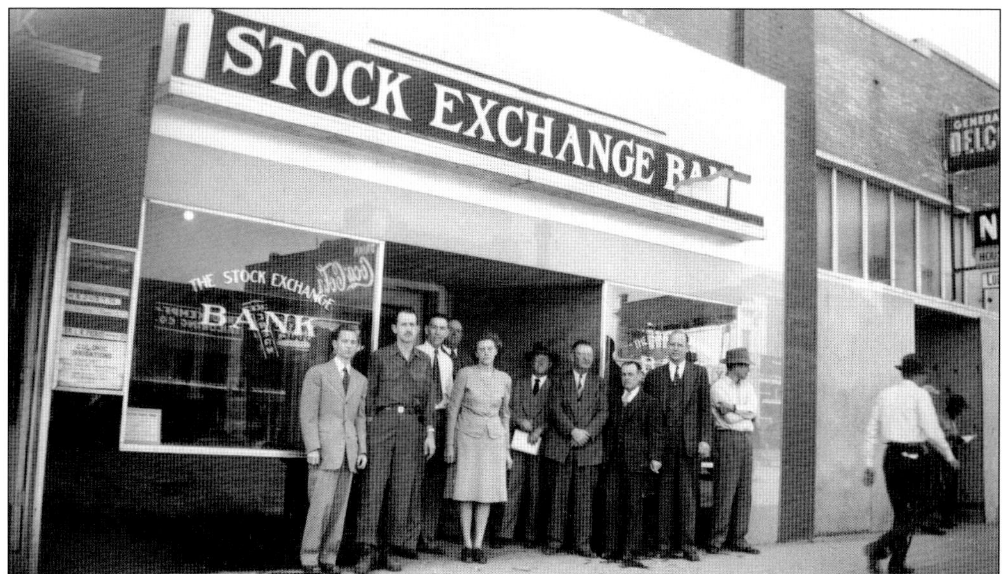

This group of individuals stands at the entrance of the Stock Exchange Bank in its first location along Main Street after moving to Woodward from Fargo in 1939. This photograph was likely taken immediately following the tornado. Note the damage to the sign above the doorway.

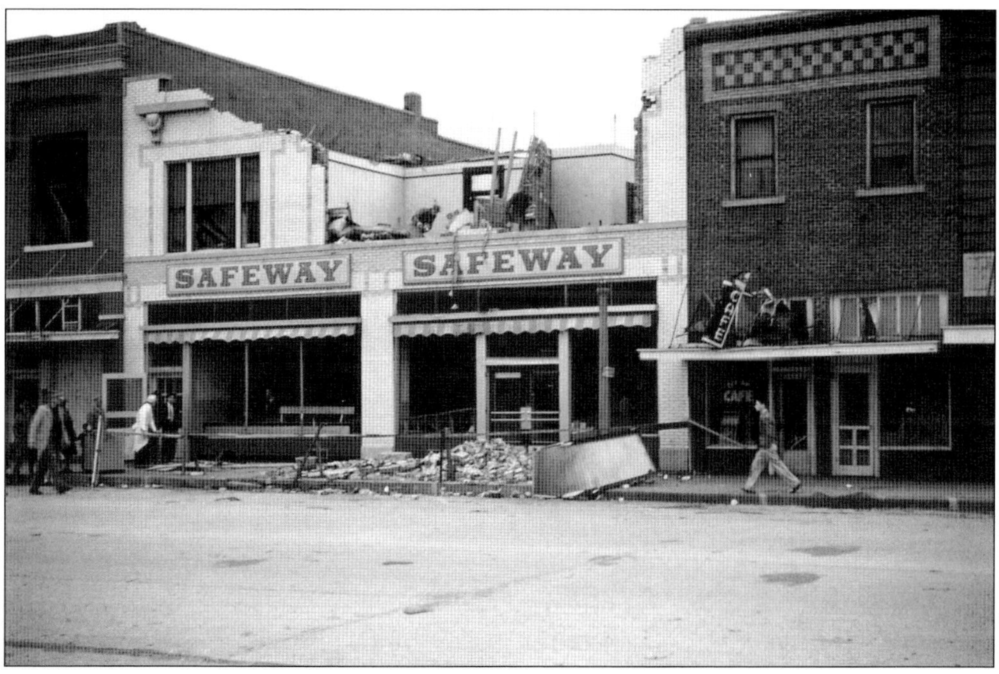

The Safeway store at 920 Main Street lost most of its brick front in the storm. The second floor was an apartment. Damage to the two buildings on either side was comparatively minor and appears to be limited to broken windows. The Safeway building was razed following the storm. The grocery store moved its location farther west down Main Street, where a new store was built.

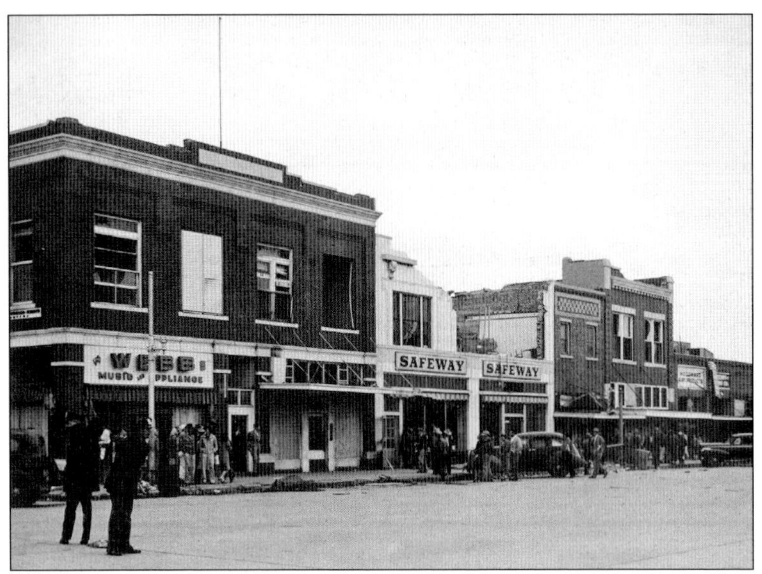

This photograph shows the Safeway store and surrounding businesses from a different angle. It makes a better visual comparison for the relatively minor damage as compared with that to Safeway. This is a good example of the randomness of damage inflicted in a tornado's path.

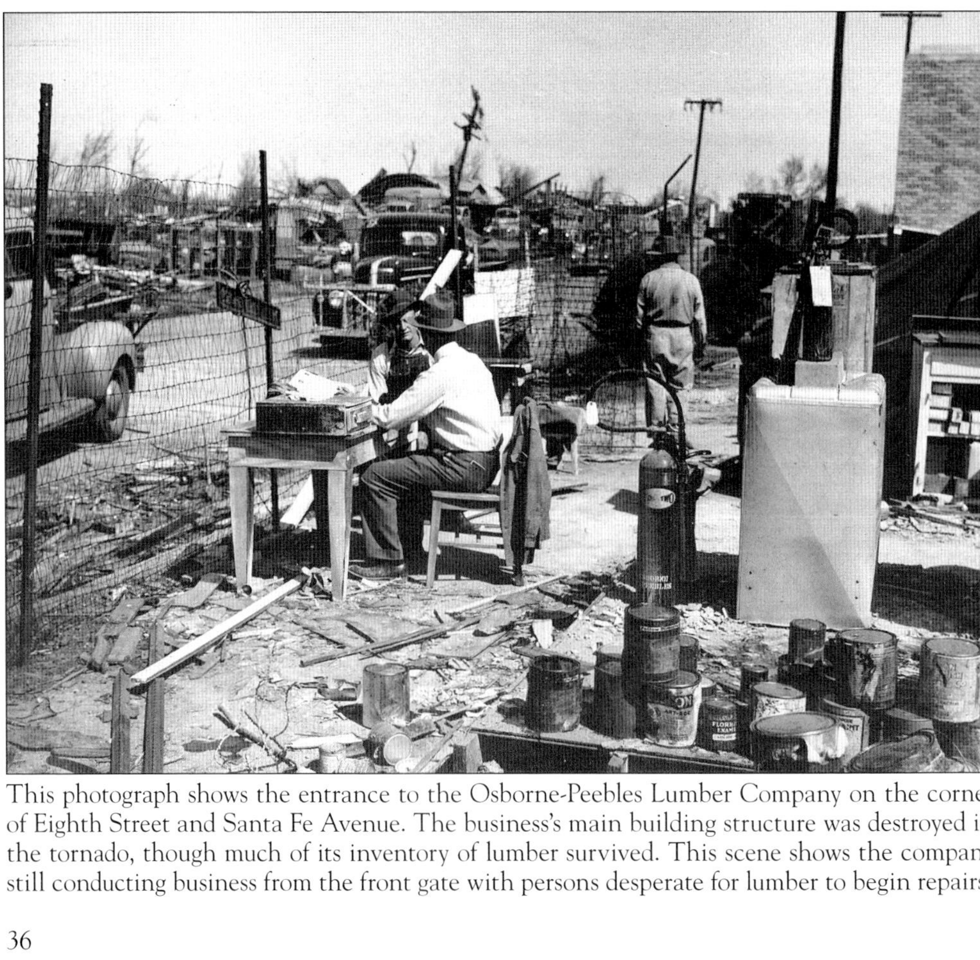

This photograph shows the entrance to the Osborne-Peebles Lumber Company on the corner of Eighth Street and Santa Fe Avenue. The business's main building structure was destroyed in the tornado, though much of its inventory of lumber survived. This scene shows the company still conducting business from the front gate with persons desperate for lumber to begin repairs.

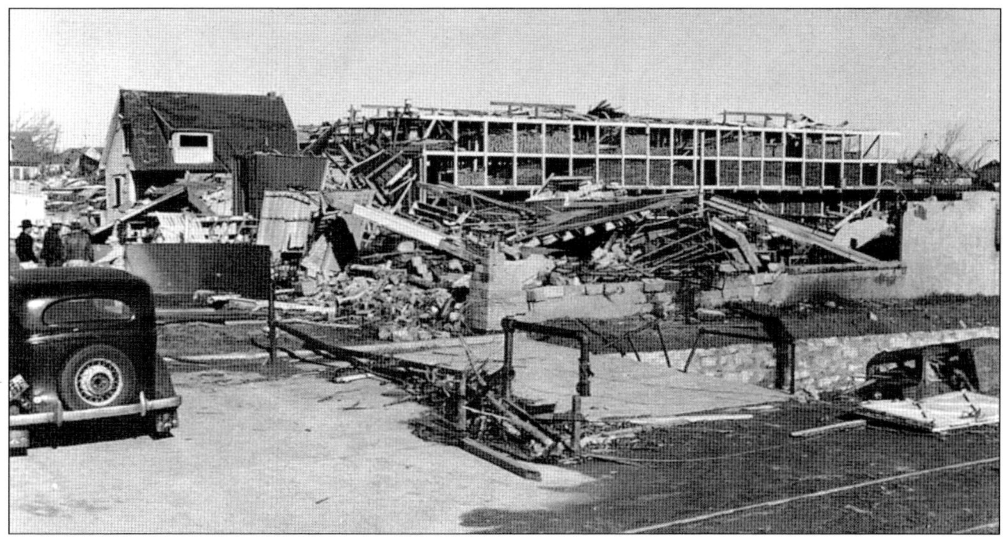

There is a lot to view in this photograph taken along Main Street just before the MKT crossing. Note the delivery van down in the drainage ditch. The building reduced to rubble was the location of a Studebaker dealership in 1947. Note the mangled guardrail across the pedestrian bridge. The lumber yard at the back of the image is Johnson Lumber Company with most of its stock intact.

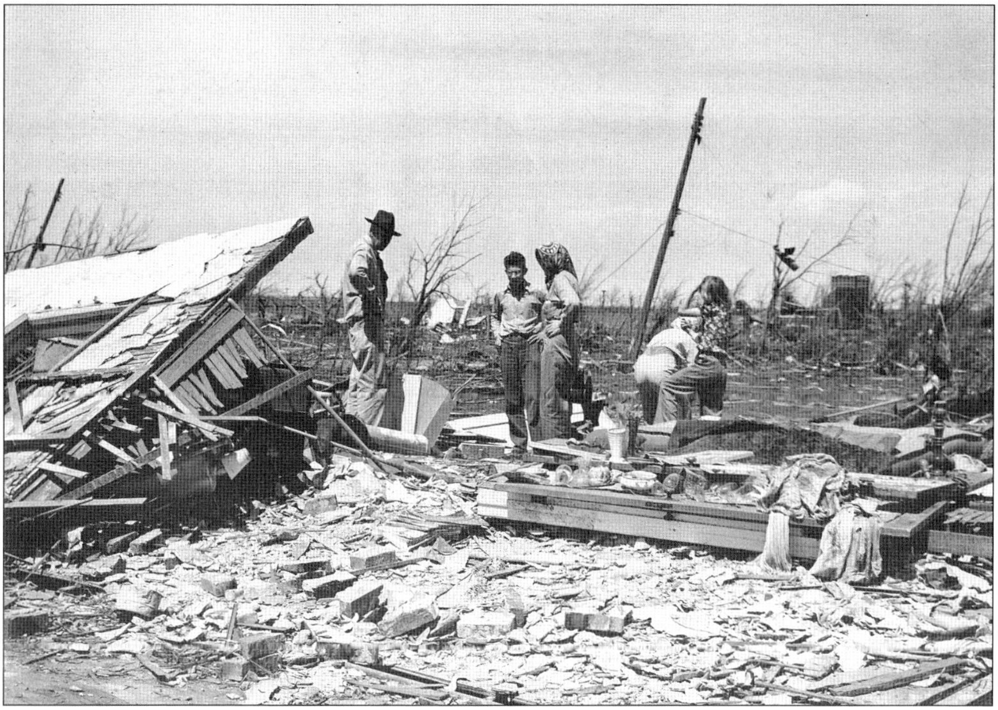

This photograph was taken at 1722 Main Street, site of the Farrand-Wood Apartments, looking north. Francis Valentine faces the camera, hands on hips. His aunt Mable Farrand-Wood is standing to the left. Others in the photograph are not identified. Mable lost her husband, Sam, to the storm. Mable and her son, George, later lived at the location when the apartments were rebuilt.

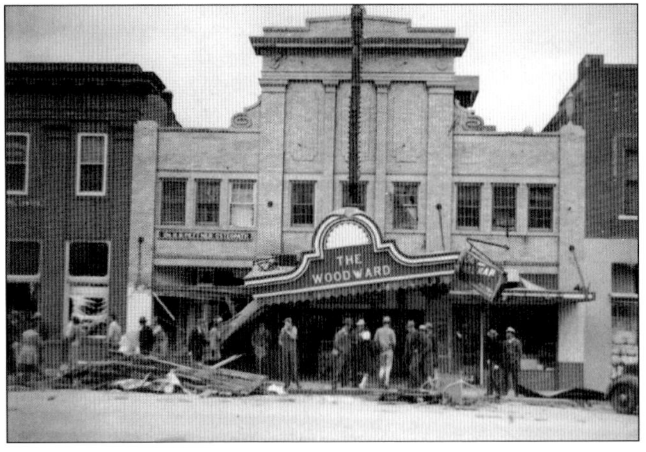

The front of the iconic Woodward Theatre shows the damage to the front marquee. When the tornado struck on April 9, the building was packed with people watching the movie *Rage in Heaven*. The manager had the presence of mind to insist that everyone remain inside the building until well after the storm passed. Built in 1929, the original building is still in use today as a performing arts venue.

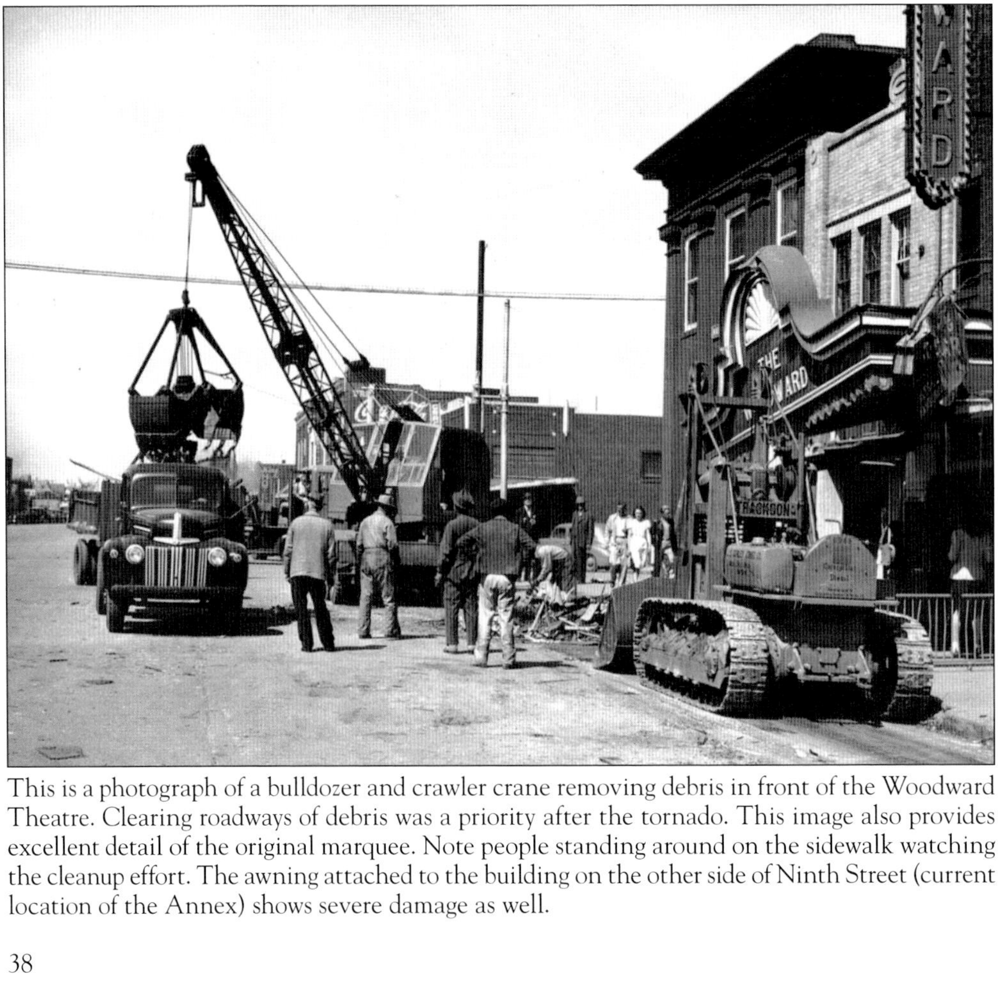

This is a photograph of a bulldozer and crawler crane removing debris in front of the Woodward Theatre. Clearing roadways of debris was a priority after the tornado. This image also provides excellent detail of the original marquee. Note people standing around on the sidewalk watching the cleanup effort. The awning attached to the building on the other side of Ninth Street (current location of the Annex) shows severe damage as well.

This scene near the Woodward Theatre looks east down Main Street. C.R. Anthony's store is visible across the street. The damaged awning and marquee of the movie house are still hanging, though the barricades seen in other photographs that were put up to keep pedestrians from walking underneath have been removed.

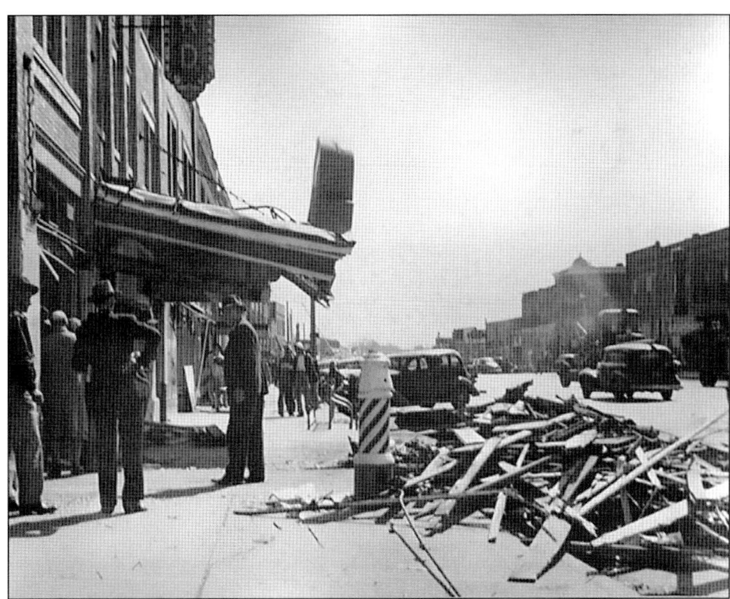

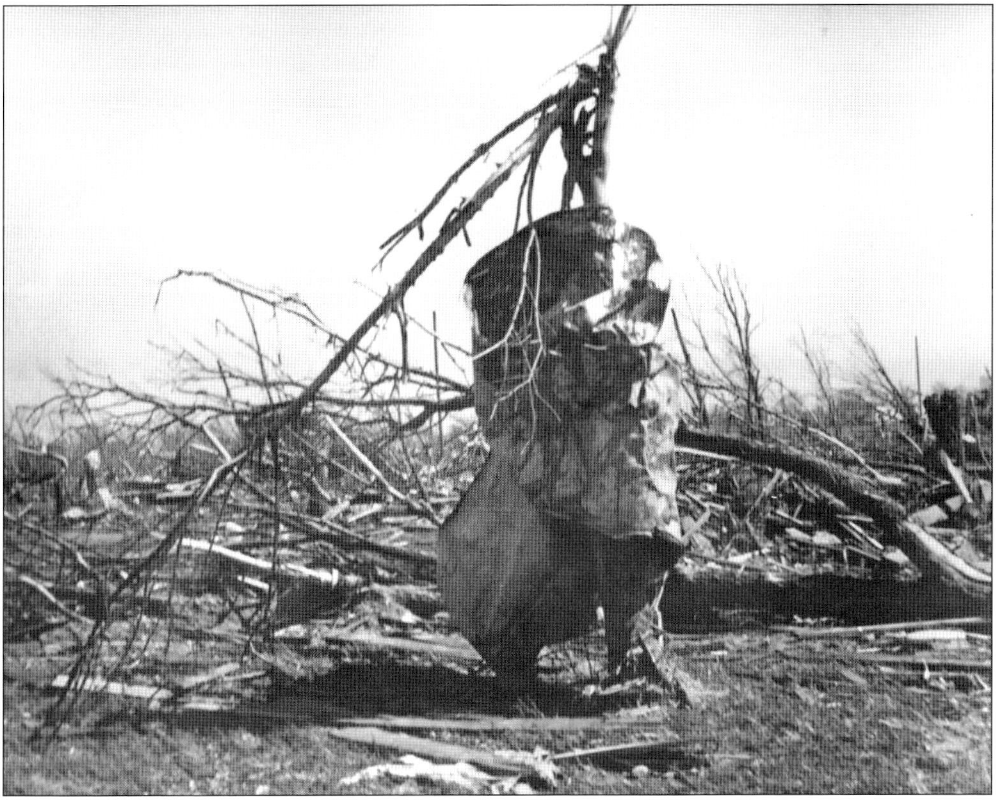

This image of twisted metal wrapped around a tree is a testament to the sheer destructive force of the winds in an F-5 tornado. According to the National Weather Service (NWS), an F-5 (Fujita scale) tornado can pack winds of between 261 and 318 miles per hour. The intensity phrase associated with an F-5 is "incredible tornado." Houses can be lifted completely off their foundations and carried for some distance.

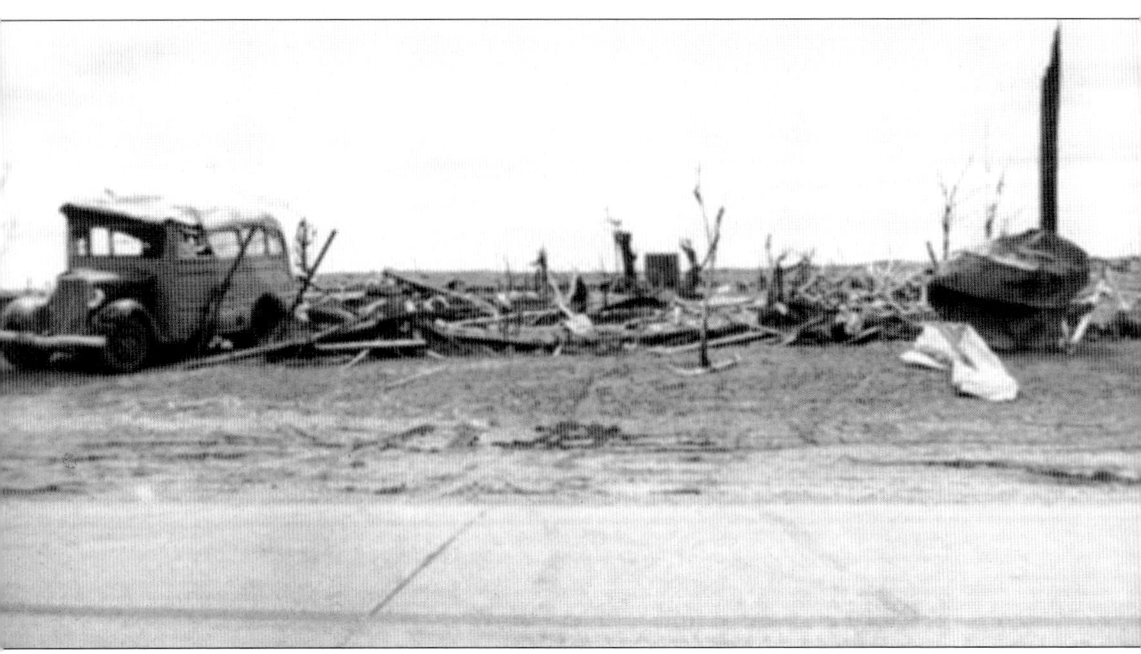

Seen here is a storm-damaged school bus. Because of damage to the North Ward School (later Madison Park Elementary) and the West Ward School (later Westwood Elementary), along with very minor damage to the East Ward School (later Horace Mann) and Old Central School buildings (razed following the tornado), classes were canceled for the remainder of the school year. High school seniors were given their diplomas. What would become the Woodward Junior High School building was rapidly constructed just to the north of the high school building and opened in 1948 to help with the overflow. In the meantime, until the damaged schools could be rebuilt, classes were held all over town in the temporary buildings, community centers, and churches.

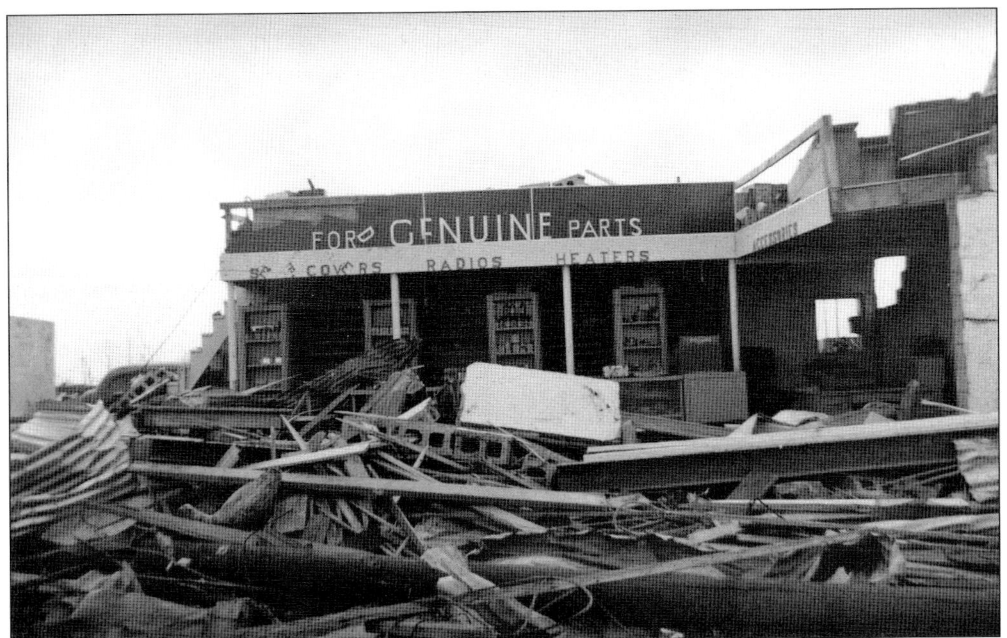

This is a photograph of damage to the Ferguson Ford Motor Company, located along Main Street and owned by Dwight Ferguson. Note the exposed stairs leading up to the second floor of the building. This image was captured the day after the tornado.

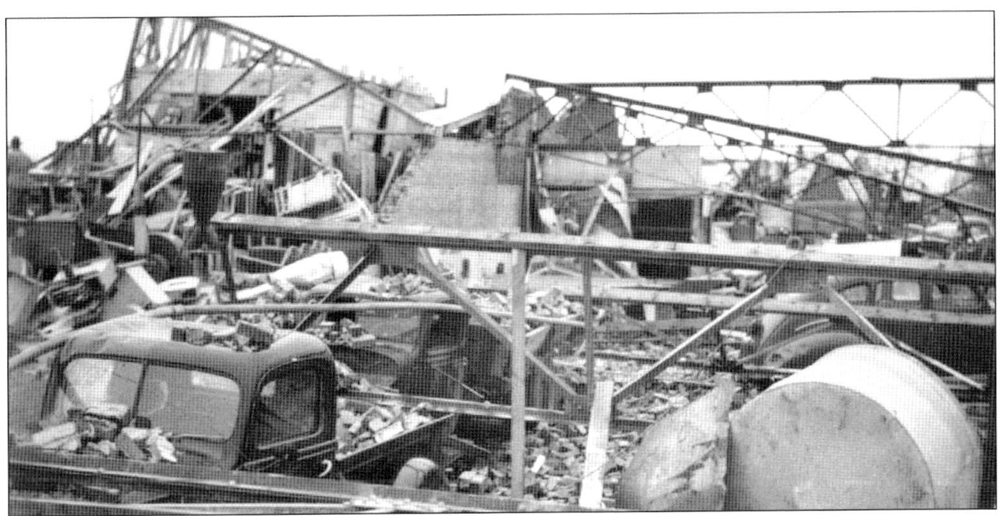

Seen here is another angle of the damage to the Ferguson Ford building on Main Street next to the Carl Ticer Equipment business. The business was completely and utterly destroyed. Of particular concern locally were the totally wrecked combines and tractors in the Ferguson inventory that would be needed for the upcoming harvest. Owner Dwight Ferguson was the brother of Congressman Phil Ferguson.

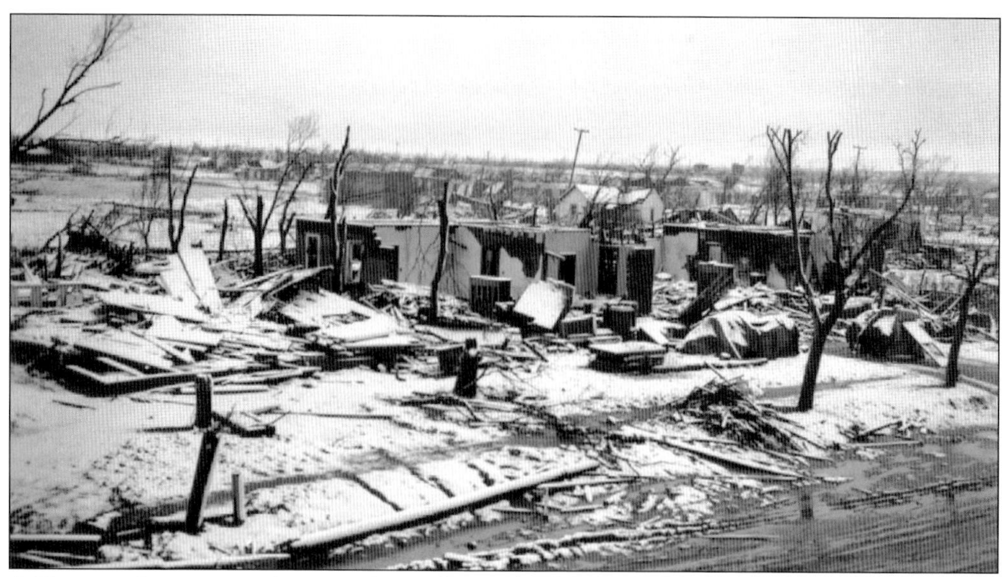

Adding insult to injury, the immediate aftermath of the 1947 tornado brought three inches of snowfall. This photograph taken early the next morning following the storm shows an unknown residence with snow on the ground. Note the snow-covered piano in the center of the picture.

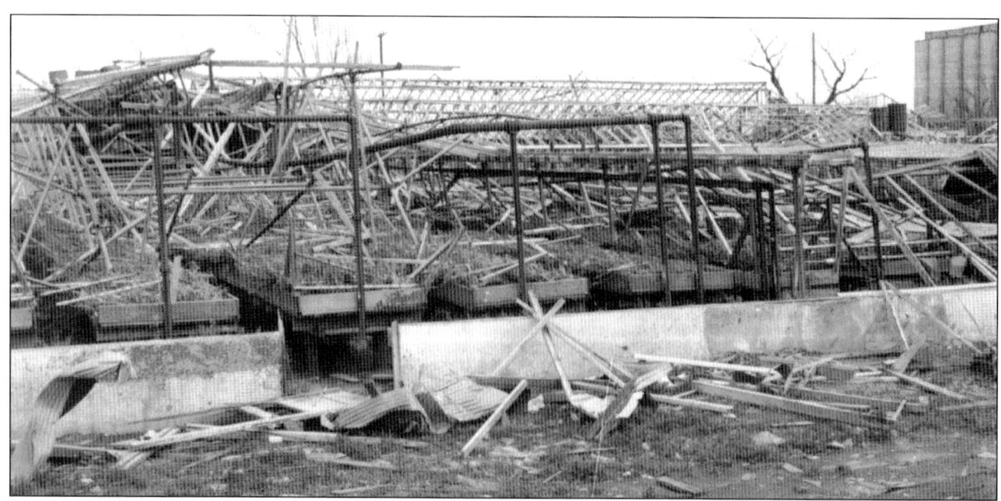

Obviously, a greenhouse is no match for the force of an F-5 tornado. This photograph shows the remains of a greenhouse that was part of a business known as Woodward Florist, owned by Ernest and Ethel Brinkman. The location was 1115 Madison Avenue in the north part of town. The Fisher Grain elevators can be seen in the background.

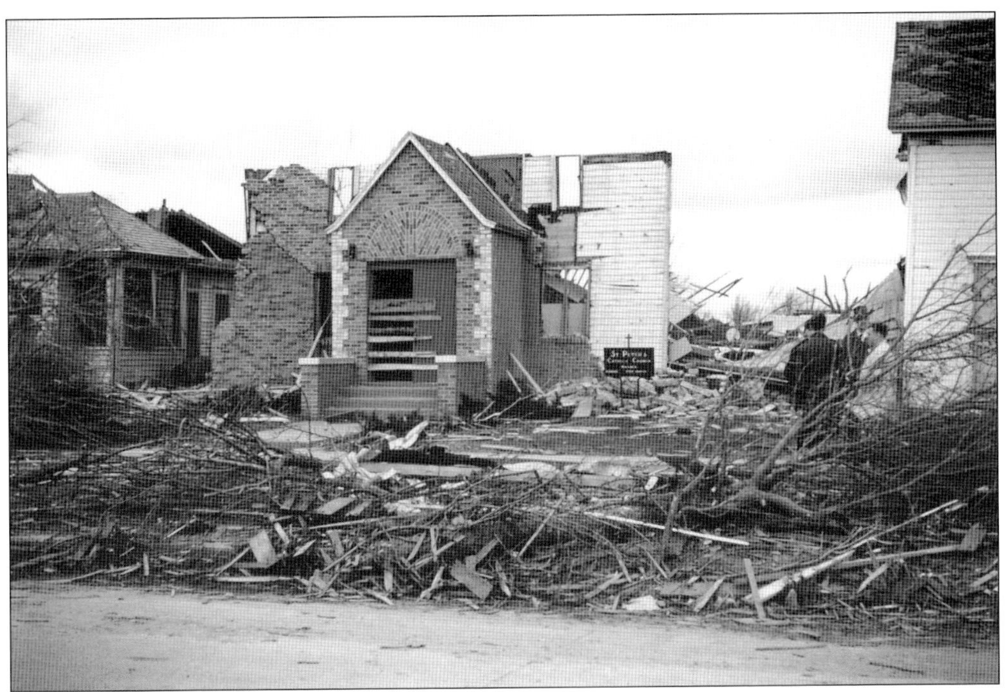

These photographs show the remains of St. Peter's Catholic Church, at that time located just to the east of the Woodward County Courthouse along Main Street. Only part of the front edifice and the entrance remained following the storm. Catholic parishioners met at the Presbyterian church for a time before moving to a Quonset hut erected on the north end of the property upon which a new church was built on the corner of Twenty-First Street and Oklahoma Avenue.

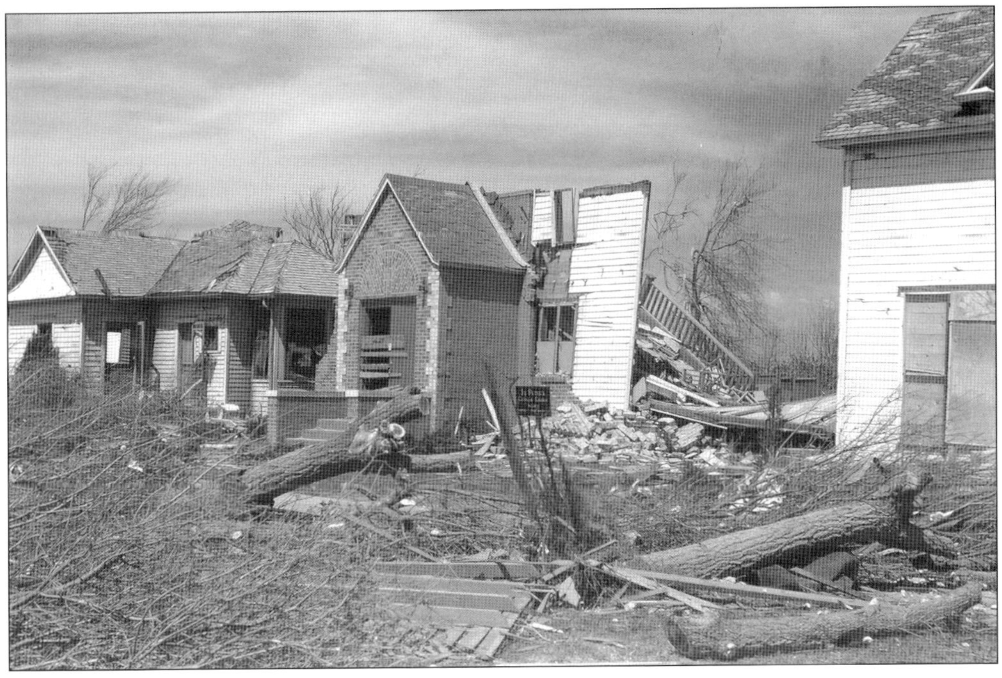

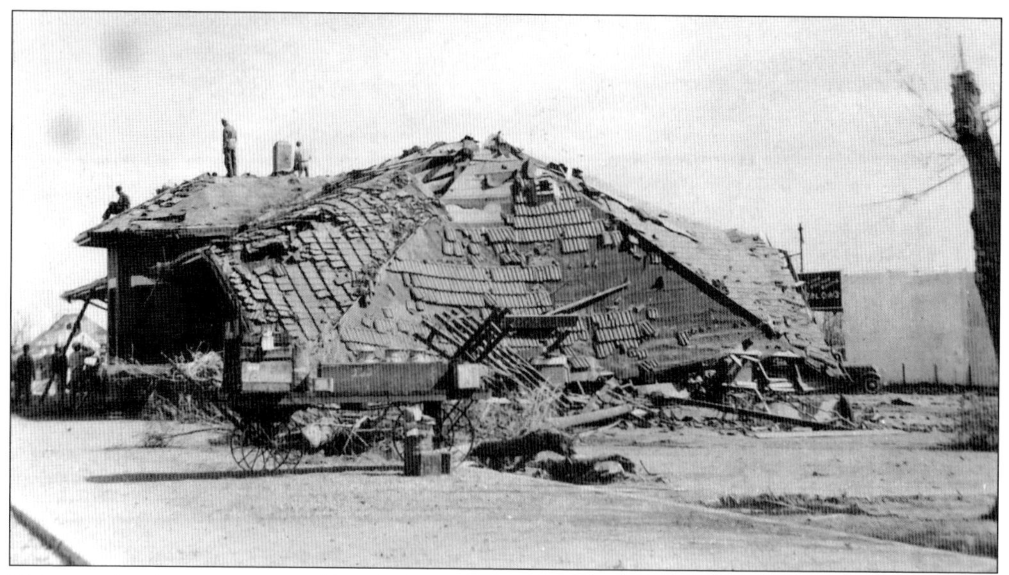

This was the damage sustained by the MKT (Katy) Railroad terminal on Main Street following the tornado. The Katy was still a viable railroad in 1947, so the building was reconstructed. The rebuilt property today has been repurposed as the Chiropractic Health Center.

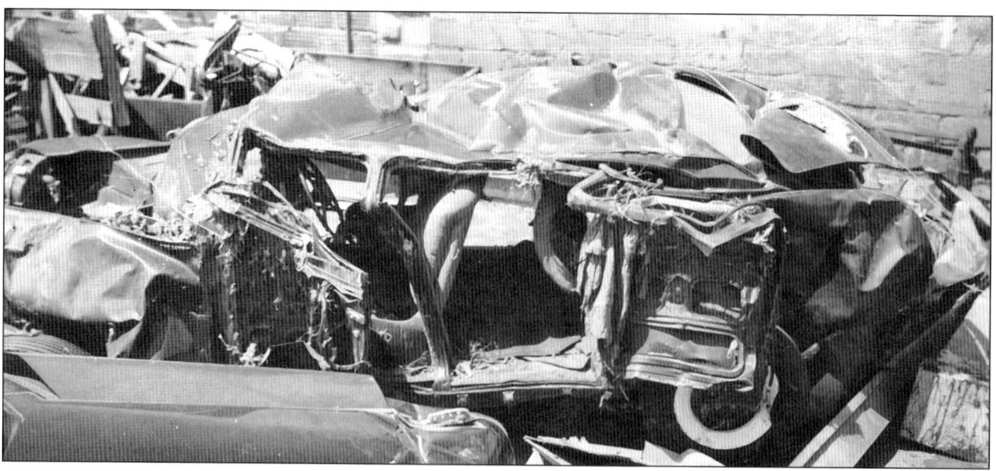

This photograph, taken by Everett McDonald, shows a 1946 Plymouth that was no match for the fury of the storm. It is a total loss. In addition to the sheer speed of the winds in the Woodward tornado, it is said that the force of those winds exerted 600 pounds per square foot. It is a small wonder that large, heavy automobiles such as this one were tossed around.

This is G.M. Williams's Pontiac upside down on the home of Thomas Baker. According to a newspaper report of the time, the car was blown from 1721 Main Street to 1701 Main Street—from Eighteenth and Main Streets to Seventeenth and Main Streets, an entire city block—before landing in Baker's dining room.

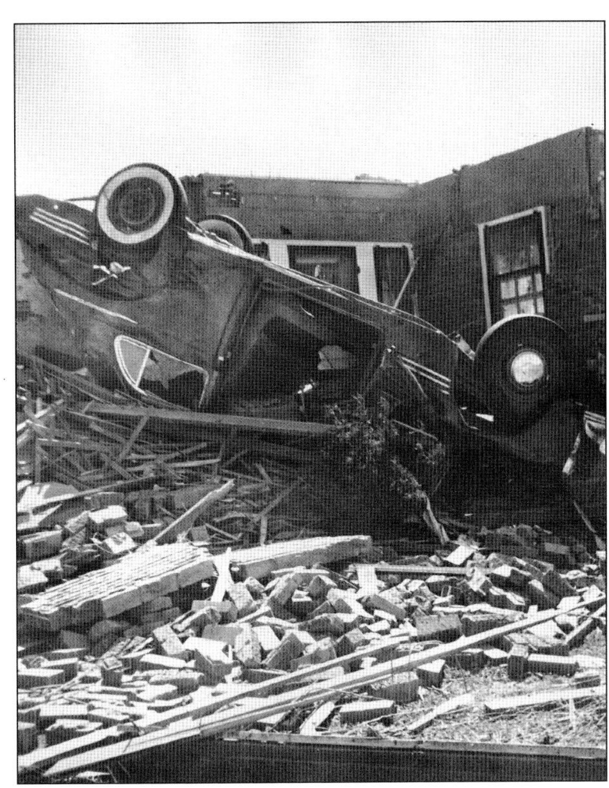

This photograph of an indeterminate location shows a debris field with three damaged homes in the background. Beyond the homes, railroad cars can be seen, so this was likely along the Santa Fe Railway line. Note the photographer with a tripod on the right side of the photograph. Tornado tourists were everywhere following the storm.

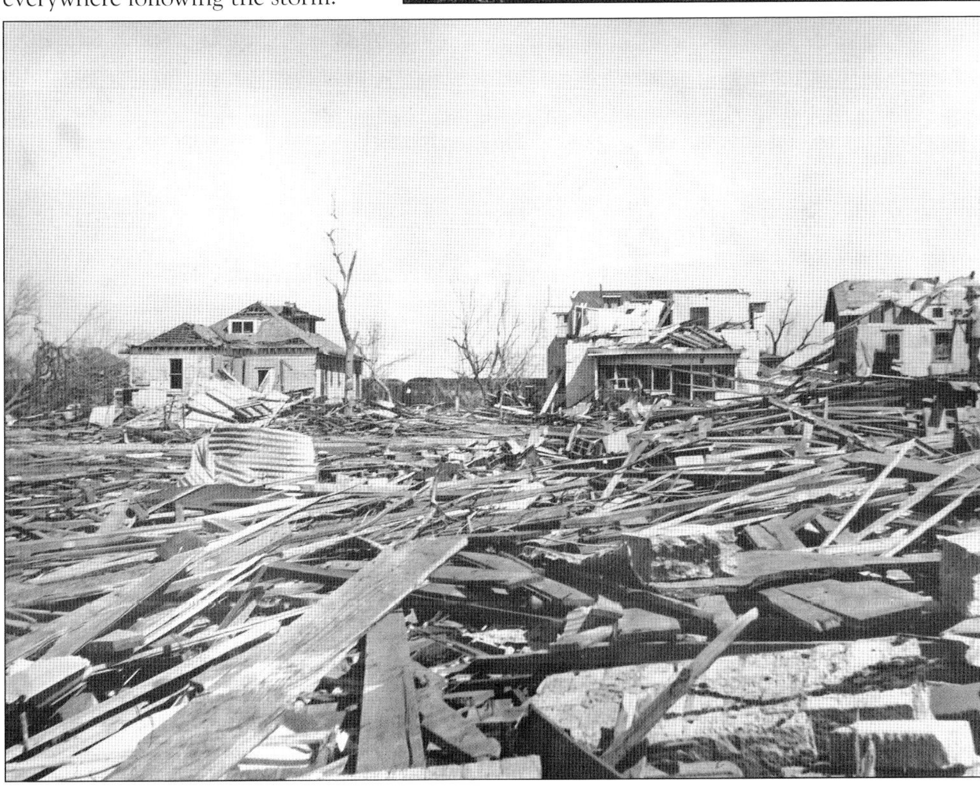

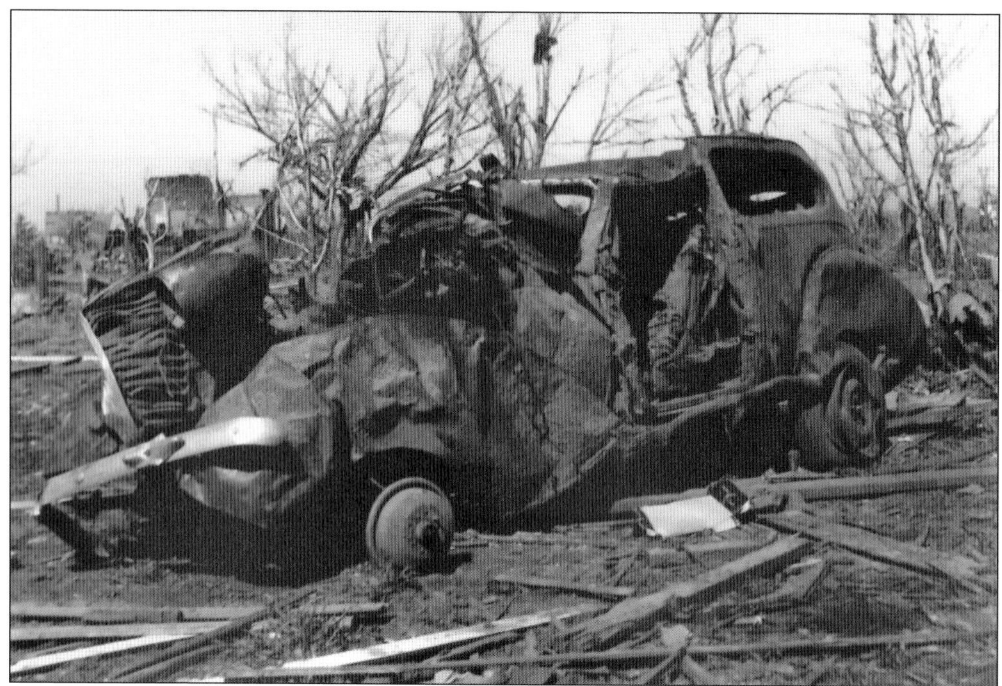

This vehicle not only suffered damage from being tossed about by tornadic winds but appears to have burned as well. A number of fires broke out as the tornado passed but were confined to a commercial area along Eighth Street just north of the railroad tracks. Fire crew efforts were hampered by the lack of water pressure due to no electricity for pumps but were aided by torrential rains.

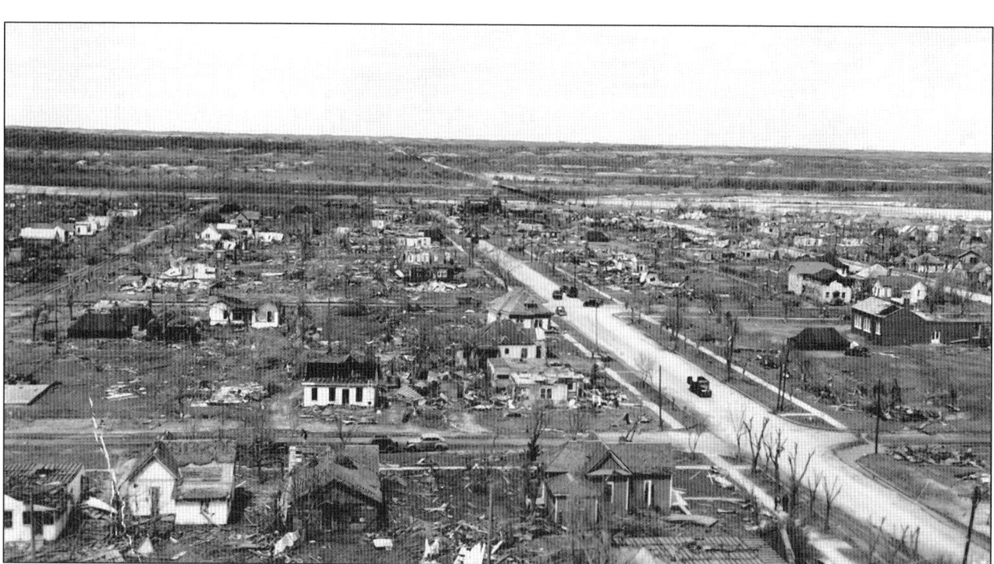

This photograph was shot from the air, possibly atop the Fisher Grain elevator headhouse, looking north toward the North Canadian River. The light-colored thoroughfare on the right side of the image is Ninth Street. The remains of the OG&E power plant can be seen at the end of the street. The heavily damaged Eighth Street bridge is to the right of the plant.

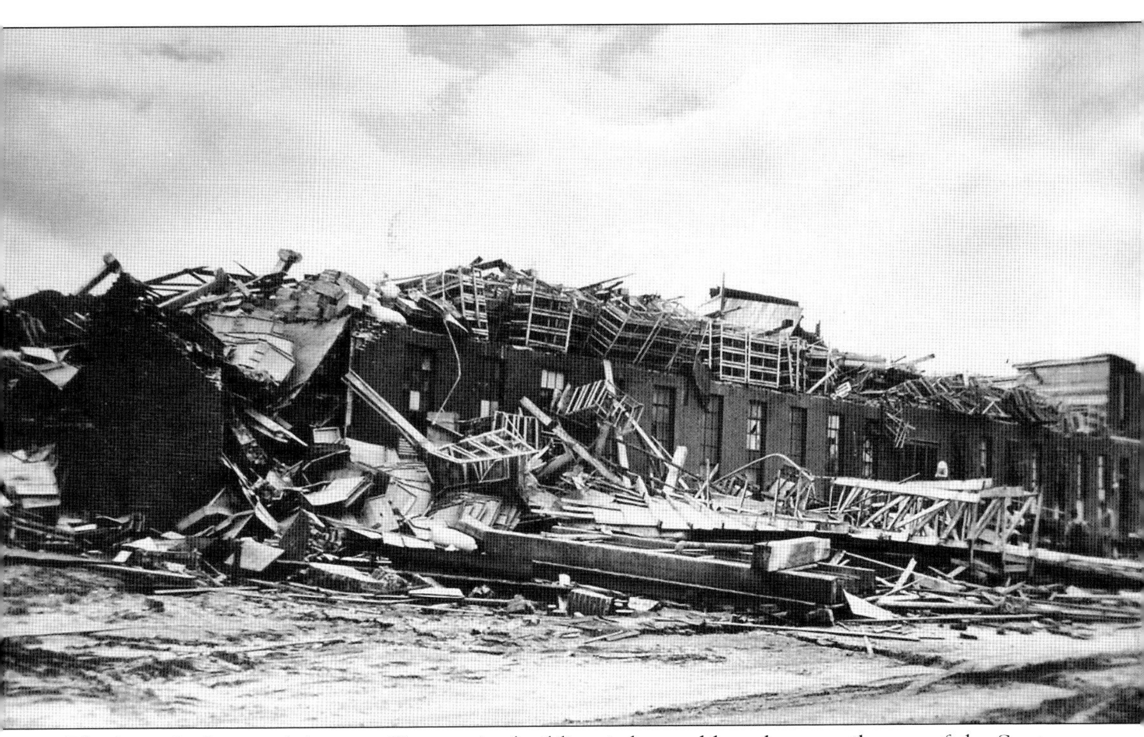

The heavily damaged Armour Creameries building is located less than a mile east of the Santa Fe Railway terminal along the railroad tracks. The creamery was rebuilt on the same spot and remains standing, though unused, today. Cream production was big business in Woodward in the first half of the 20th century with millions of pounds of cream shipped annually via rail to different areas of the country. The manager of the Woodward Armour Creameries plant was instructed to remove all meats and dairy products from the building and donate them to relief organizations.

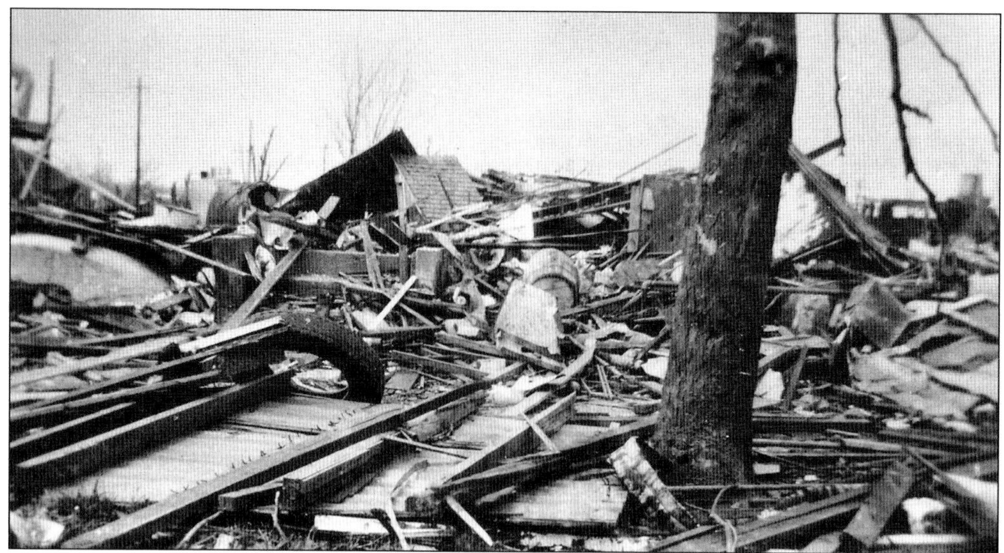

Inscribed on the back of this photograph are the words "Why bulldozers and cranes are needed after a tornado," as it shows a heavy debris field in an unidentified location. Note the panel with exposed nails sticking up. Hazards like that would have been commonplace, making yet another case for heavy machinery to assist in cleanup.

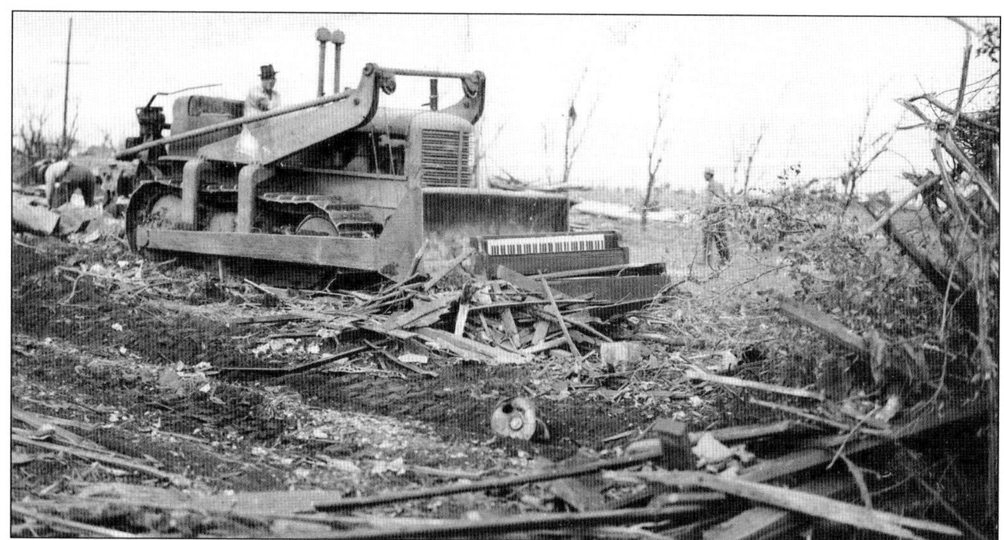

Trash and debris from the storm were piled by bulldozers for easier pickup by the cranes (in this case including someone's piano). All of the debris picked up after the storm was hauled away by trucks to a location along Thirty-Fourth Street where it was dumped and later covered. The site is currently occupied by the Woodward Convention Center and Northwestern Oklahoma State University (NWOSU) Woodward Campus.

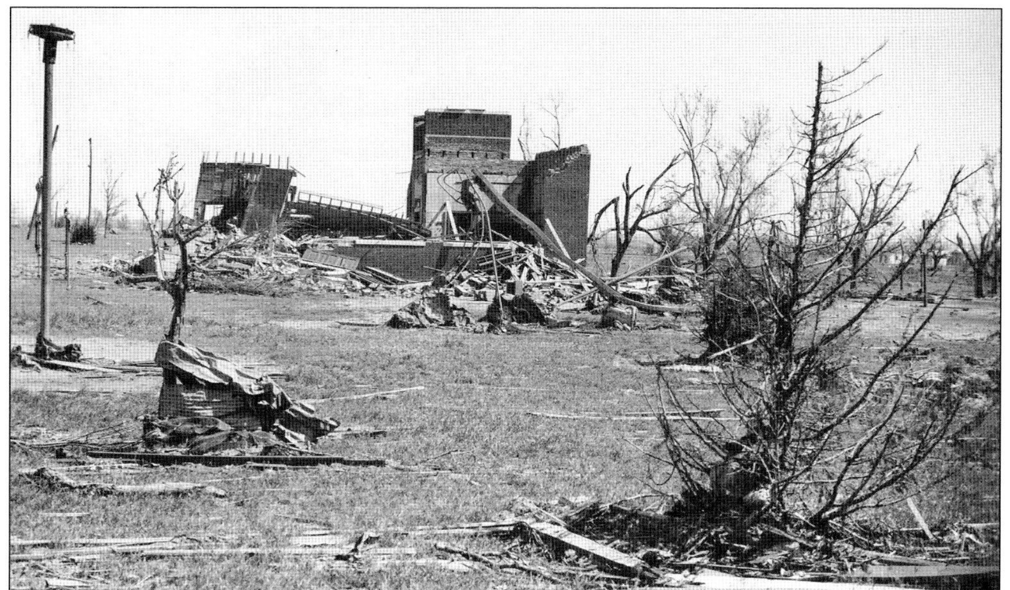

This building, identified as the West Ward School (elementary school) on the northwest corner of Kansas Avenue and Nineteenth Street, was later rebuilt and named Westwood Grade School. The rebuilt structure remains today and serves as the Woodward Christian Academy. This was one of four schools that experienced severe damage in the storm and had to be reconstructed quickly to accommodate area children.

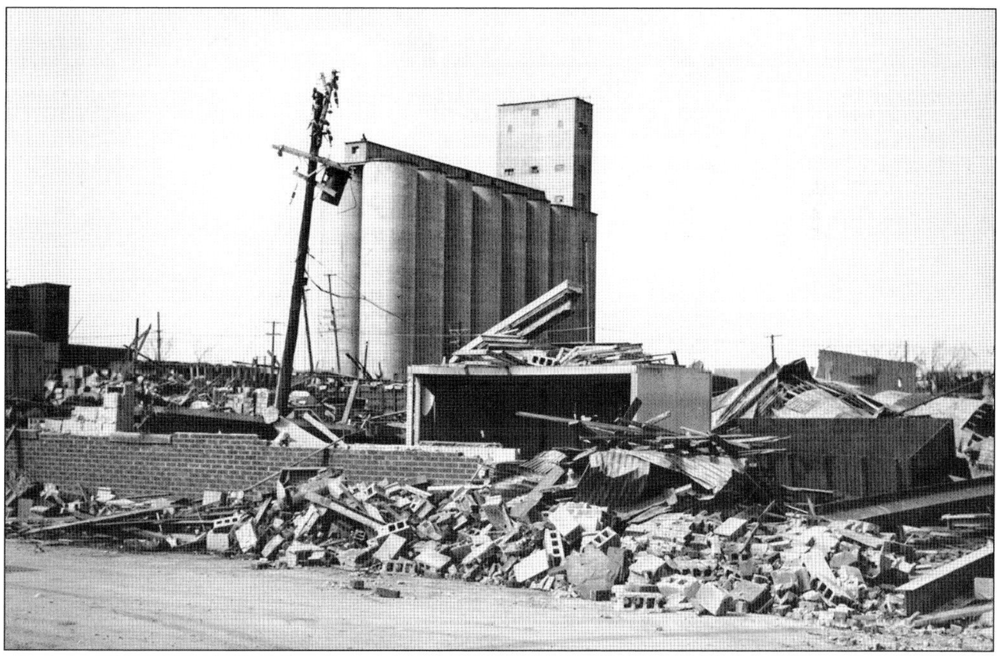

This view looks southwest toward the Fisher Grain elevators, possibly from Webster Avenue and Eighth Street. The photograph is a particularly good example of the destruction wrought on structures north of the railroad tracks in Woodward. Note the steel I-beams lying on the ground, completely torn loose from whatever building they were supporting. Despite broken windows to the upper headhouse of the grain elevator, the large concrete structure remained intact.

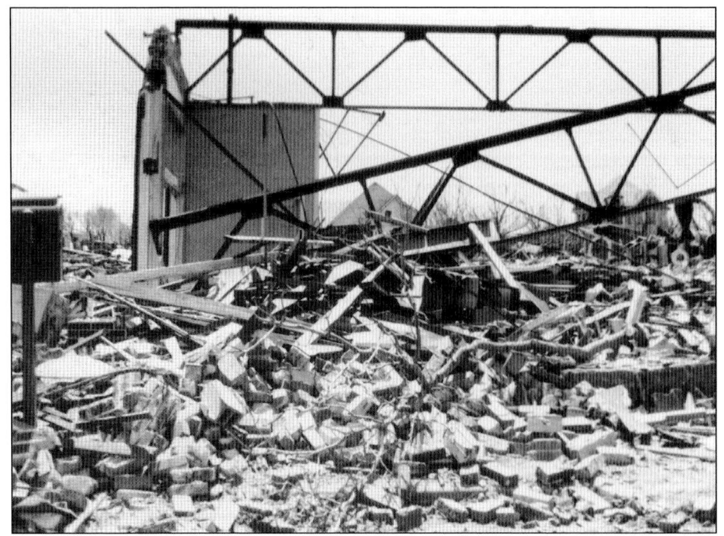

This photograph shows an unidentified commercial building with its metal framing exposed. The home with gables in the background was built by prominent businessman John Gerlach and located on the southwest corner of Eleventh Street and Texas Avenue facing north. The authors believe that this would have put this building along Main Street in the 1000 block.

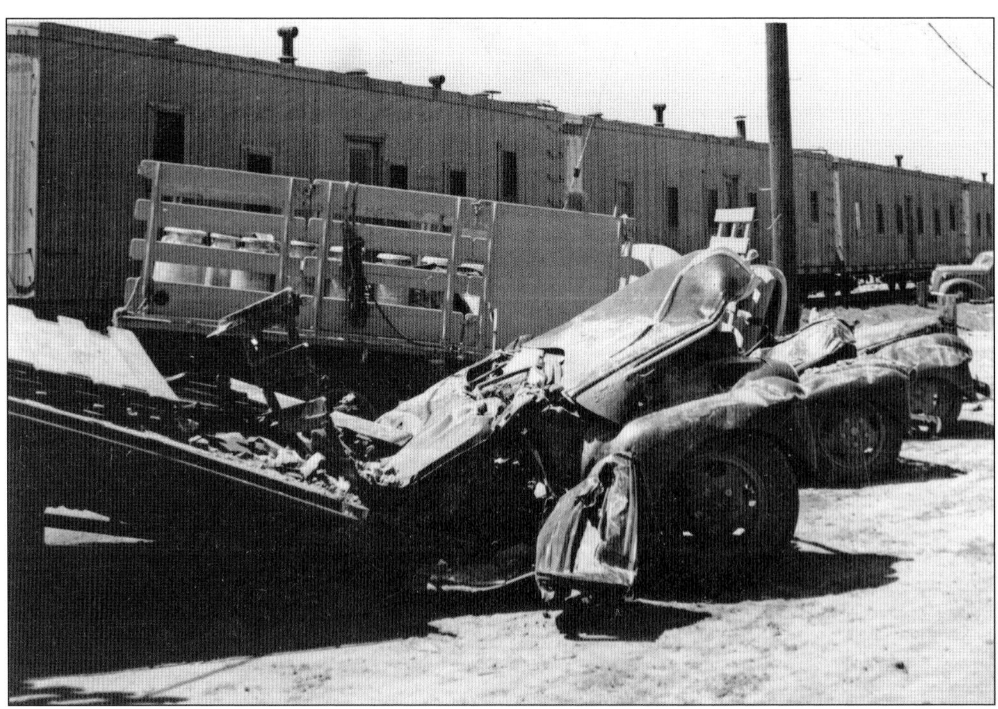

Several wrecked trucks are lined up near the railroad tracks, possibly near the creamery—note the truck with milk cans in the back. Also, the boxcars appear to be refrigerated railway cars. The Armour Creameries building was located just to the east of the Santa Fe depot with its own side rail for loading cream cans onto trains for transport.

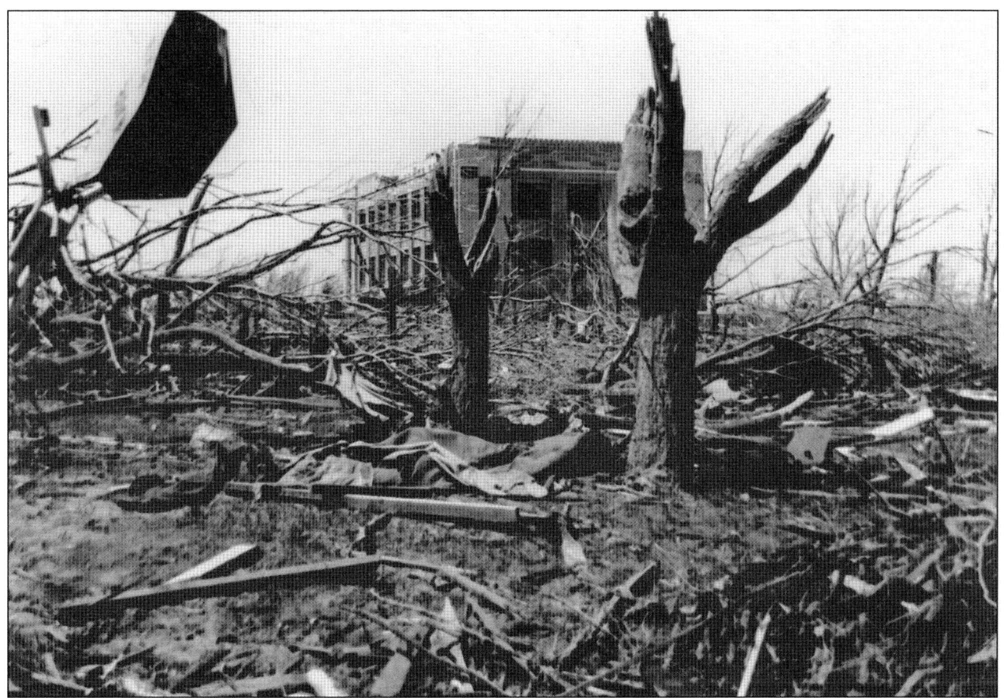

This photograph shows the debris field, which appears to be a combination of downed trees, twisted metal, and scraps of wood, to the east of the Woodward County Courthouse. This image was likely captured from the northwest corner of the intersection of Main and Fifteenth Streets (the current location of the Woodward Public Library).

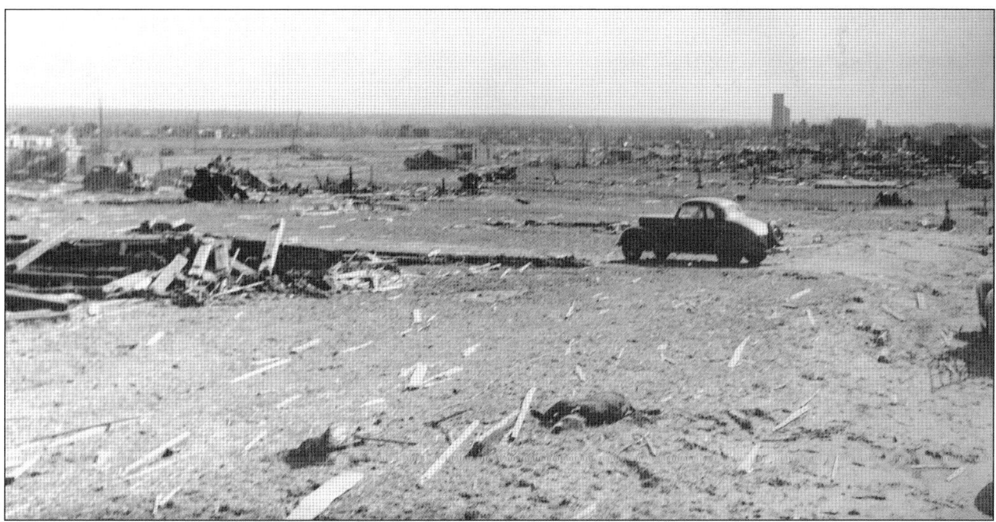

This scene looks northeast on the west end of Woodward in the Highland Park Addition. There is a dead calf in the foreground, most likely picked up by the tornado and dropped where it lay. The Fisher elevator and courthouse are in the distance. Note the scraps of wood on the ground pointing in the same direction, indicating wind direction as they were blown.

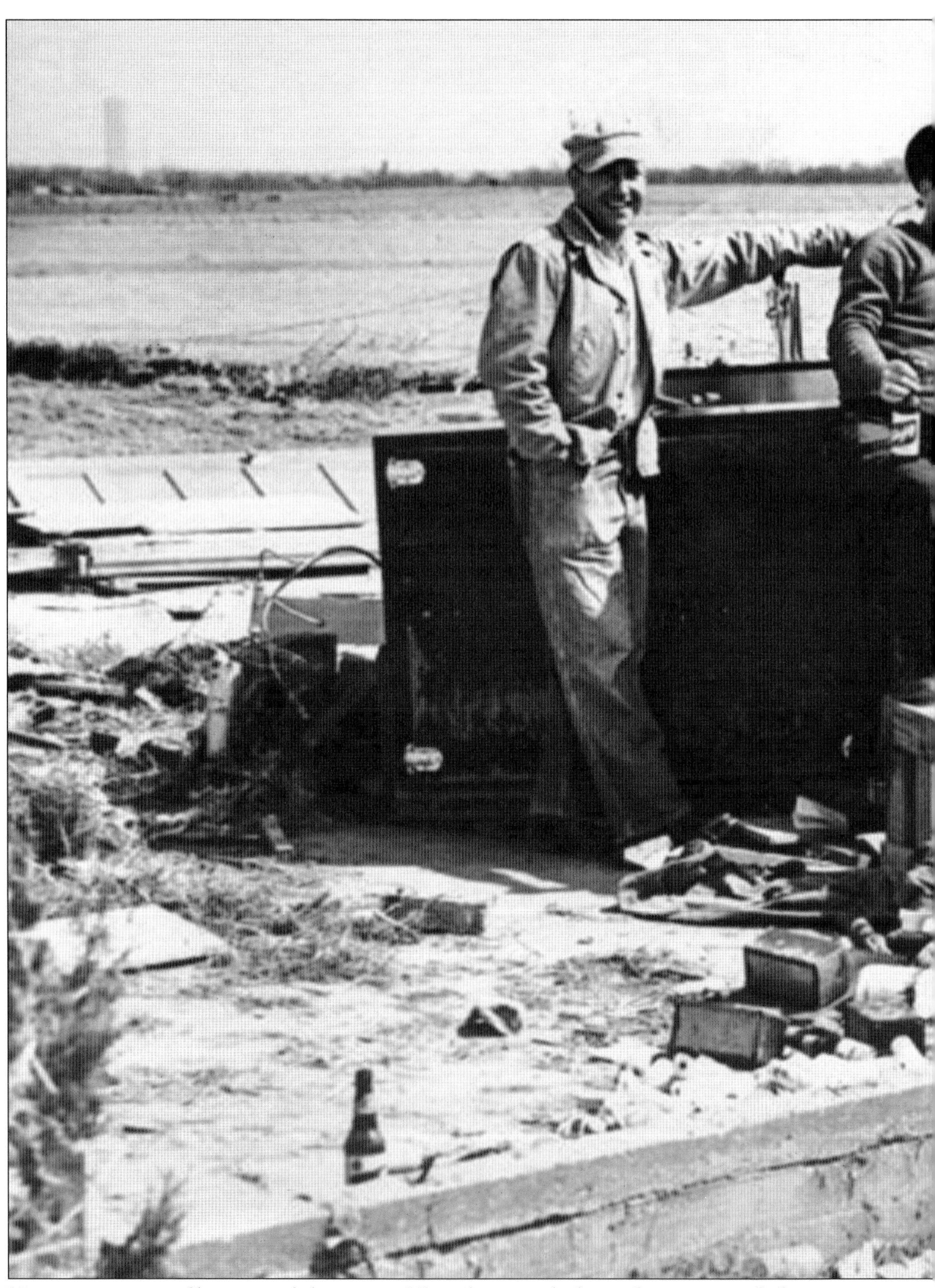

Here is a moment of levity amid the misery. This photograph shows the remains of a beer tavern on West Main Street called the Bele-Ve-Dere. The men are identified as co-owners Hubert Feese (left) and Alexander "Sauce" Wassenmiller (right). Hubert and Sauce lean against the bar, the only remaining piece of the business. Feese and Sauce were in the bar when the tornado hit and

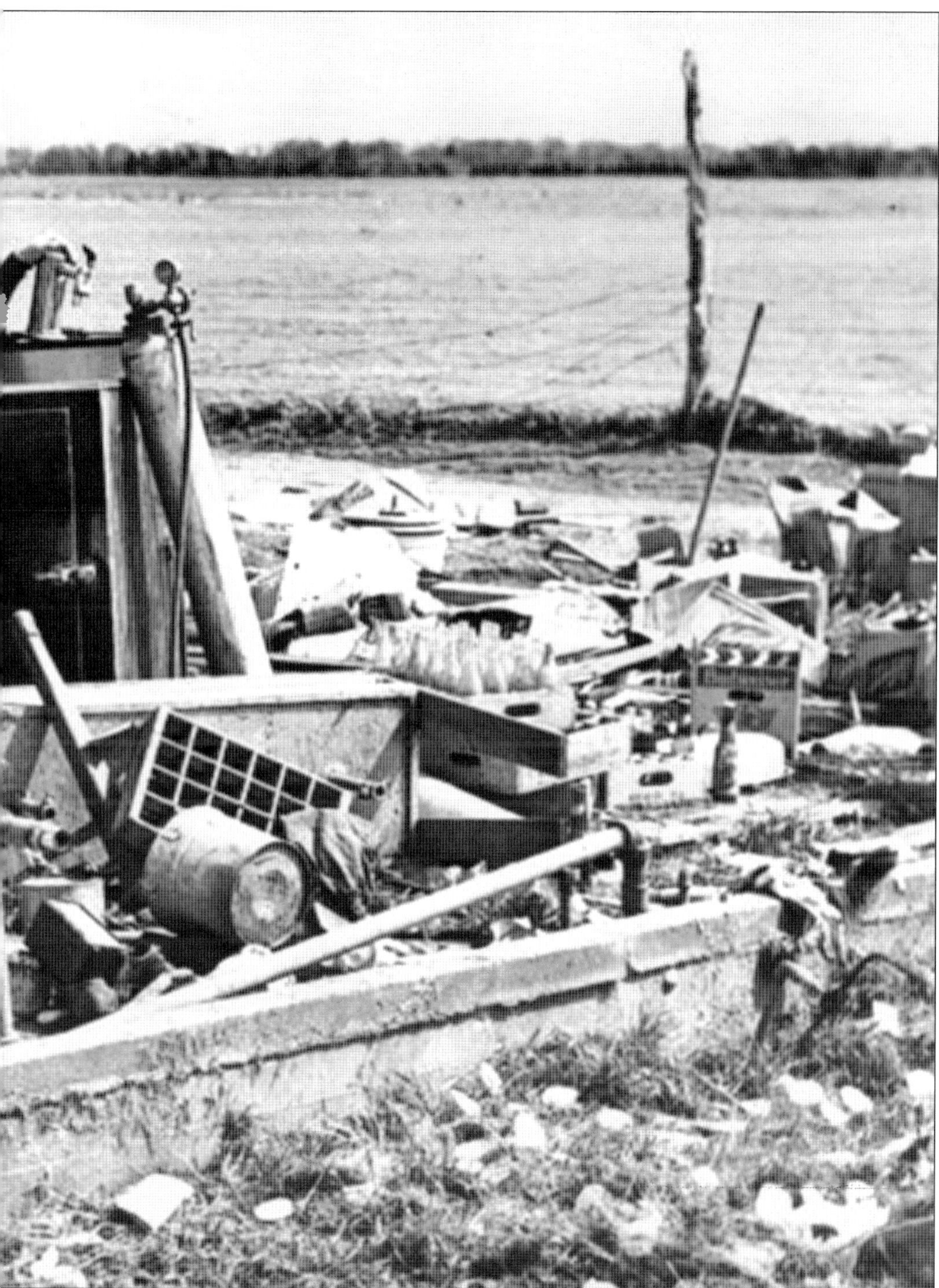

ducked down behind the bar for cover. Feese worked as an announcer at KSIW radio. He had, only a month or so before, been involved in an aircraft accident from which he walked away. Sauce and his wife, Pearl, left Oklahoma in the 1950s and moved to California. He passed away in 2004 in Palm Desert, California. After the tornado, Feese and Sauce moved their bar to Shattuck.

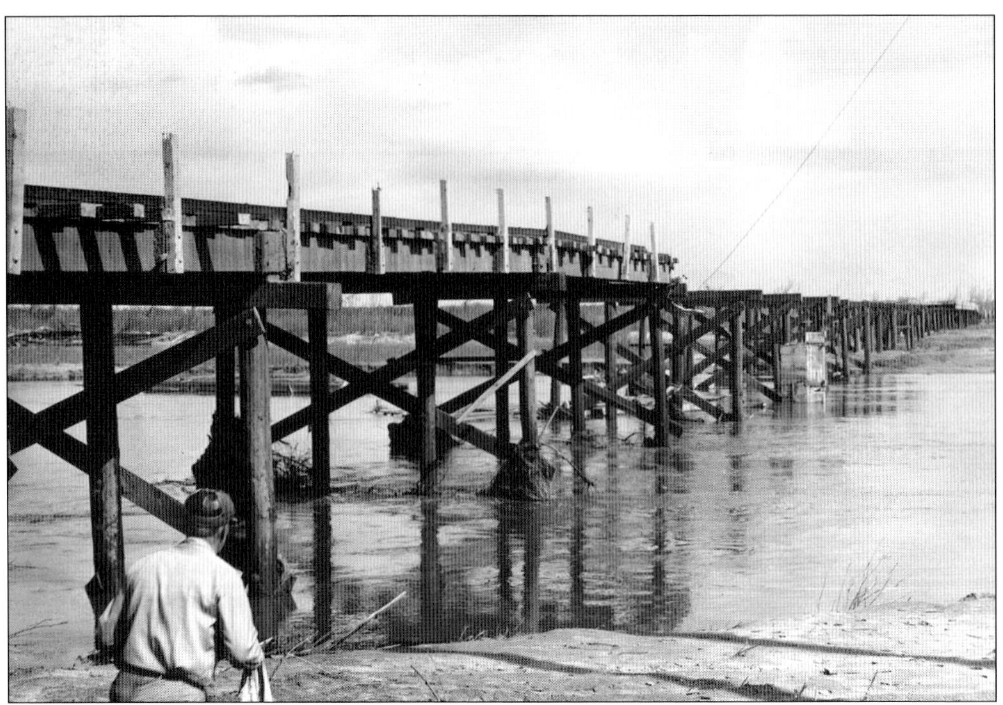

These photographs show the severe damage incurred by the Eighth Street bridge over the North Canadian River, which was part of the highway leading north out of town. Loss of the structure effectively cut off the city of Woodward from the north without having to travel several miles east or west to locate a way across. The bridge deck was rebuilt soon after the tornado and then replaced in the 1970s by a more modern concrete bridge that extended from Ninth Street.

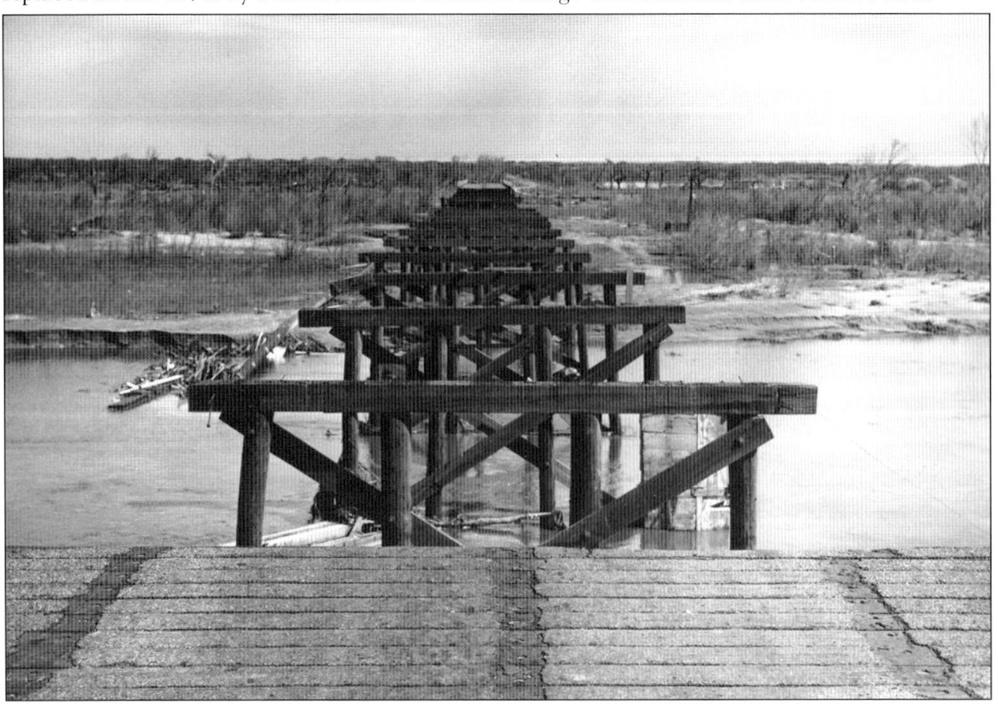

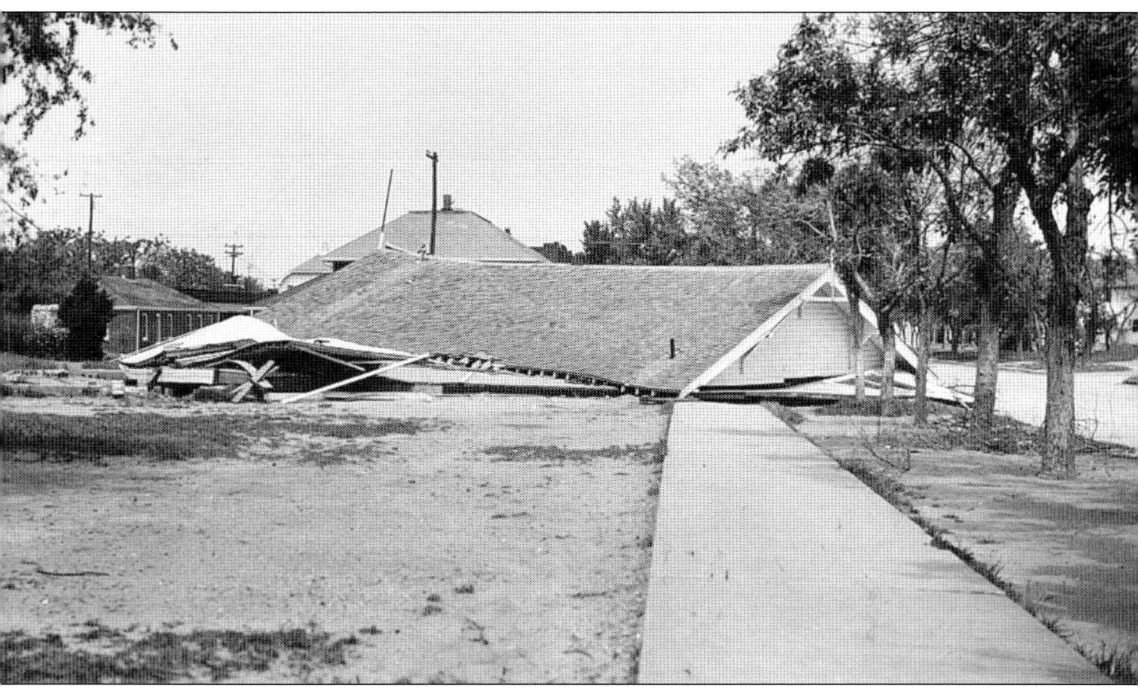

This image, captured by Everett McDonald, shows the remains of the school band building. The location appears to be the corner of Tenth Street and Maple Avenue. There is a gymnasium on the site now. This is one of at least two documented examples (the other on page 82) of entire roof structures being torn loose but remaining remarkably intact and landing on the ground. Meteorologists at the time said that winds on the edge of the tornado were moving at 75 miles per hour, but the core was estimated to have been as much as 450 miles per hour.

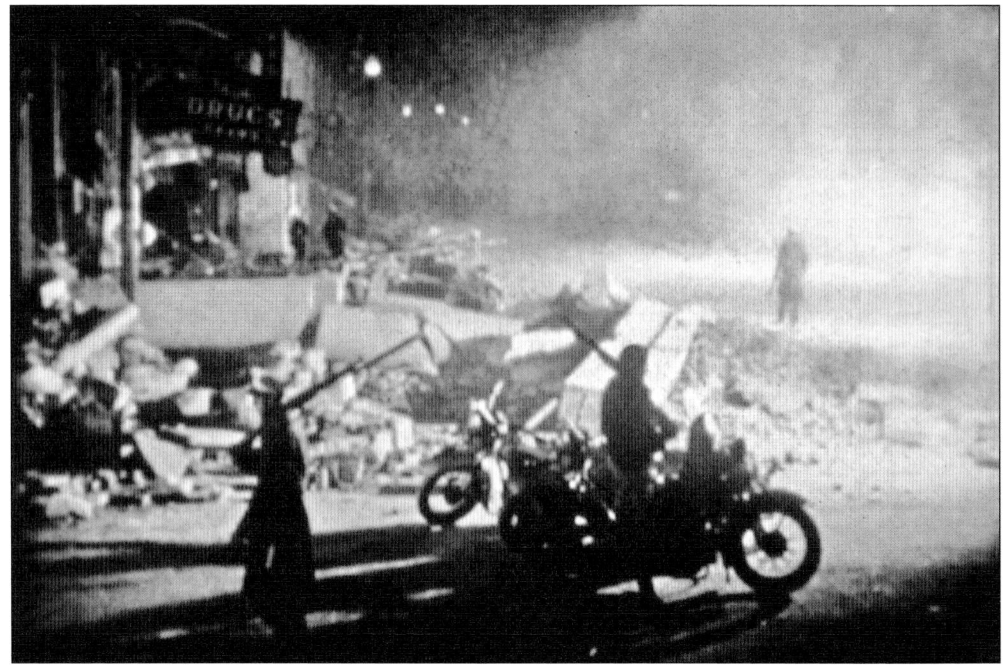

This image, taken at night, shows two military guards on duty, most likely along the 700 block of Main Street. Looting, or concerns about looting, became prevalent in the immediate aftermath of the storm. One newspaper in Chicago reported on April 10 that citizen vigilante committees had formed because of reports of looting of damaged and unoccupied shops and homes.

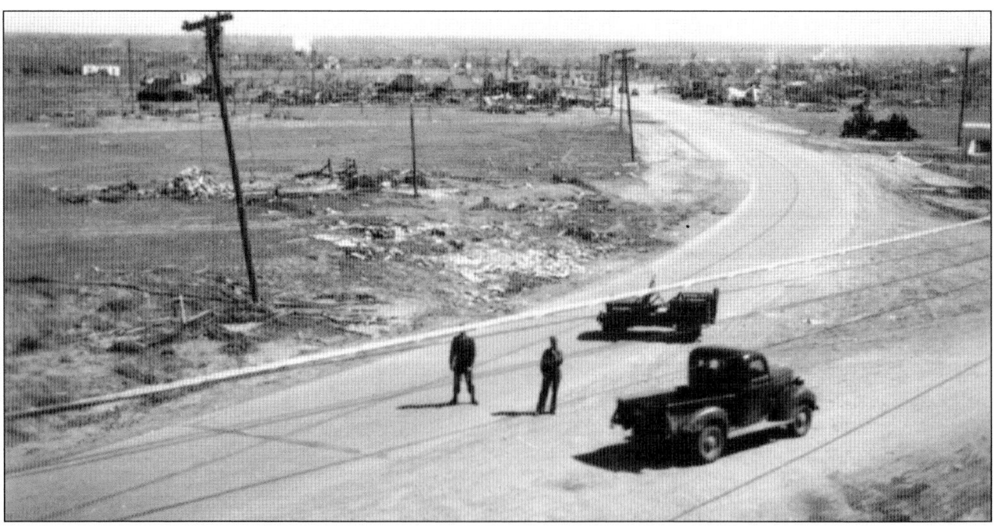

This is a photograph of what is apparently military police preventing curious sightseers or those with malicious intent from entering the city. As word of the destruction in Woodward reached Oklahoma City and other places in the region, there was a steady stream of tornado tourists trying to see the area for themselves. (Courtesy of the Oklahoma Historical Society.)

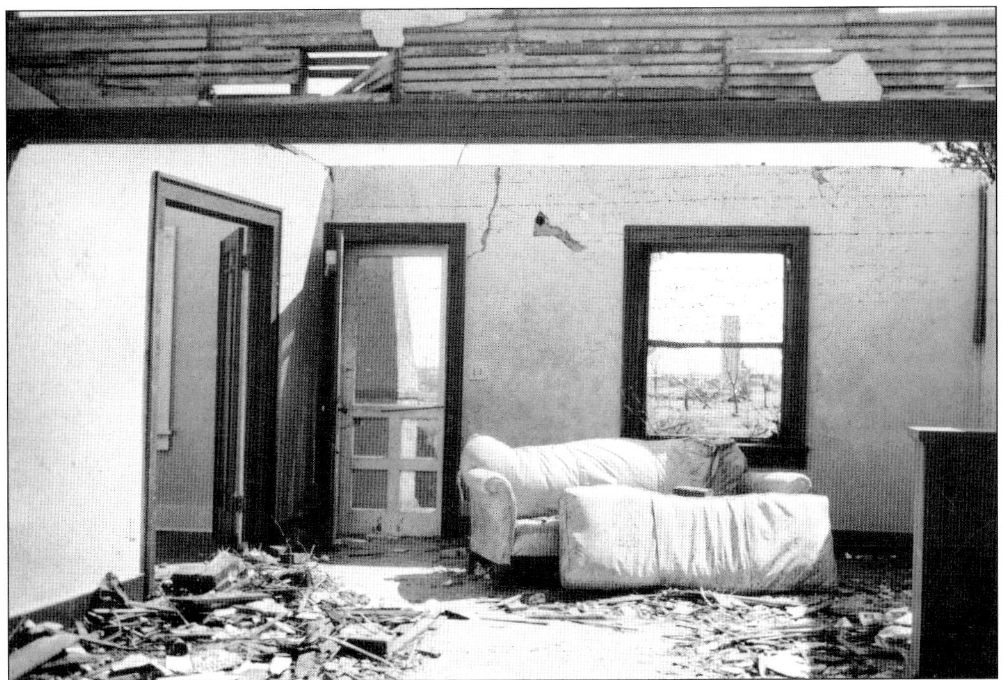

Like a scene from a surrealist painting, the interior of this home, despite the rubble on the floor, seems an oddly peaceful view. There is a lot to see in this image—the path through the living room; the missing roof; the load-bearing beam; and the Fisher Grain elevator in the background.

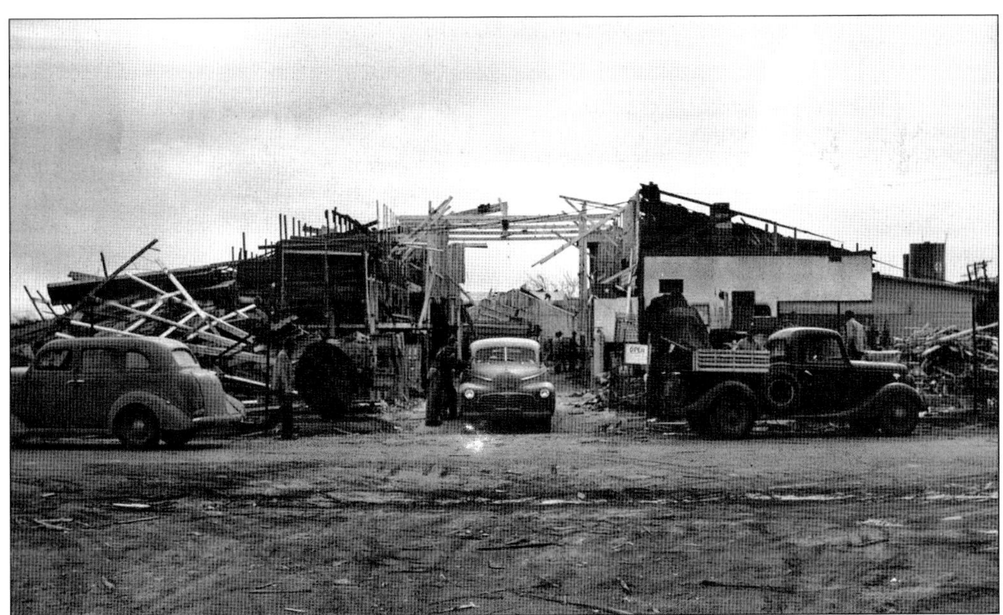

A photograph shows the front of the Osborne-Peebles Lumber Company along Eighth Street just north of the railroad tracks. Note the "Open" sign to the right of the entrance. Despite severe damage to the main office of the business, the lumberyard remained open, providing a critical service to those seeking to repair or begin rebuilding their homes.

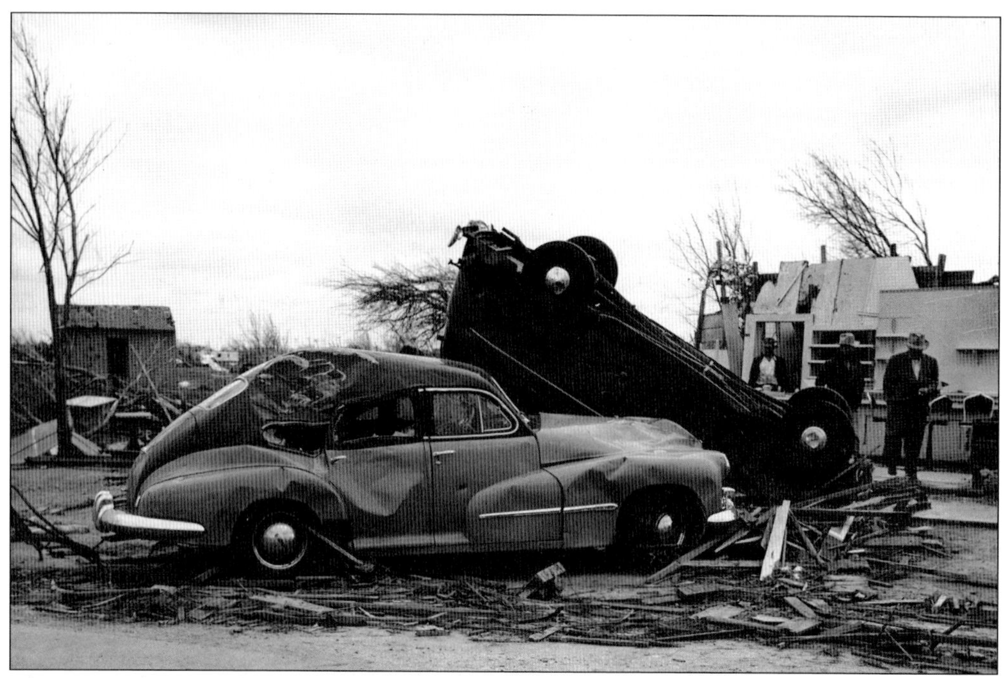

These two photographs show the extensive damage to the Oasis Steak House in Woodward after the 1947 tornado. The Oasis was founded by John Shelby, a Syrian immigrant, sometime around 1940. He sold the restaurant to Charles Pappe (later of Sonic Drive-in fame) on January 10, 1947, just months before the tornado. Pappe rebuilt the restaurant and then sold it in 1951. The restaurant was sited on an unusual triangular piece of land, with Twenty-Second Street to the east and South Main Street in front. A law office now occupies the rebuilt space.

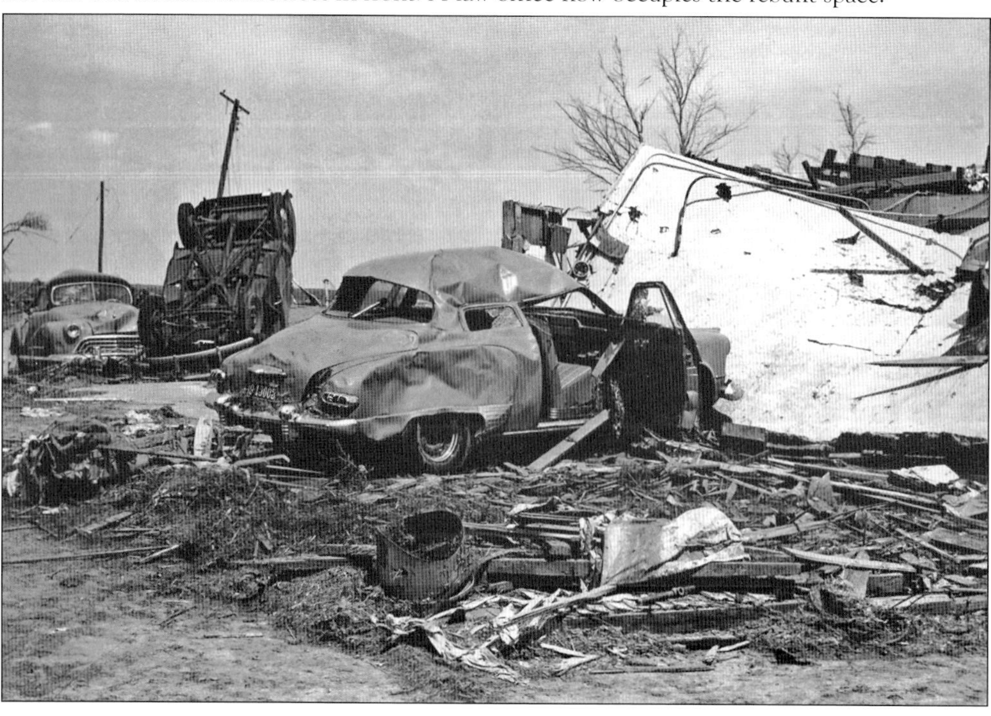

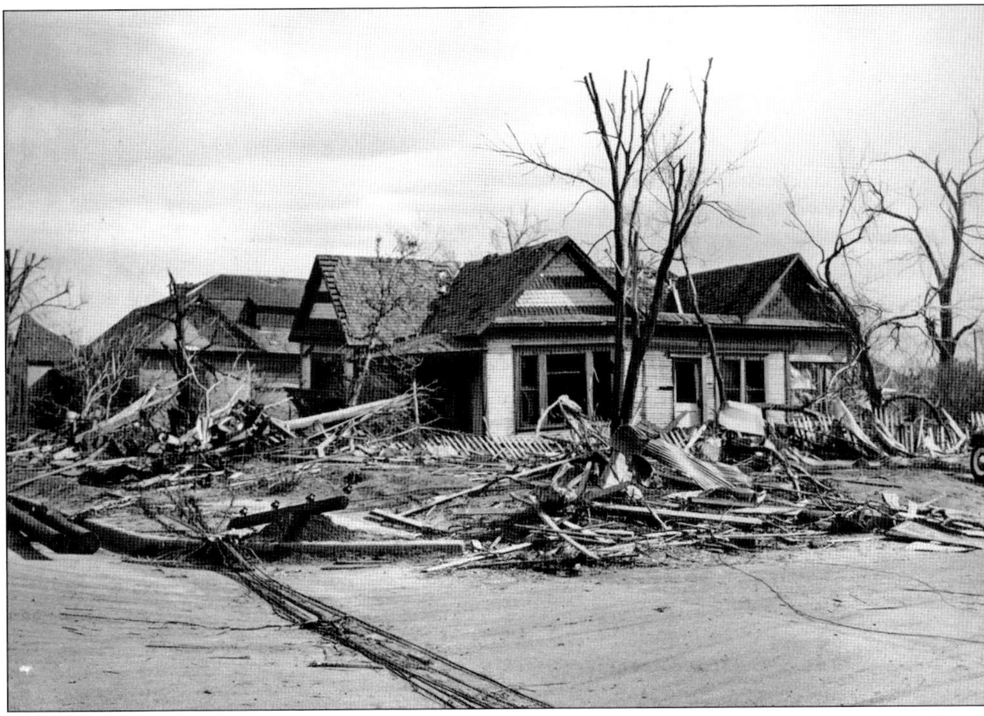

Seen here is an unidentified multigabled home located in the Cline Addition of the city (north of the railroad tracks). Note the picket fence blown back against the house, indicating the site was on the east side of the street in front. Power lines lay strewn across the ground.

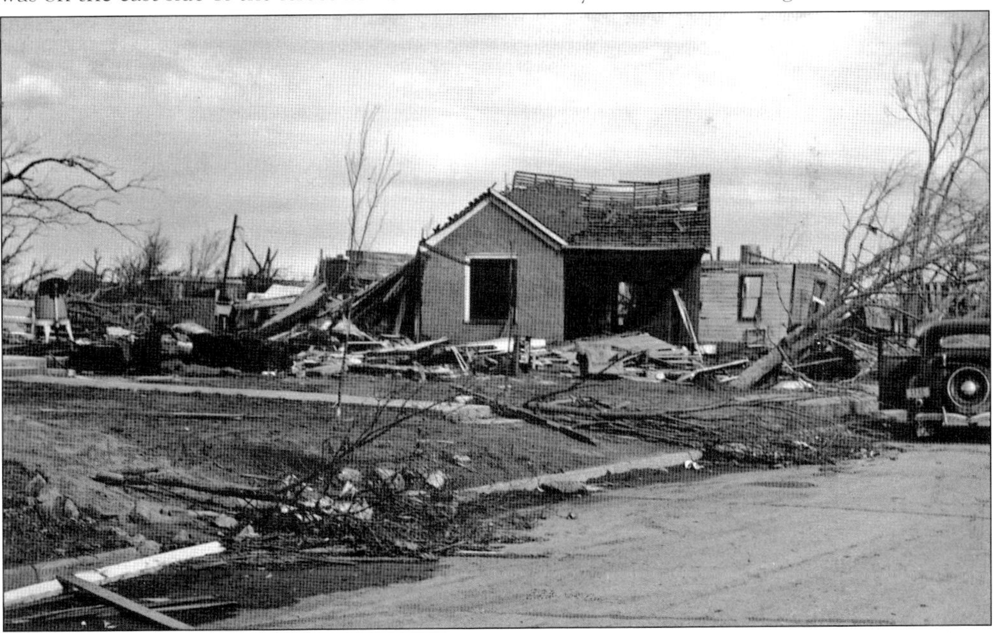

This is another unidentified home located in the Cline Addition. The structure appears to have been blown completely off its foundation. The sidewalk on the left side of the photograph leads to steps where a home used to stand. It is possible that the shell of a structure seen in the image was that home blown several feet to one side.

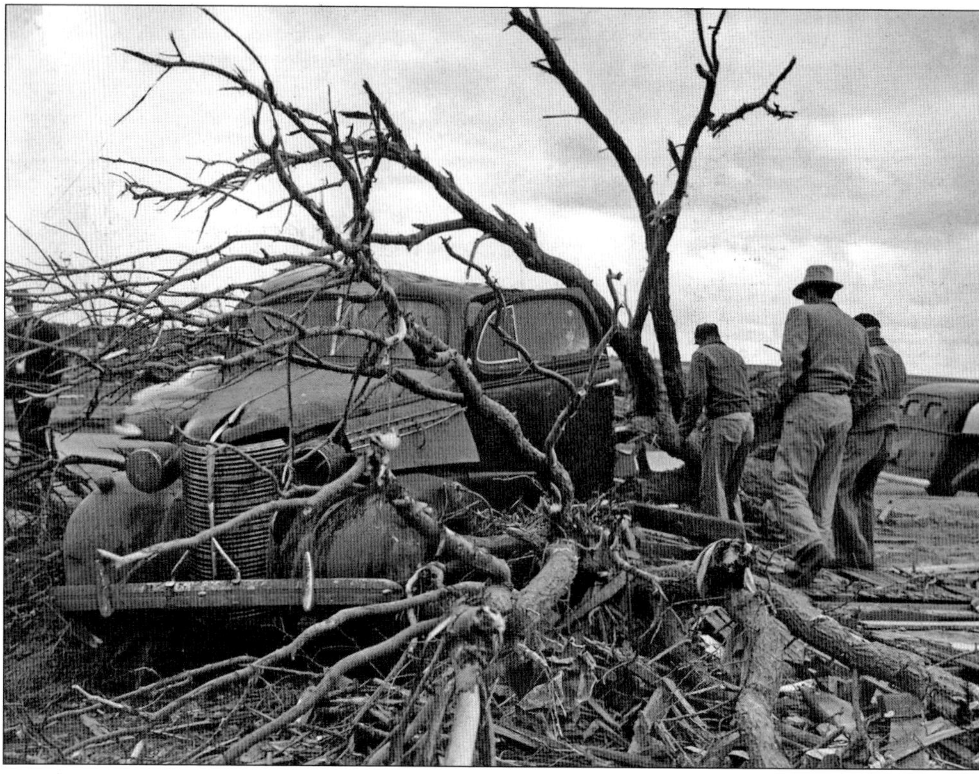

It is difficult to say whether this is a tree wrapped around a vehicle or a vehicle wrapped around a tree. Regardless, it is a tangled mess. The location was only identified as being the Highland Park Addition in the west end of the city. Several men appear to be looking for something around the vehicle.

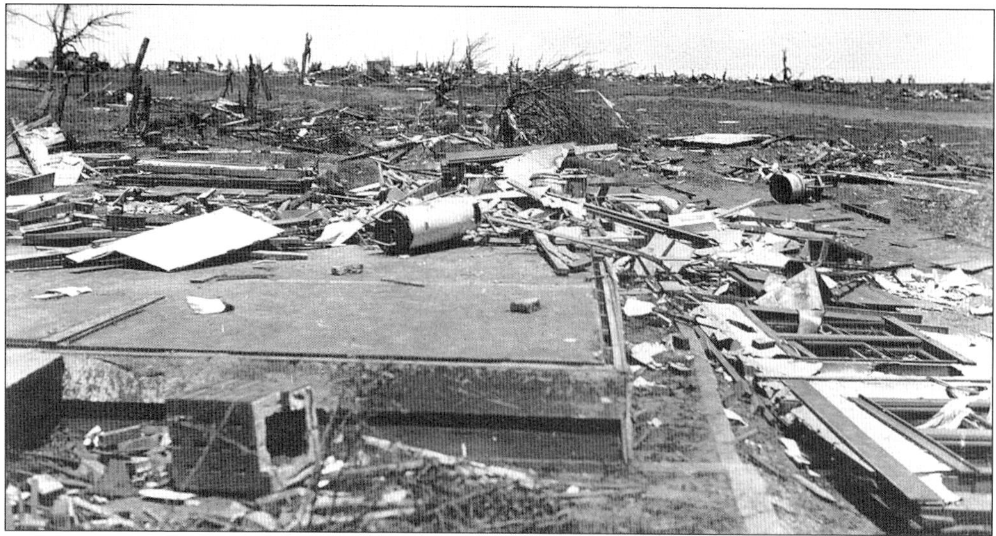

This photograph is a good example of the barren landscape left in the wake of the 1947 tornado, particularly on the west side of town. The leveled home in the foreground was identified as Marvin Ervin's home. Note that the house appears to have exploded, with entire walls lying on the ground on the right side and at the back.

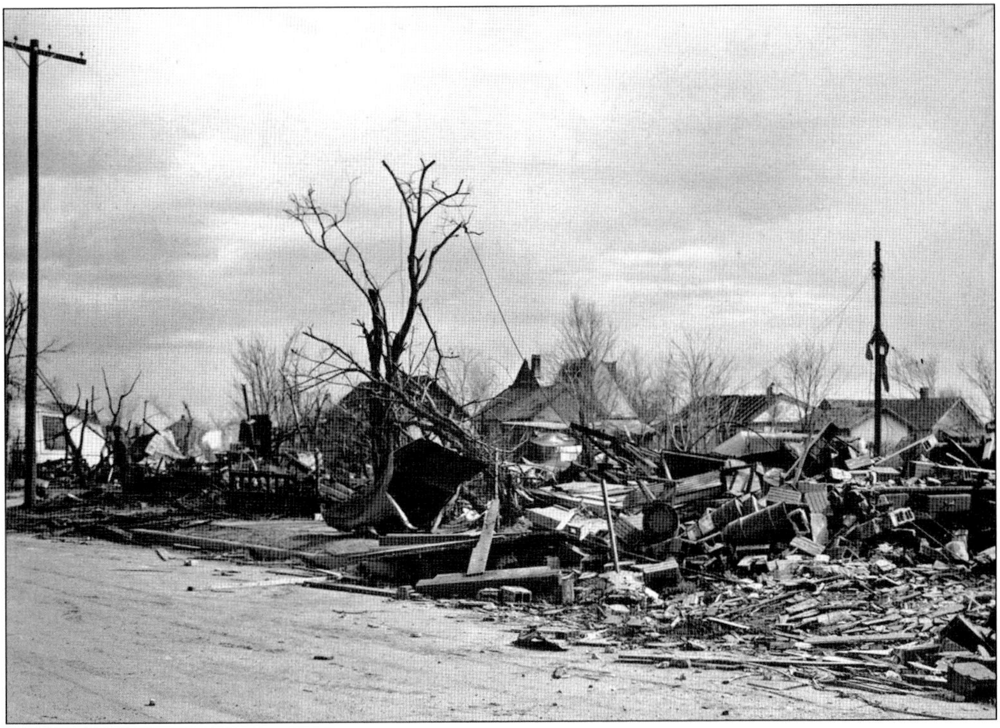

It is hard to look at destruction such as this and comprehend that it represents someone's life and material possessions. The neighboring homes appear to have much less damage. This home was located in the Cline Addition in the north end of the city. Note the chest of drawers on the far right side of the photograph.

This image is of several people searching through the debris of what was their home. Only one partial wall remains standing. This was likely taken on the west end of the city. Local newspapers published lists of where the homeless were staying for friends and family to locate loved ones more readily. Lists of names were also published for those admitted to area hospitals.

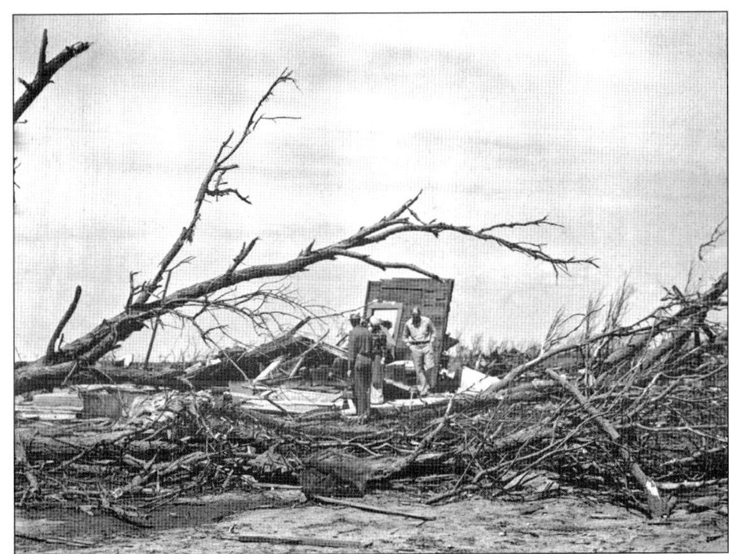

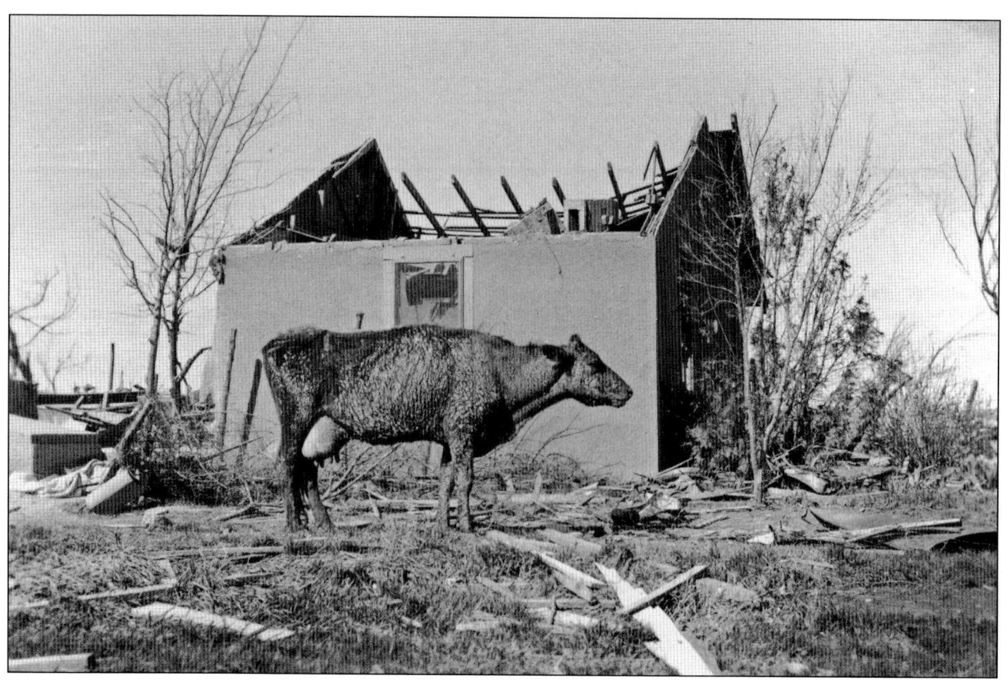

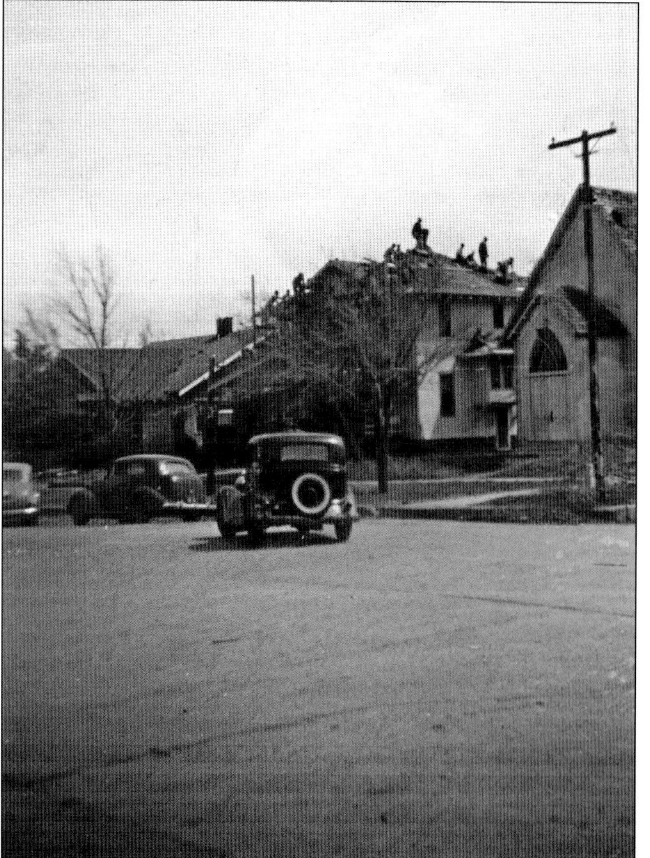

This cow covered in what may be mud (it rained mud as the storm passed) is probably searching for her calf. Several photographs taken on the west side of the city show bovines wandering amid the rubble of homes and structures. The fences that contained them in their pastures were likely destroyed by the storm. Among the animals were many with horrific wounds. State troopers worked as quickly as possible to dispatch the injured animals.

In this image, a vehicle turns east onto Texas Avenue in front of St. John's Episcopal Church. Several men are on the roof of the house next door, apparently making repairs. Both structures remain standing today.

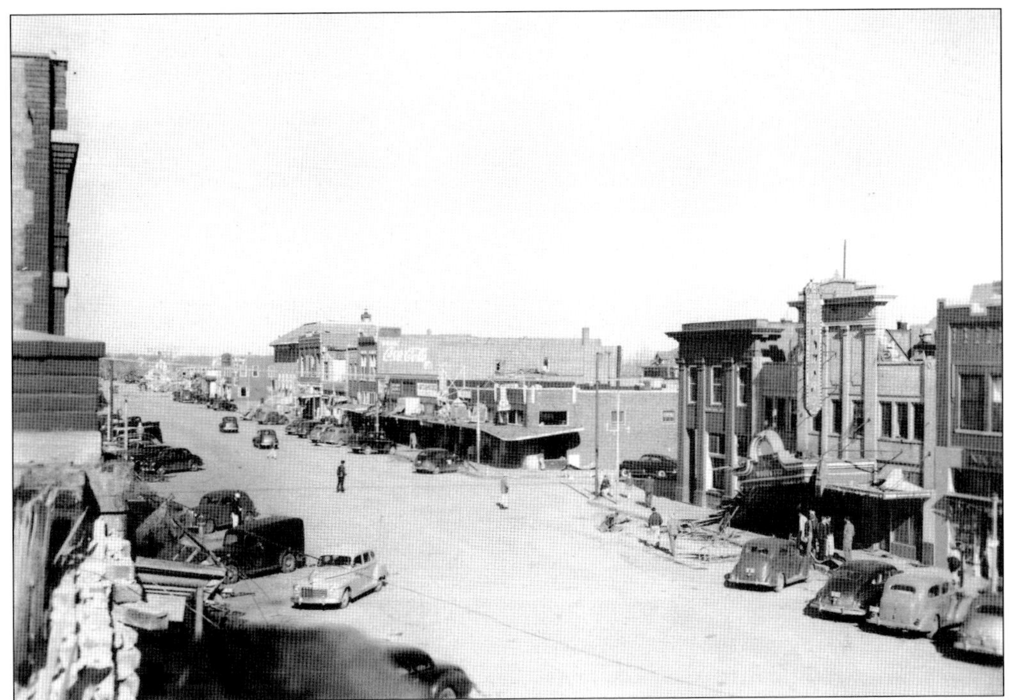

This image was captured atop the C.R. Anthony store building in the 800 block of Main Street (south side of the street), looking to the northwest toward Ninth Street. The damage to the Woodward Theatre is apparent, as is an awning on the building on the northwest corner of Ninth and Main Streets, then the location of Grace's Shoppe (a dress store).

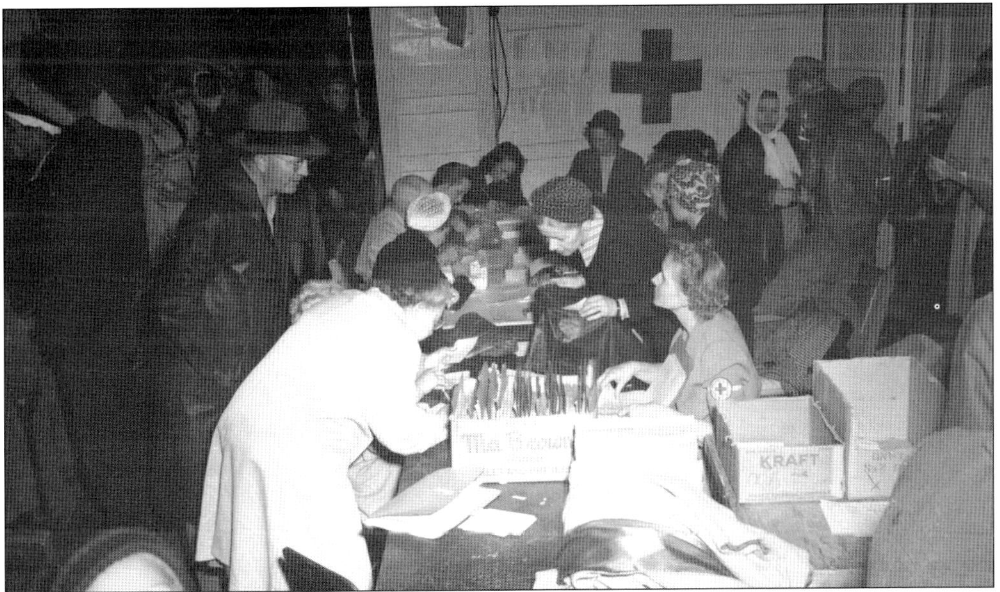

This image shows people in the community building at Ninth Street and Texas Avenue seeking aid from Red Cross workers. The Red Cross sent 10 social workers from Oklahoma City to Woodward the day following the storm to assist in creating lists of the dead and injured. They also assisted in initiating requests for aid from needy families.

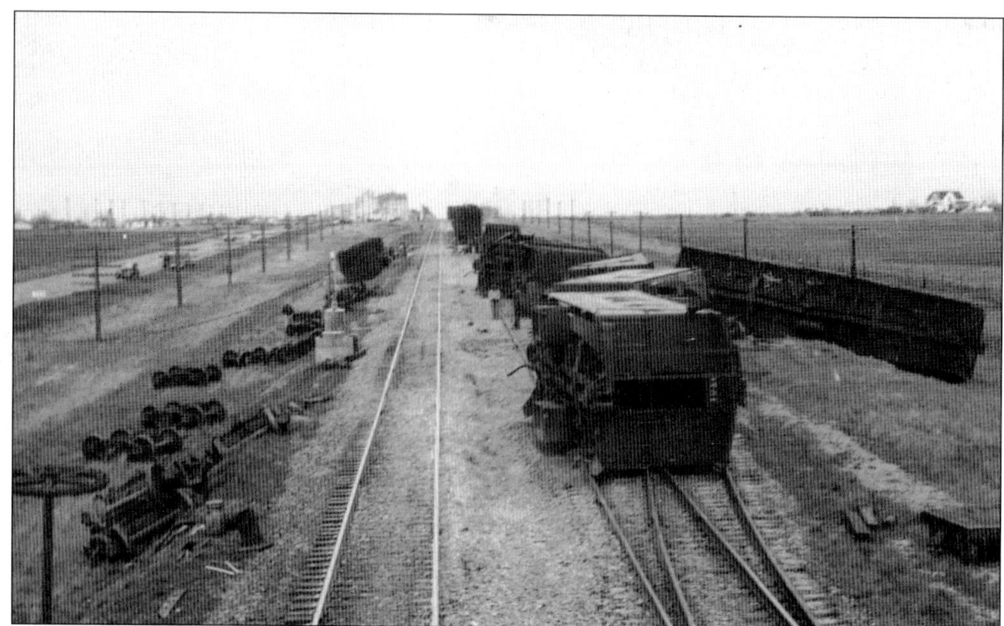

The exact location of these tornado-derailed train cars is not known, but news reports of the day indicated that the tornado straddled the tracks of the Santa Fe Railway for some time and blew a moving freight train with 21 cars completely off its tracks.

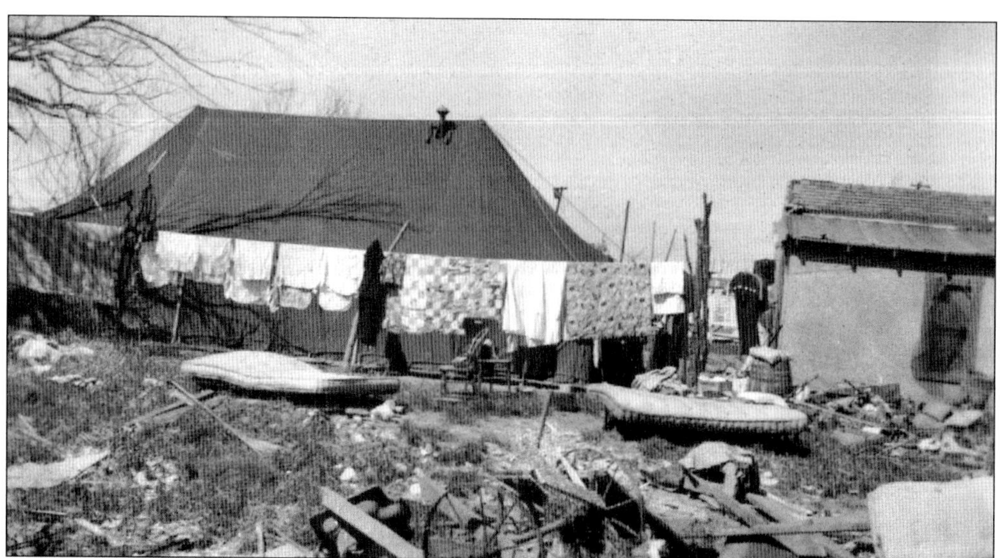

This photograph, taken by Everett McDonald, shows a large family-sized tent and clothesline hung with quilts and other bedding. Two mattresses are drying in the sun. The back of this image is inscribed, "Woodward is a city of tents since the tornado."

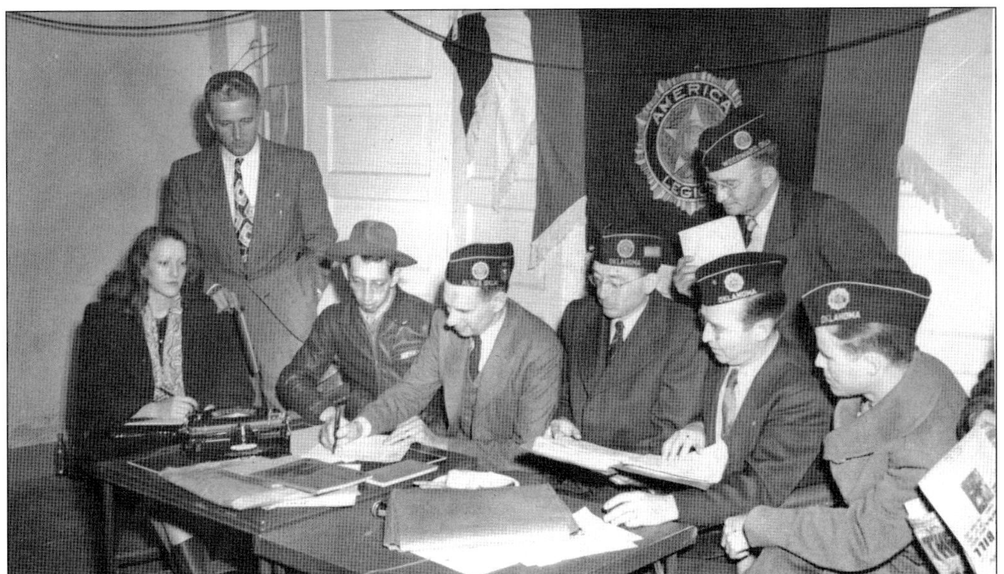

Members of the American Legion descended upon Woodward and set up an office in the community building to assist veterans in filling out the paperwork necessary to receive needed aid. They also shuttled veterans to medical appointments as needed.

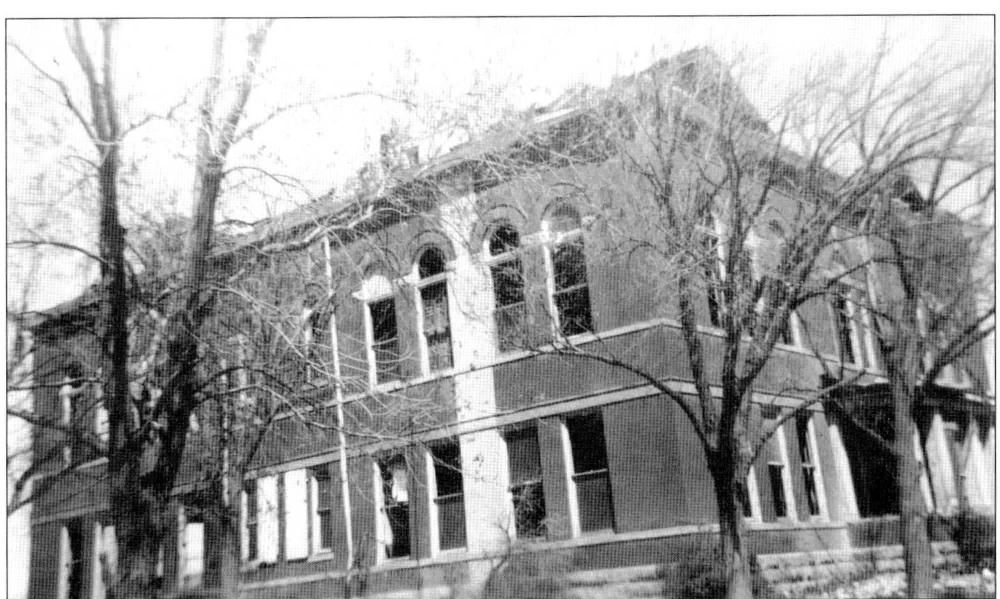

Woodward County's first real courthouse (pictured) was built in 1901 facing east along Tenth Street. The cupola on top of the building was a unique feature in its day and offered spectacular panoramic views of the city and surrounding area. A newer courthouse was built along Oklahoma Avenue in 1935. Both buildings were severely damaged in the storm. In the end, this building was razed.

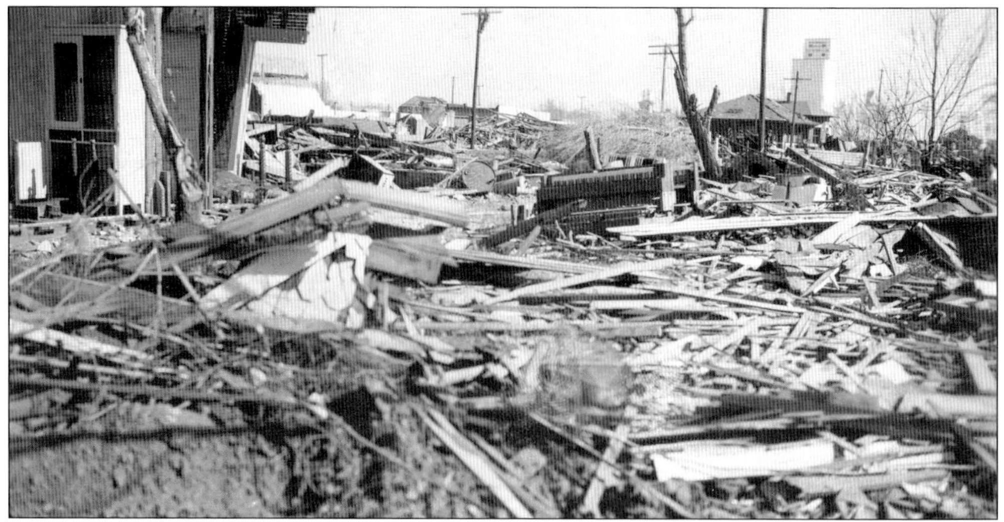

A handwritten note on the back of this photograph indicates that the view looks south from Kansas Avenue. In the foreground is a house with a wall missing. A piano is out in what was a yard. The Katy Railroad depot is viewable in the near distance. That is the Farmer's Co-Op grain elevator in the far distance.

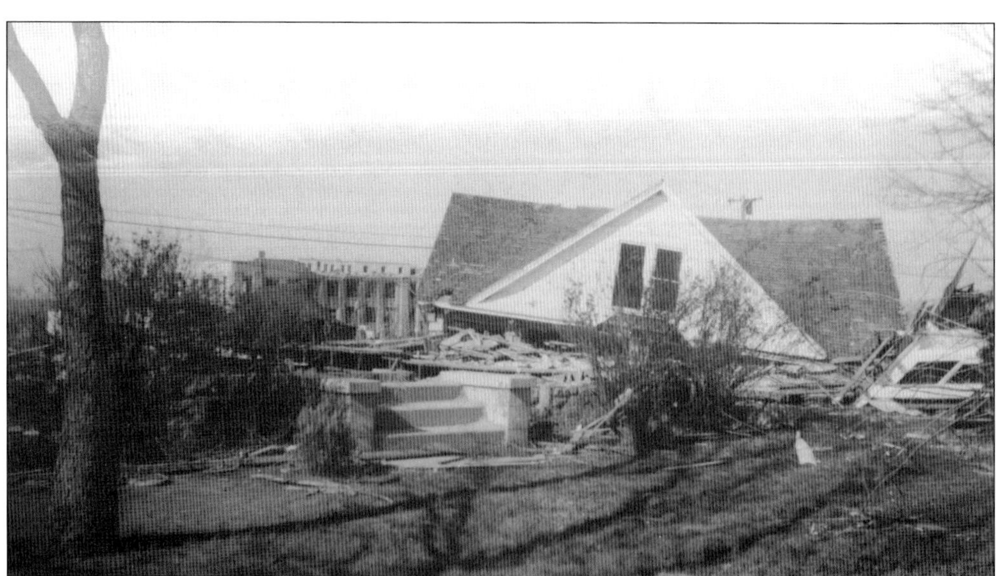

This home was identified as that of Joe Kaelan. Given the proximity to the Woodward County Courthouse in the distance, this is likely along Texas Avenue. The Kaelan home was not only blown off its foundation, it appears to have collapsed, with the second story remaining seemingly intact on the ground.

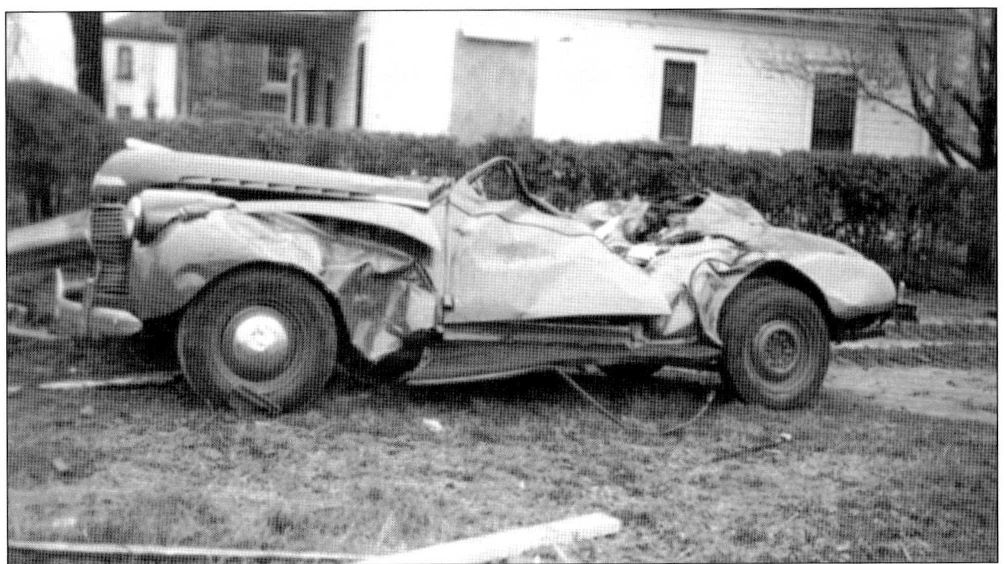

This particular vehicle became something of a celebrity when the wire services picked up this photograph and printed it in newspapers around the country. Authorities at the time believed it was blown down the street, turning end over end during the height of the storm.

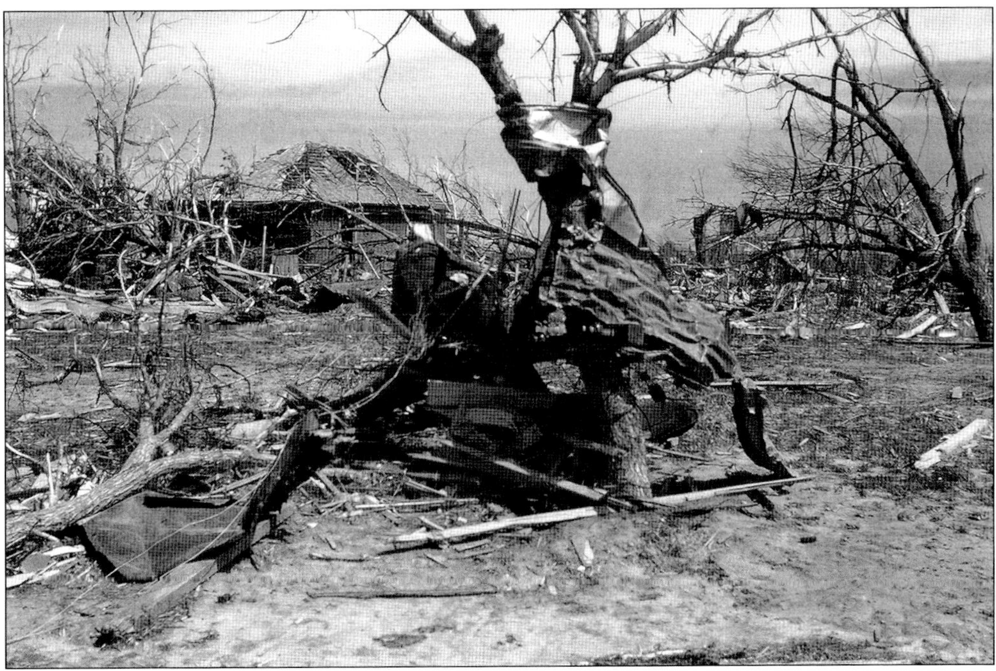

This image is typical of many made in the days and weeks following the 1947 Woodward tornado. This and the remaining photographs of this chapter were shot in color (though published in black and white), mostly by people who visited Woodward after the storm.

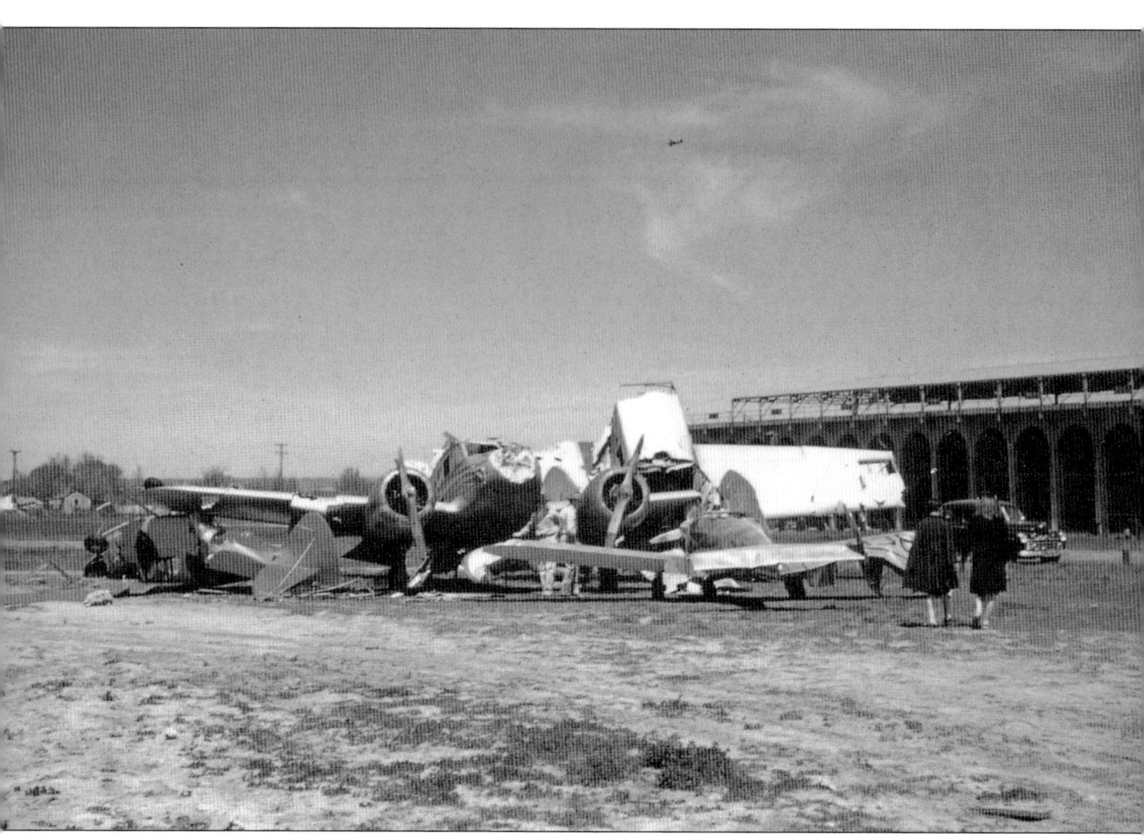

This image shows planes at Woodward Municipal Airport mangled by the monster tornado. The airport in 1947 was located on the site of the present-day Woodward Municipal Golf Course at Crystal Beach. A few individuals can be seen moving around the wrecked aircraft. Note the arena grandstand in the background. This photograph was taken by Dr. Clayton Young, a physician from Alva who flew to Woodward to view the damage.

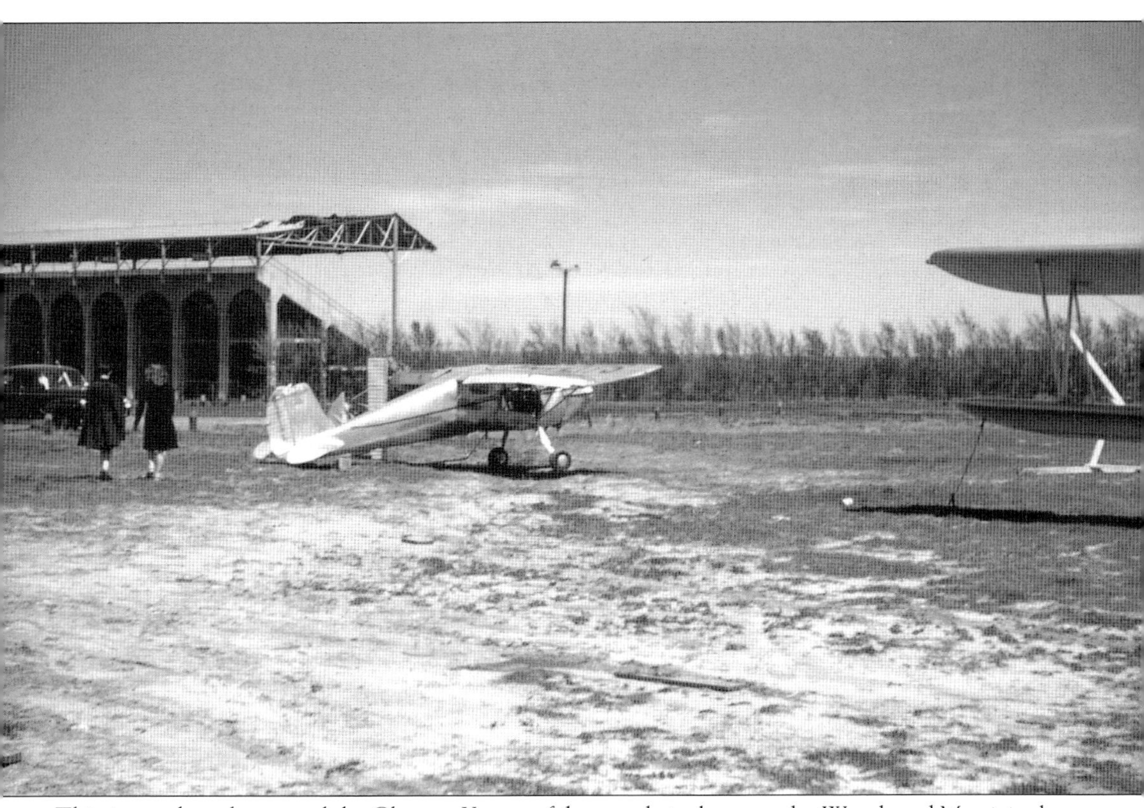

This is another photograph by Clayton Young of damaged airplanes at the Woodward Municipal Airport. Damage to the roofline of the arena grandstand is apparent in this image. The airport moved to the location of the former Army air base west of town in the 1950s and became known as West Woodward Airport.

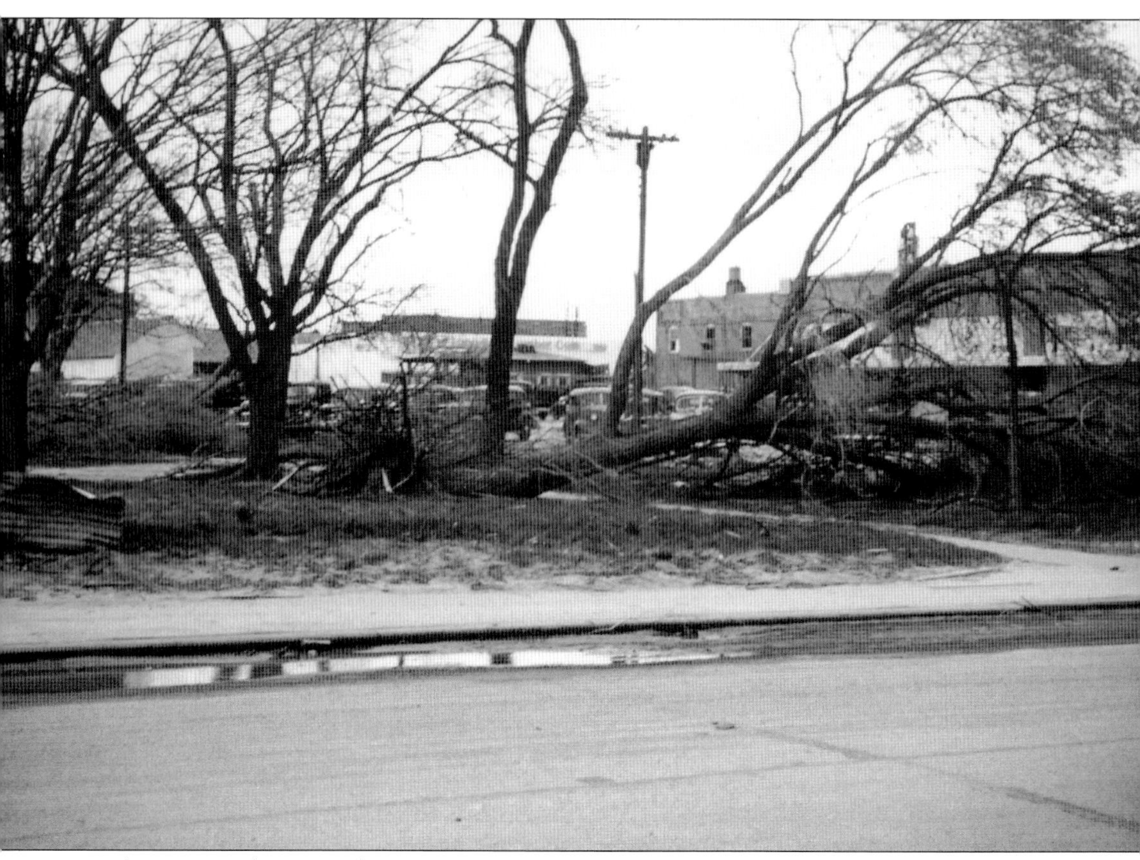

This image taken near the intersection of Eighth Street and Texas Avenue on the east side of Central Park (present-day Centennial Park) shows the damage suffered by the many elm trees growing in the park. In the background across the park, the edifice of Long-Bell Lumber Company can be seen. The Adams Brothers Grocery is on the right-hand side of the image, partially obscured by the downed tree.

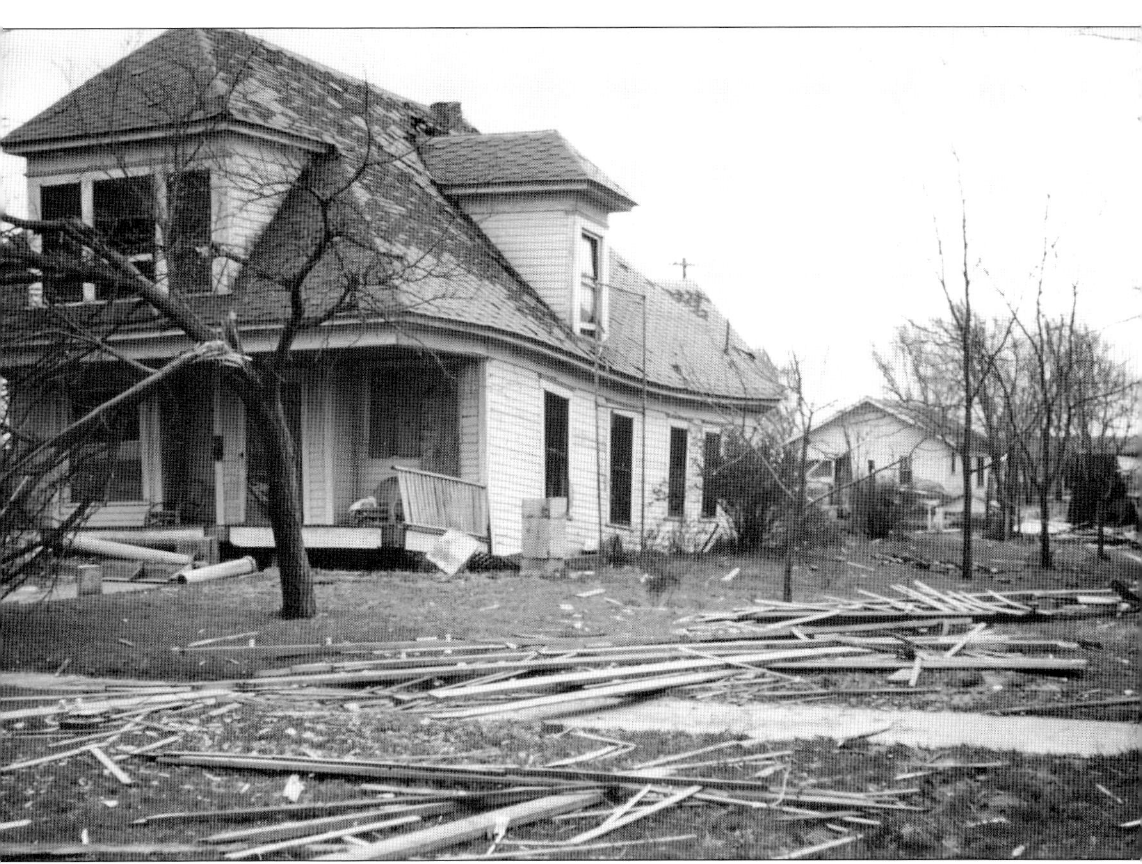

The damage to this home located in the 1200 block of Texas Avenue is extensive and includes what appears to be a damaged foundation on its west side. Note how the roofline and siding on the side facing the camera sag. Interestingly, this home remains standing at 1203 Texas Avenue. This was another photograph taken by Dr. Clayton Young of Alva.

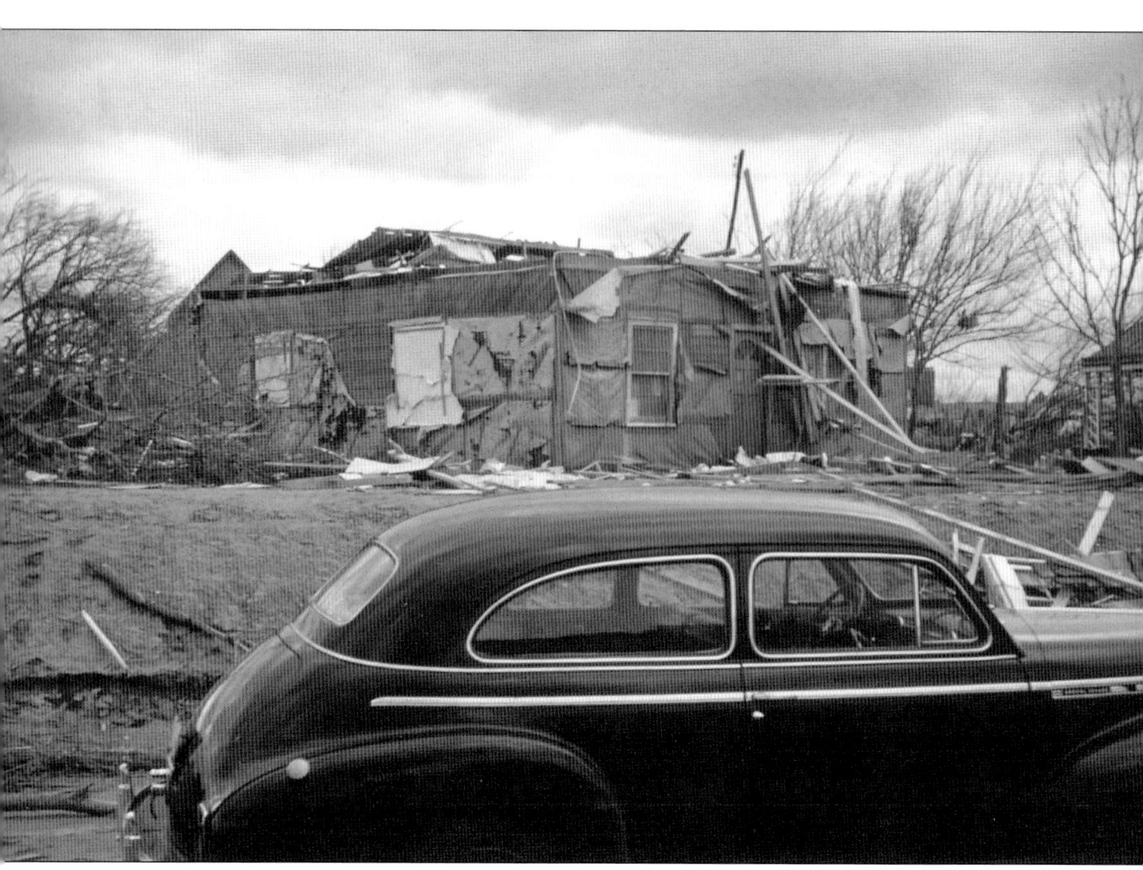

This home was almost certainly a total loss. The siding has been torn off, completely exposing the home's wood lathe wall substructure beneath. What appears to have been the second story on the home has been completely torn off. In fact, if one considers the angle of the home next door, this house may have been blown completely off its foundation. The address of this structure was not identified in this image.

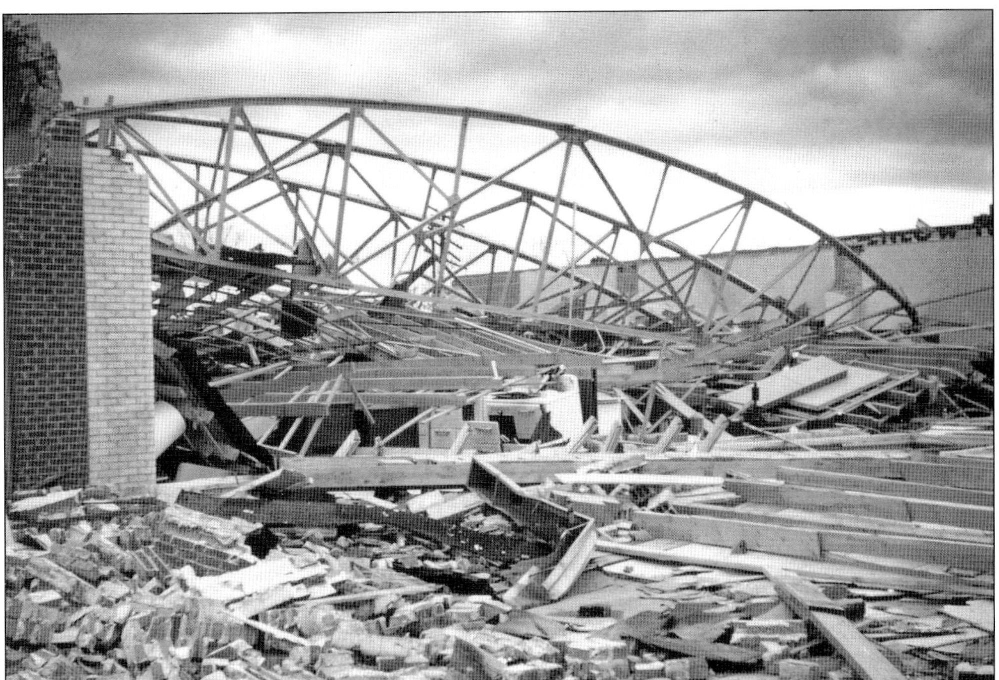

This completely destroyed building was the location of the Carl Ticer Equipment Company in the 1100 block of Main Street, near the corner of Eleventh and Main Streets. Despite the loss of several commercial structures throughout the city, most were rebuilt and operating again before the end of 1947.

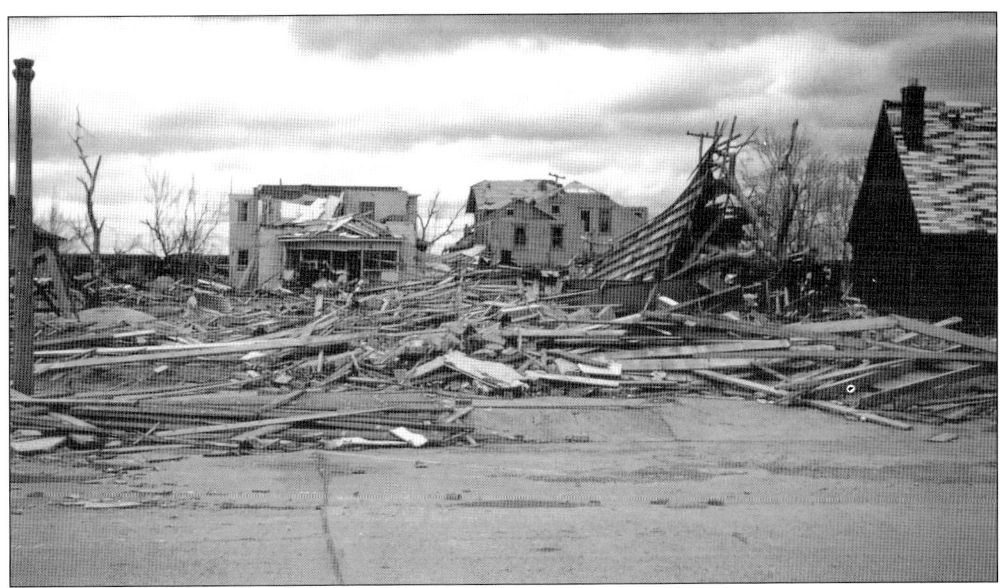

This view is looking north from Main Street toward the Santa Fe Railway tracks. The structure at the right side of the photograph was a gas station and is today the headquarters for Woodward Main Street. The severely damaged homes in the background are along Kansas Avenue.

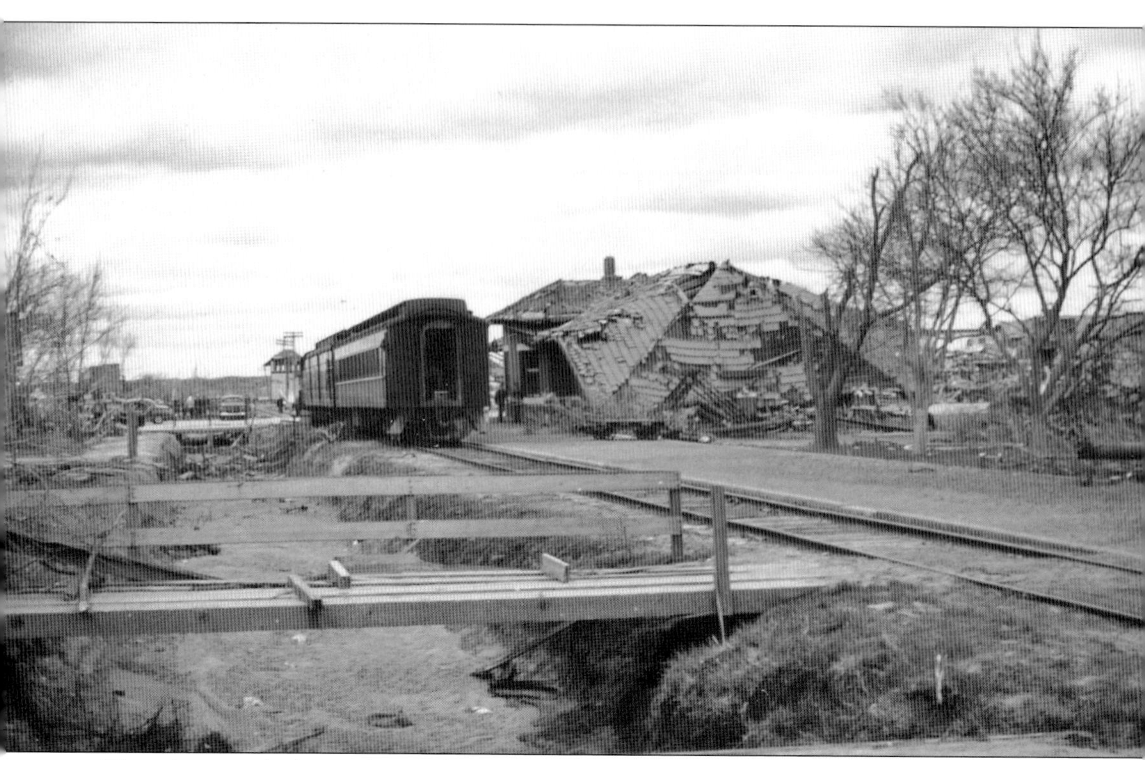

This photograph shows the nearly total destruction of the MKT Railroad depot. A passenger train is shown stopped by the depot, located on the south side of Main Street. The structure was rebuilt and today serves as the Chiropractic Health Center.

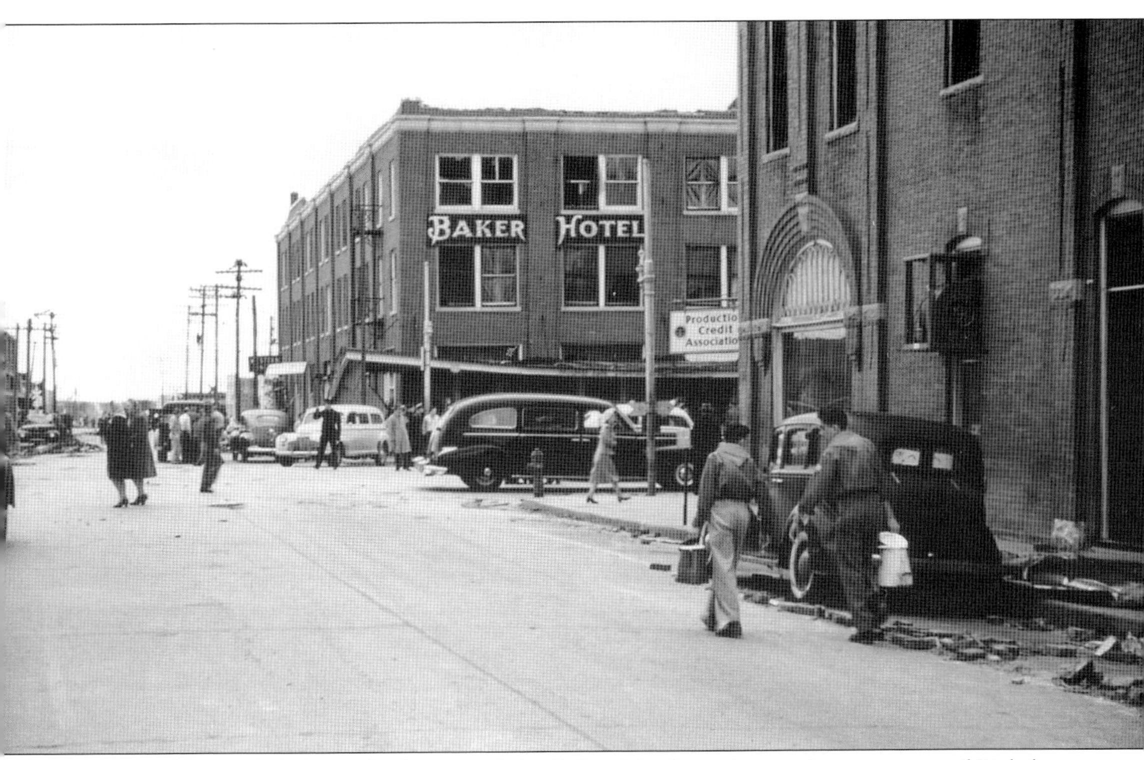

This view from Eighth Street looks toward the Baker Hotel on the northwest corner of Eighth and Main Streets. There are two Boy Scouts carrying pails along the street, possibly containing food from the community center for workers on Main Street. Despite considerable damage to the upper floors of the hotel, including broken windows, the overflow from the Woodward Hospital was moved to the Baker for further transport to other area hospitals.

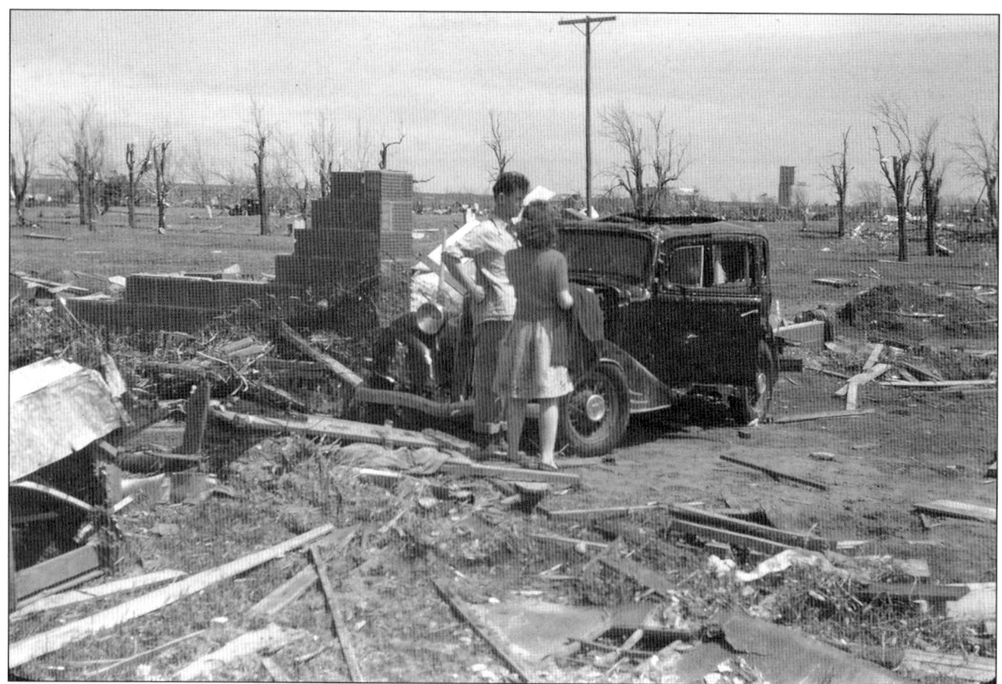

A young couple surveys the damage to their property located somewhere on the west end of Woodward, where the destruction was most severe. The Woodward County Courthouse is partly visible behind a tree, and the Fisher Grain elevators are in the background.

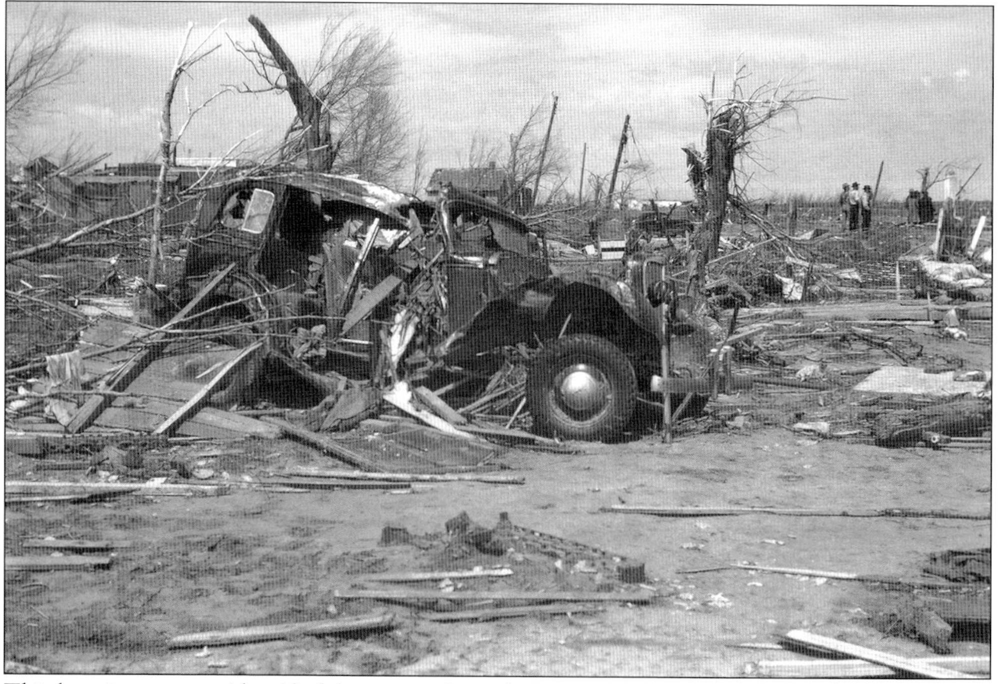

This location was not identified, but given that a few structures are remaining in the background, it may be in the North Ward area of the city. The wrecked automobile in the foreground was not only severely damaged in the storm but appears to have become a catch-all for blowing debris.

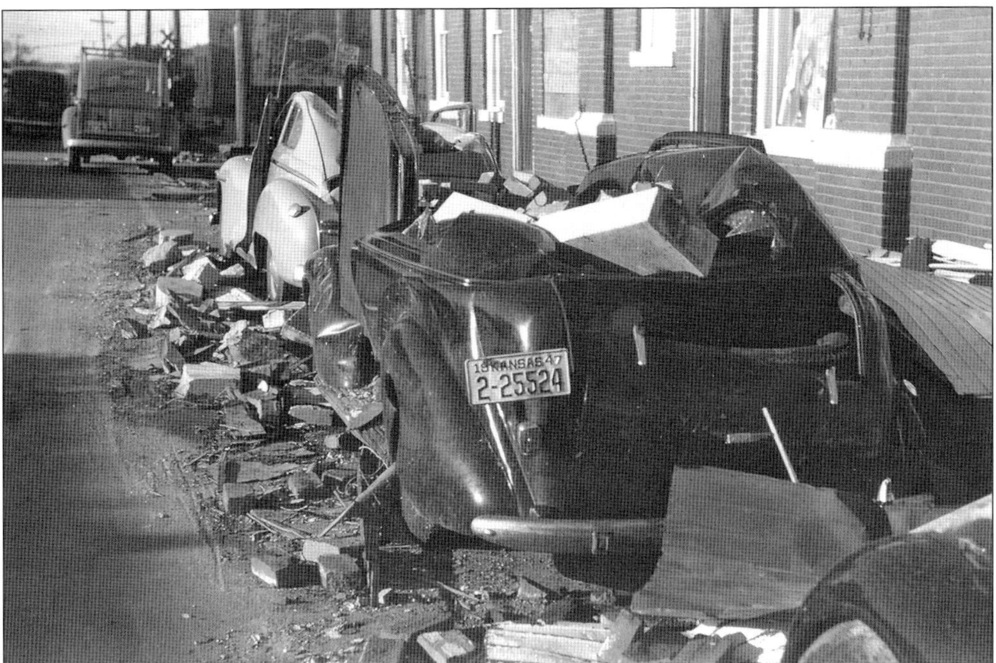

This photograph was taken near the intersection of Eighth and Main Streets and looks north along Eighth Street on the west side of the Baker Hotel. A visitor from Kansas who parked his car along Eighth Street had the roof completely smashed from debris torn loose in the storm. Note that a grader or bulldozer has already made a pass along the street to clear debris from the roadway.

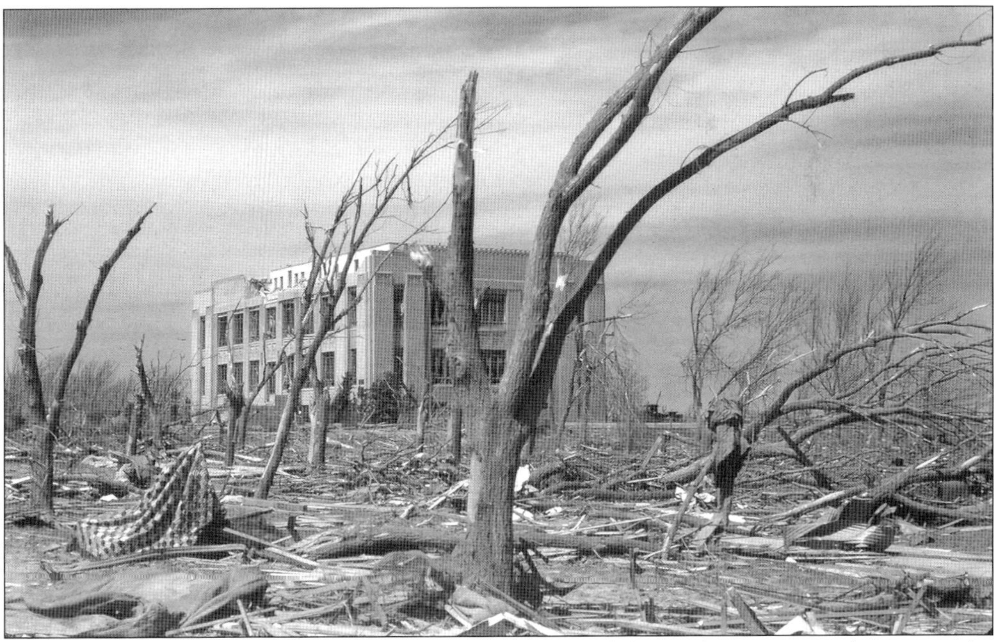

This image was taken looking toward the northwest and shows the extensive damage to the Woodward County Courthouse. In the foreground, debris litters the ground, including a piece of tin bent around a tree, a large number of splintered boards, and even someone's blanket. Note the horizon behind the courthouse building—there are no structures that appear to remain standing.

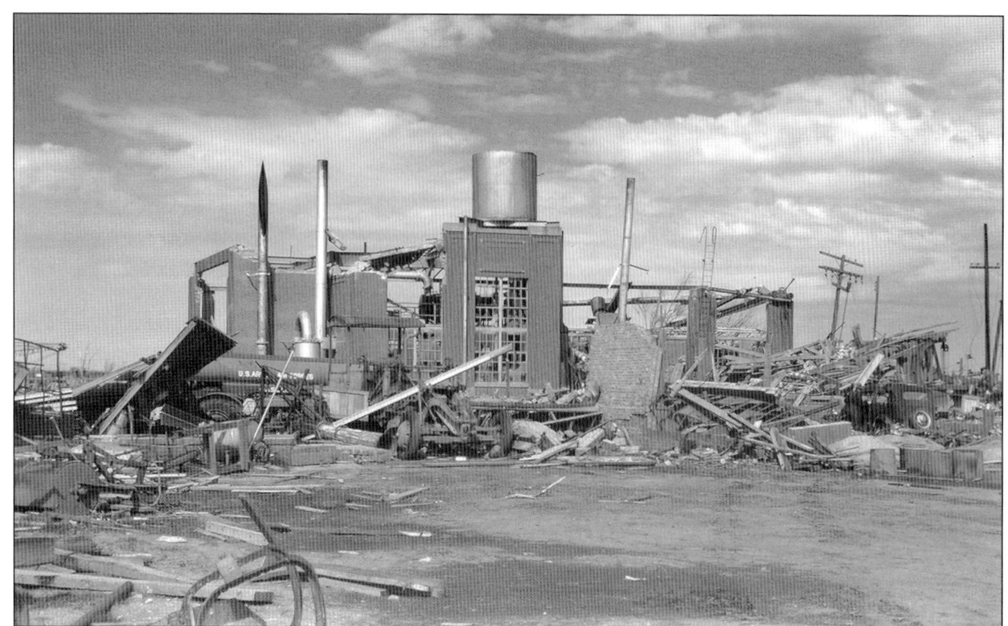

This is another view of the OG&E power plant on the north end of the city along the North Canadian River. Erwin "Jack" Walker lost his life staying at the control panel and attempting to shut down the power supply. Note the US Army Air Forces tanker visible through the debris. This may indicate a fuel source for generators brought in to restore power to the city.

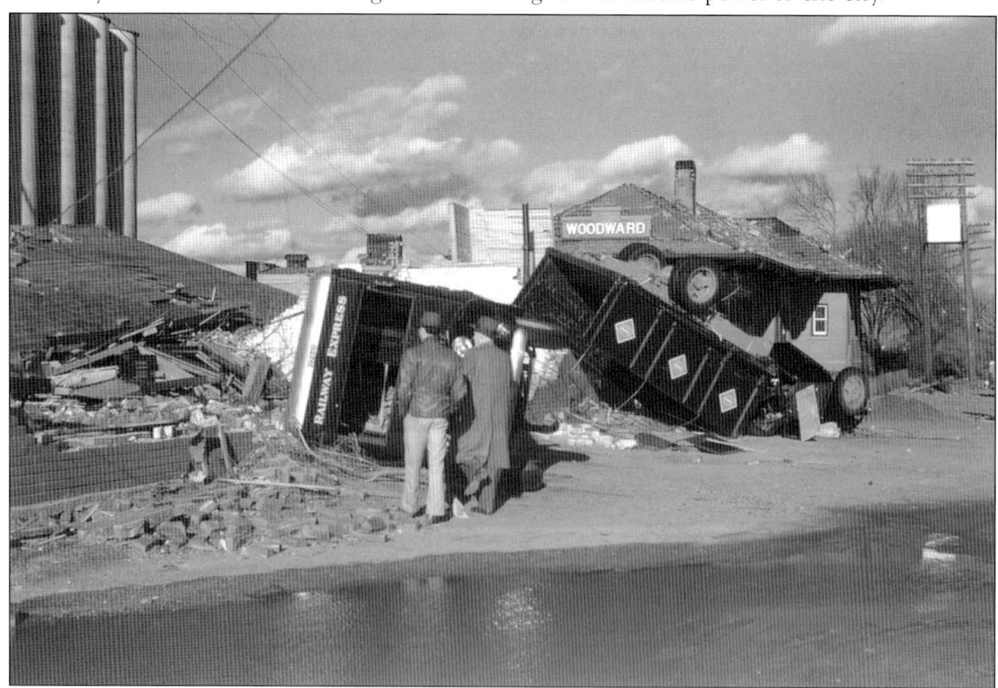

This photograph is a bit disorienting to look at, but thankfully, the Fisher Grain elevator structure helps place it in perspective. This is the west end of the Santa Fe depot complex looking toward the east. The collapsed building in the foreground is the freight building, which was just to the west of the passenger depot. A Railway Express vehicle and another truck are inverted.

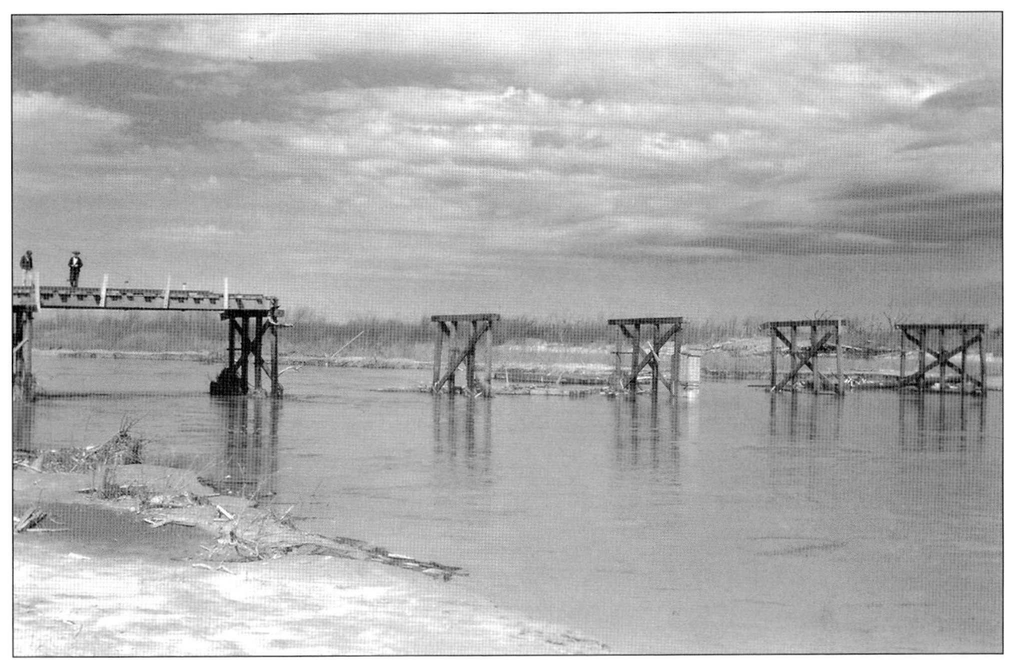

The loss of the Eighth Street bridge across the North Canadian River essentially cut off Woodward from traffic moving to or from the north. These photographs show a portion of the bridge deck in the water abutted against the support pylons. Remarkably, the bridge deck was rebuilt, and the bridge reopened inside of one month.

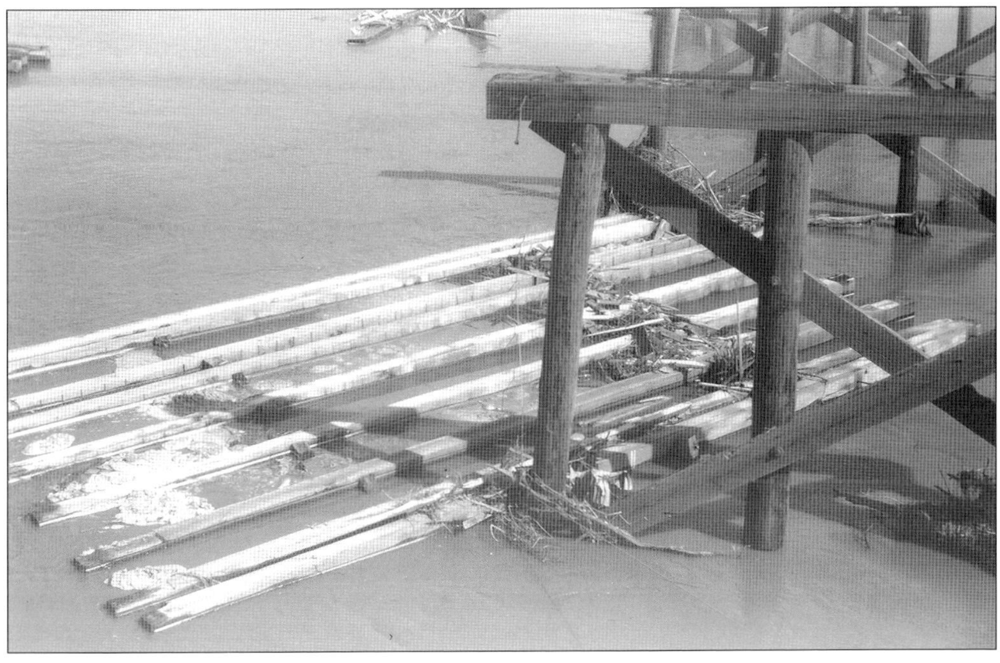

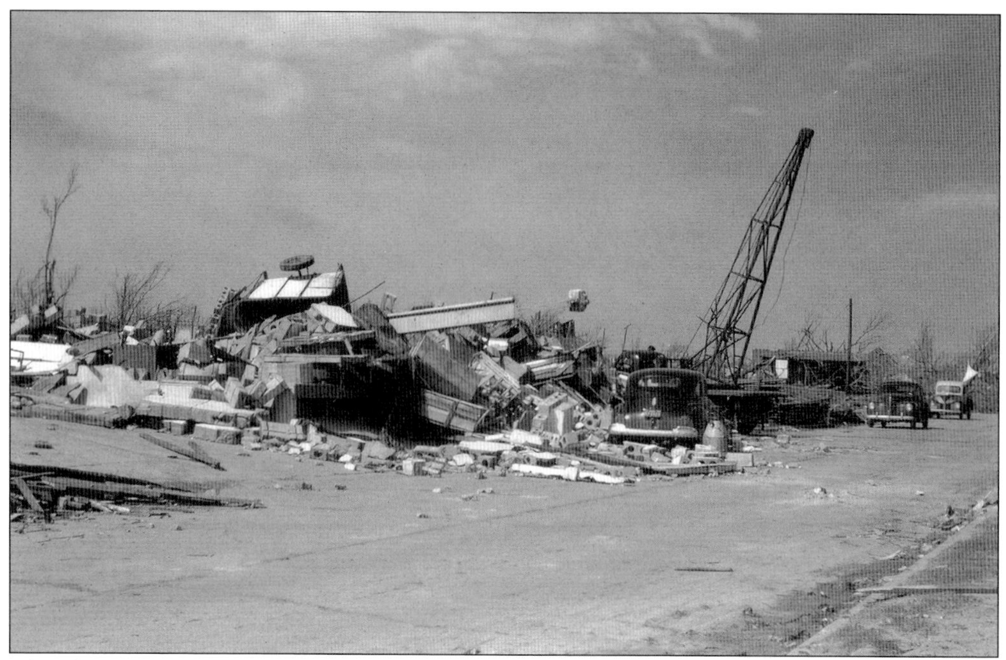

This photograph contains no point of reference as to the location of destruction or purpose of the building, but it appears to have been a warehouse of some sort. Note the banded crates scattered among the rubble.

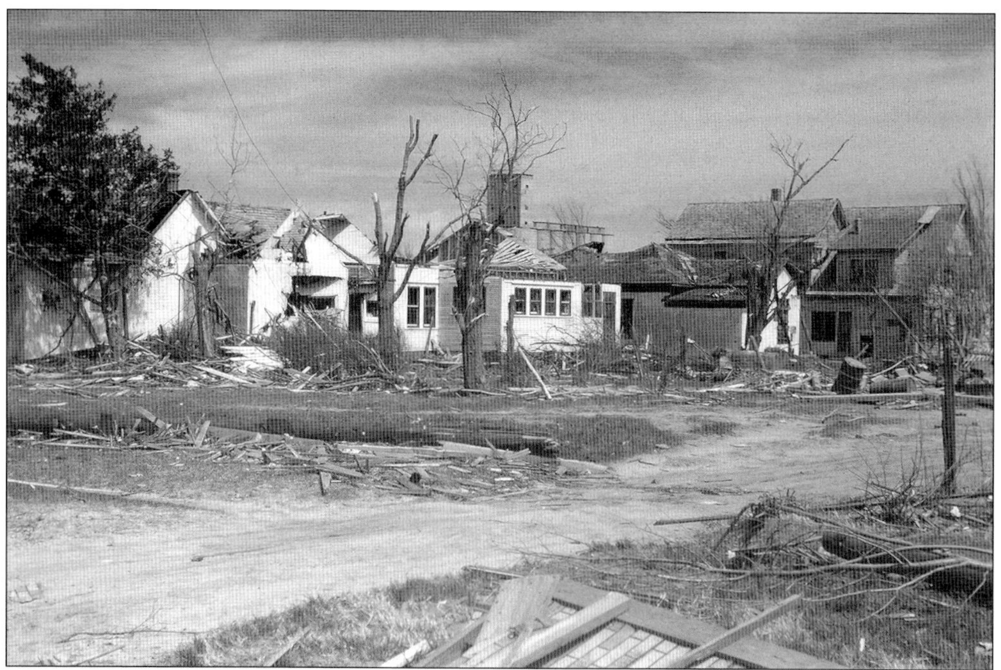

A row of residential structures shows varying degrees of destruction after the storm. The location is not identified but appears to be south of Main Street looking toward the northeast. Scientists at the time calculated that the tornadic winds at their greatest velocity (near the core) exerted 600 pounds of pressure per square foot.

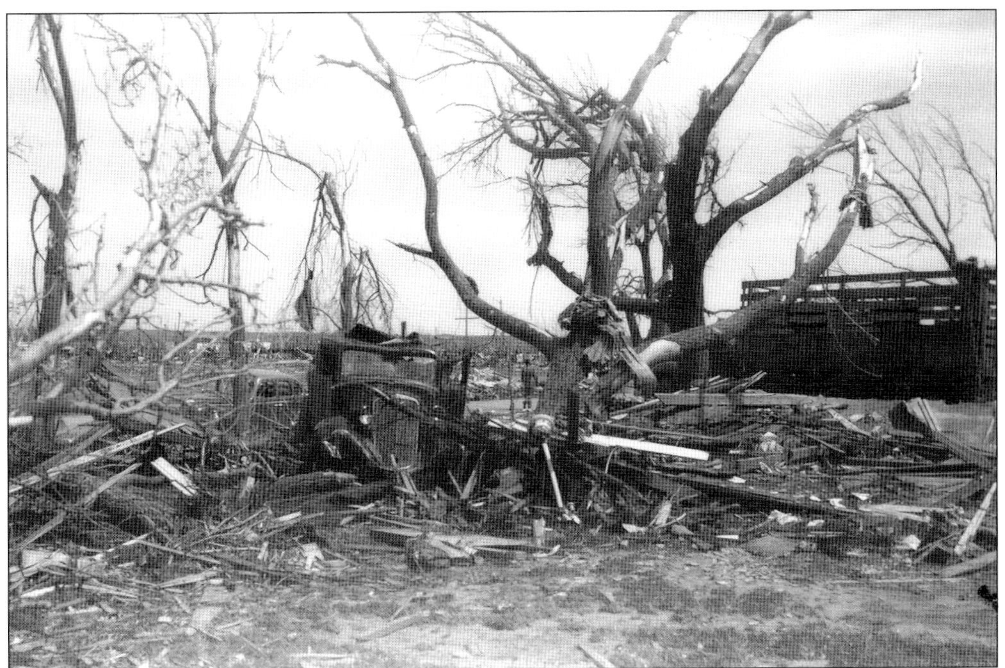

Two stark landscapes laid barren by the 1947 Woodward tornado are shown in these photographs. No specific location was attached to these photographs, but it would appear that the image above was captured in the North Ward given the number of old-growth trees. Note that a good deal of bark has been stripped from the trees forming an arch over yet another smashed vehicle that could be seen throughout the storm-damaged area. The photograph below was taken from the Highland Park section of Woodward in the west looking to the northeast. The Woodward County Courthouse can be seen framed between two utility poles. The smaller, more immature trees have a large amount of corrugated tin wrapped around their trunks.

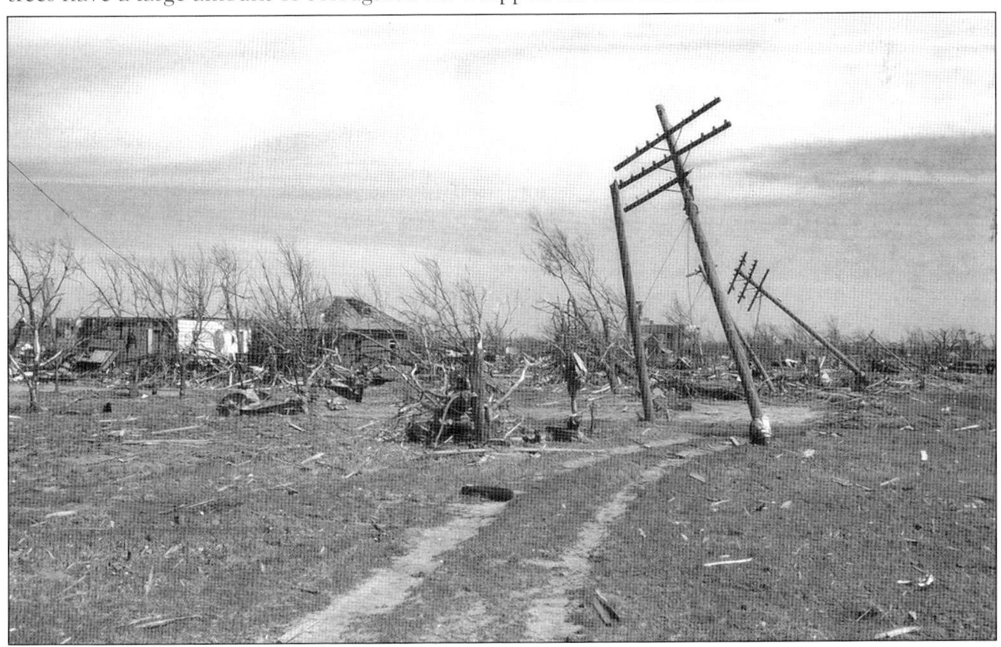

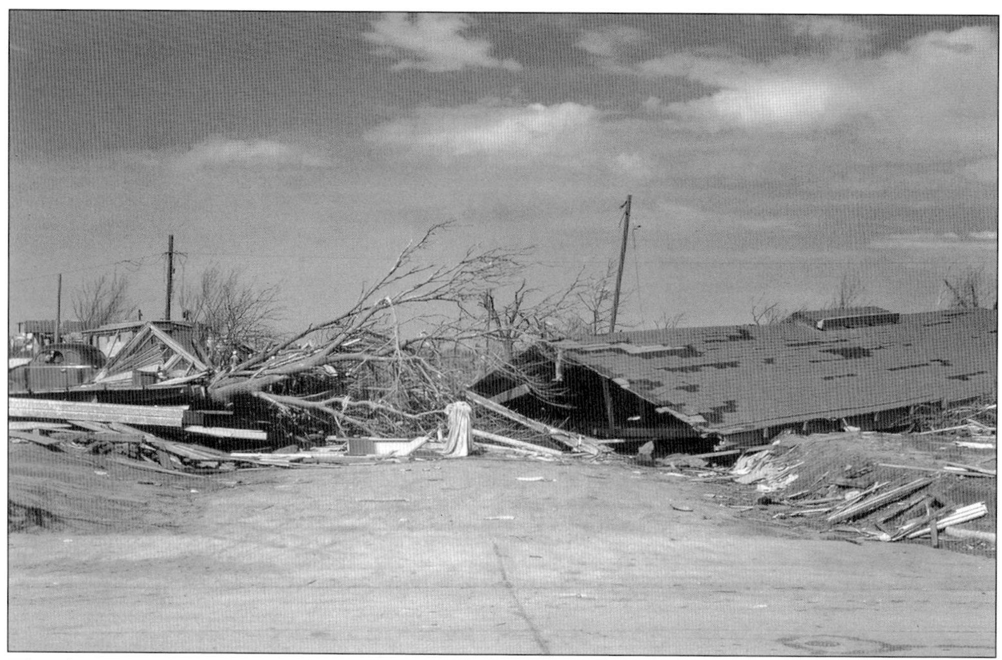

The dominant feature in this photograph, believed to have been taken at the intersection of Eighth Street and Jefferson Avenue (looking east) in the North Ward, is the entire roof structure of what was most likely a commercial building.

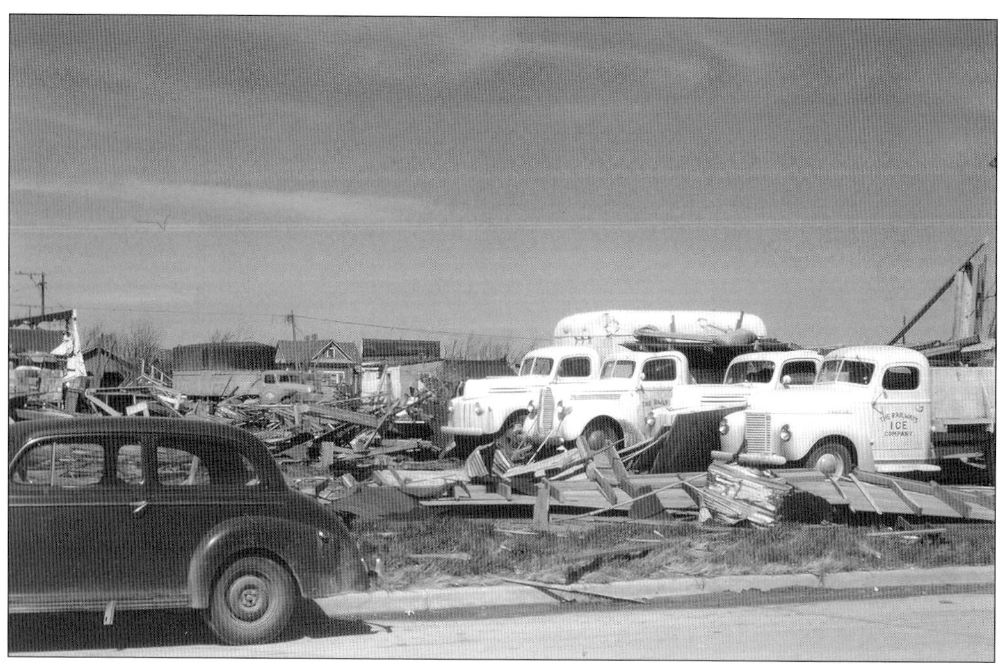

Four brightly colored trucks from the Railways Ice Company make a brilliant contrast and stand out against the backdrop of rubble. The ice plant was located along Ninth Street in the area of Santa Fe Avenue, just to the northeast of the Fisher Grain complex.

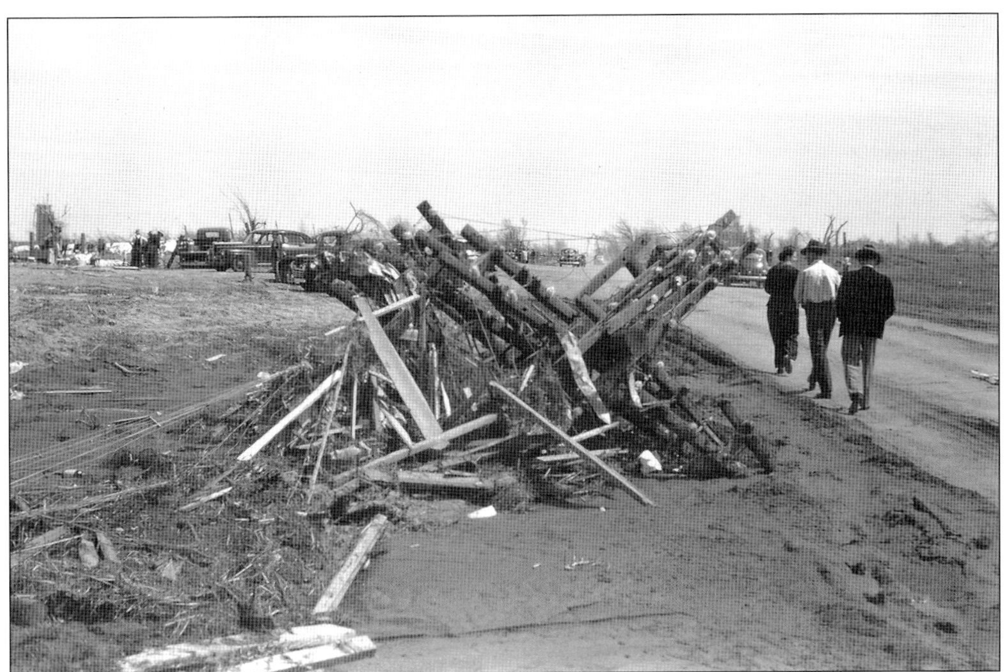

Three people are shown walking single file past a bulldozed jumble of utility poles and wires. The street they are on has been recently plowed as well. Although the location of this photograph is unknown, it is believed to have been in the Highland Park section (west side) of town.

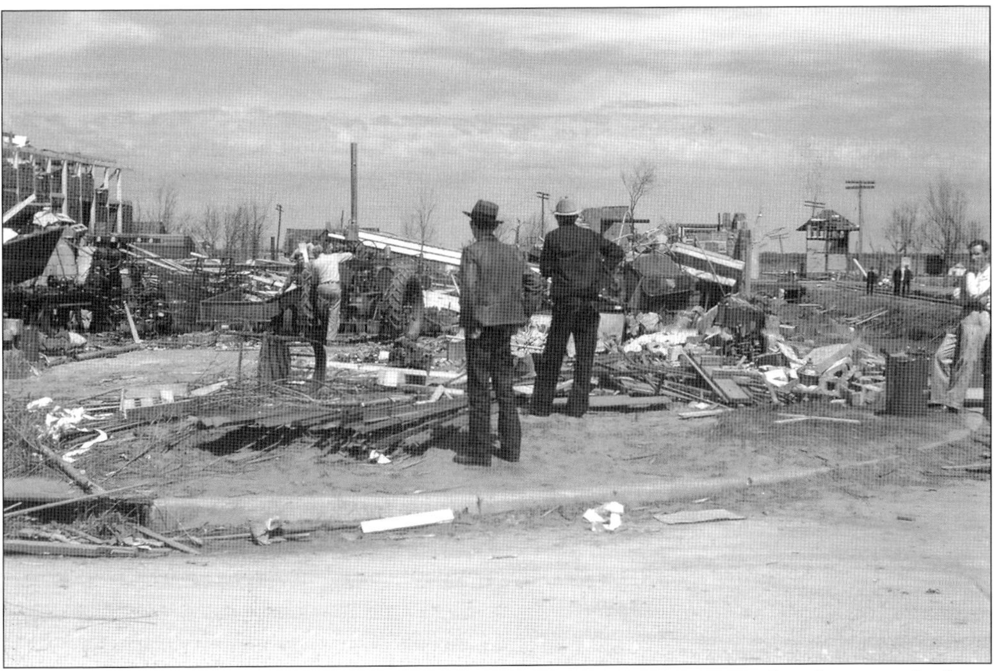

This photograph was taken on Main Street just to the west of the MKT Railroad crossing looking toward the northwest. A tractor is attempting to plow a path through the rubble. The Johnson Lumber storage is on the left side of the image. The railroad switching tower is on the right side.

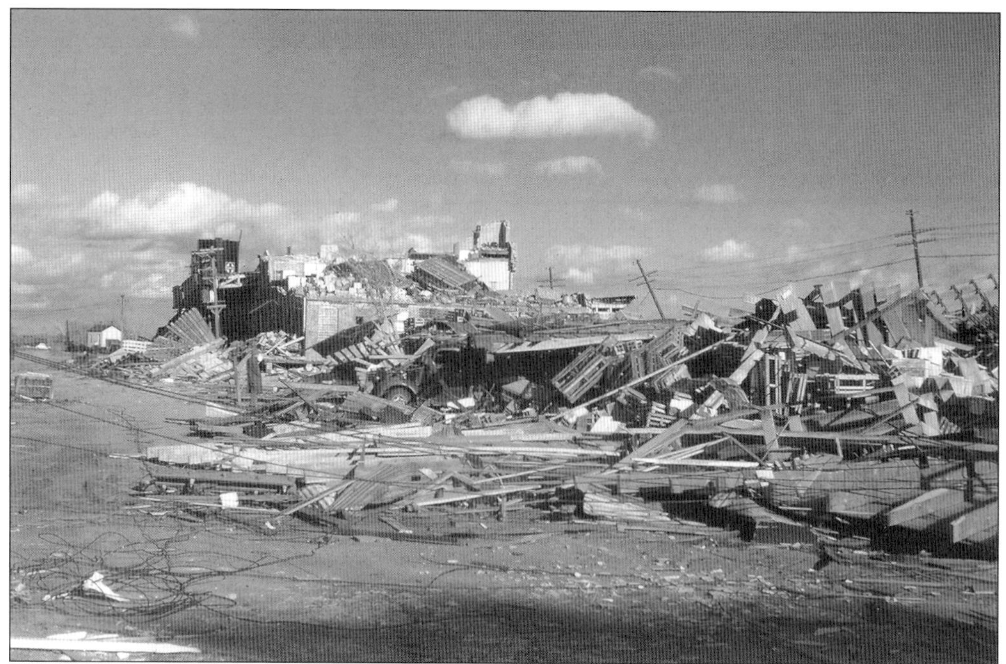

This image was captured from the northwest corner of an unidentified warehouse building looking southeast. One of two Santa Fe Railway towers is seen just beyond the building. A jumble of utility lines lies across the roadway. Note the exposed product boxes on the second floor.

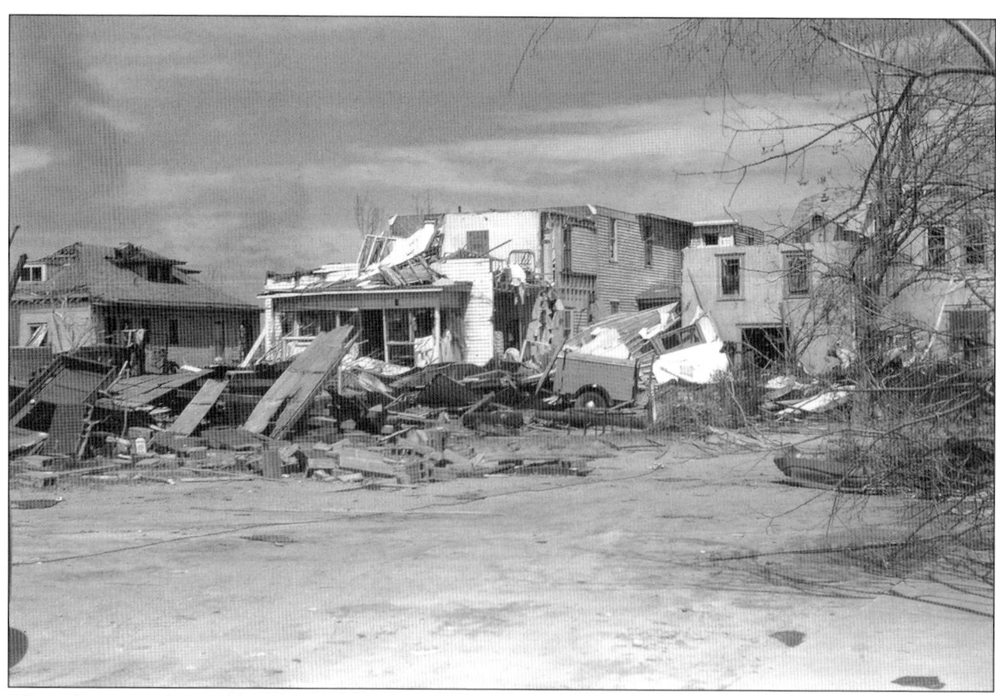

This photograph is of large homes or possibly apartments in a residential area of the city. Note the bed frame remaining on the second floor of the white structure in the middle. Wisps of black smoke can be seen on the right side, probably from rubbish being burned. The location of this photograph was not identified.

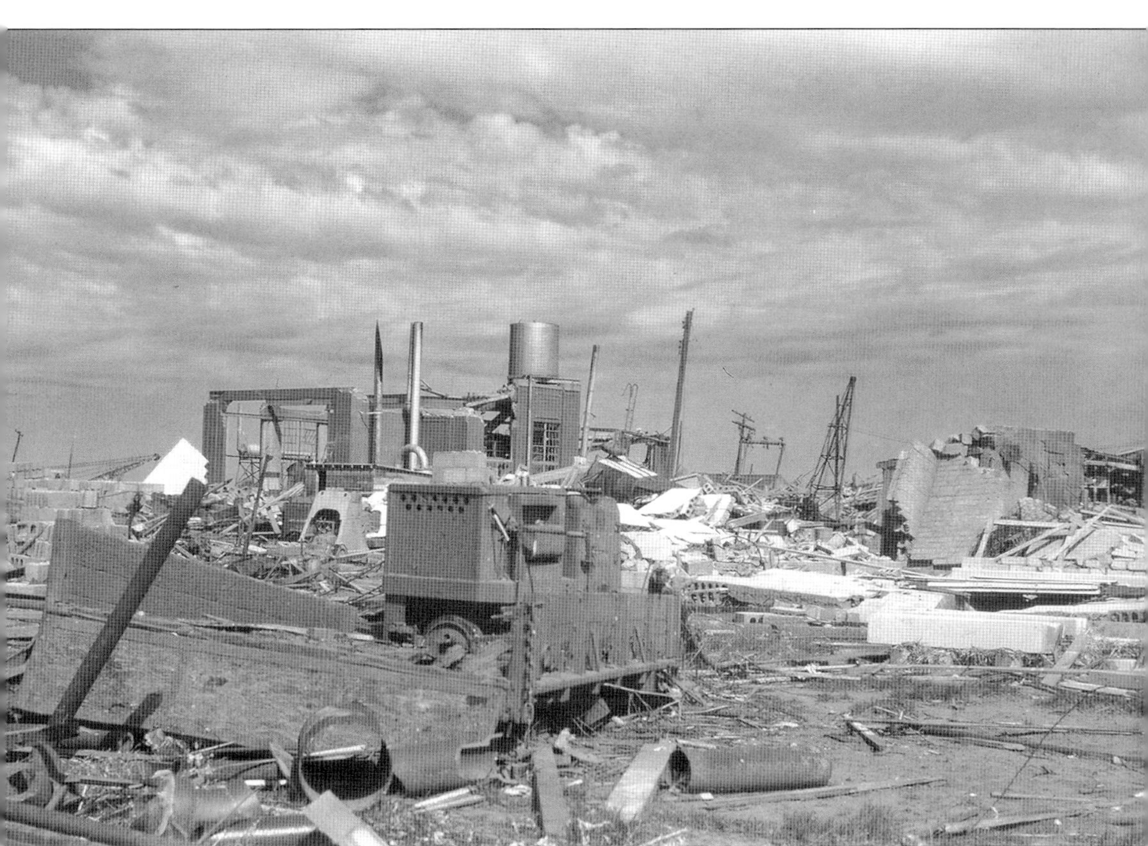

This is a wide shot of the complete destruction viewable at the end of Ninth Street looking to the northeast. The OG&E plant is visible in the background. Note the number of cinder block walls that have been torn loose from their foundations. Amid all the destruction, there is a sign of hope in the form of a crane truck visible in the middle of the image. It was possibly pulling down unstable walls to allow cleanup to begin.

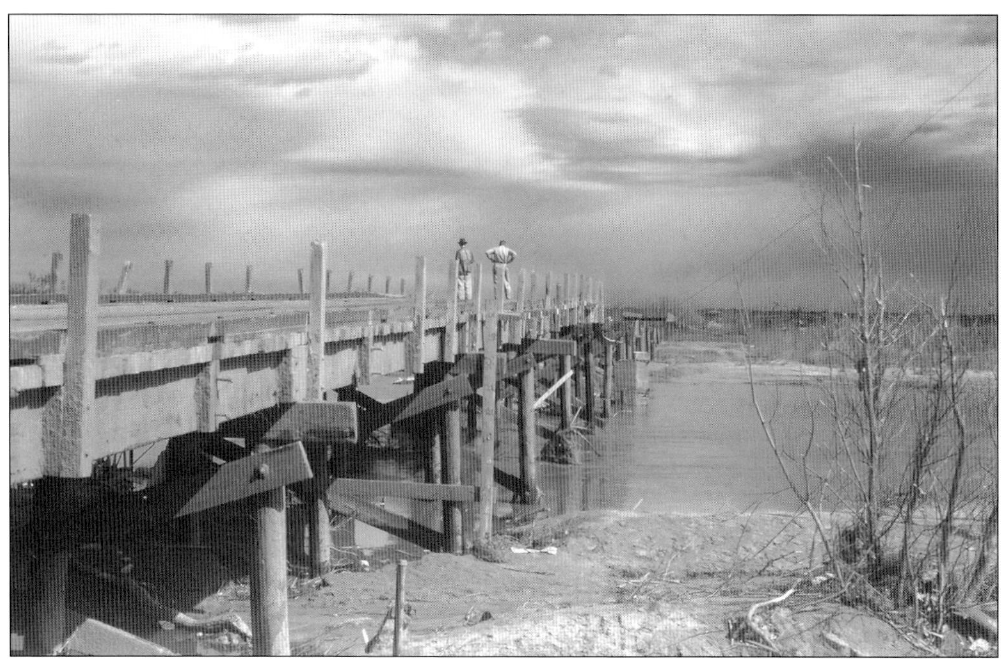

Two men survey the destruction of the Eighth Street bridge deck spanning the North Canadian River. Note the utility line seemingly tossed across the river to the far side. Years later, the bridge was shifted to Ninth Street, where it remains today, and built of concrete.

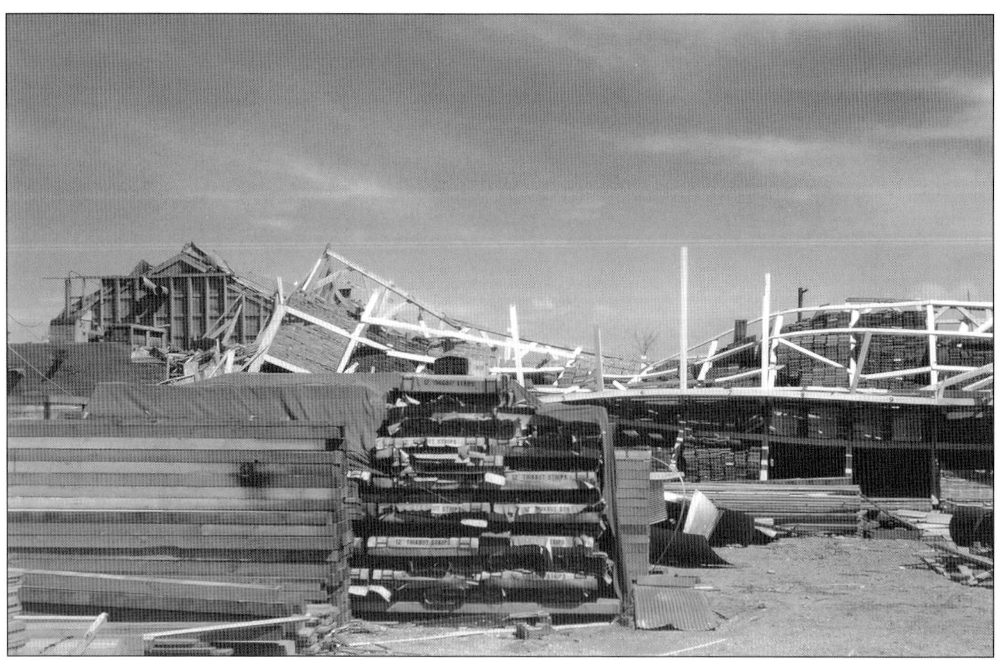

Another shot from a different angle shows damage to the Osborne-Peebles Lumber Company on the corner of Eighth Street and Santa Fe Avenue. It appears that much of the lumber stock in both this location and Johnson Lumber Company on Main Street was spared damage. This was a good thing for homeowners who needed the lumber to make repairs or rebuild their homes.

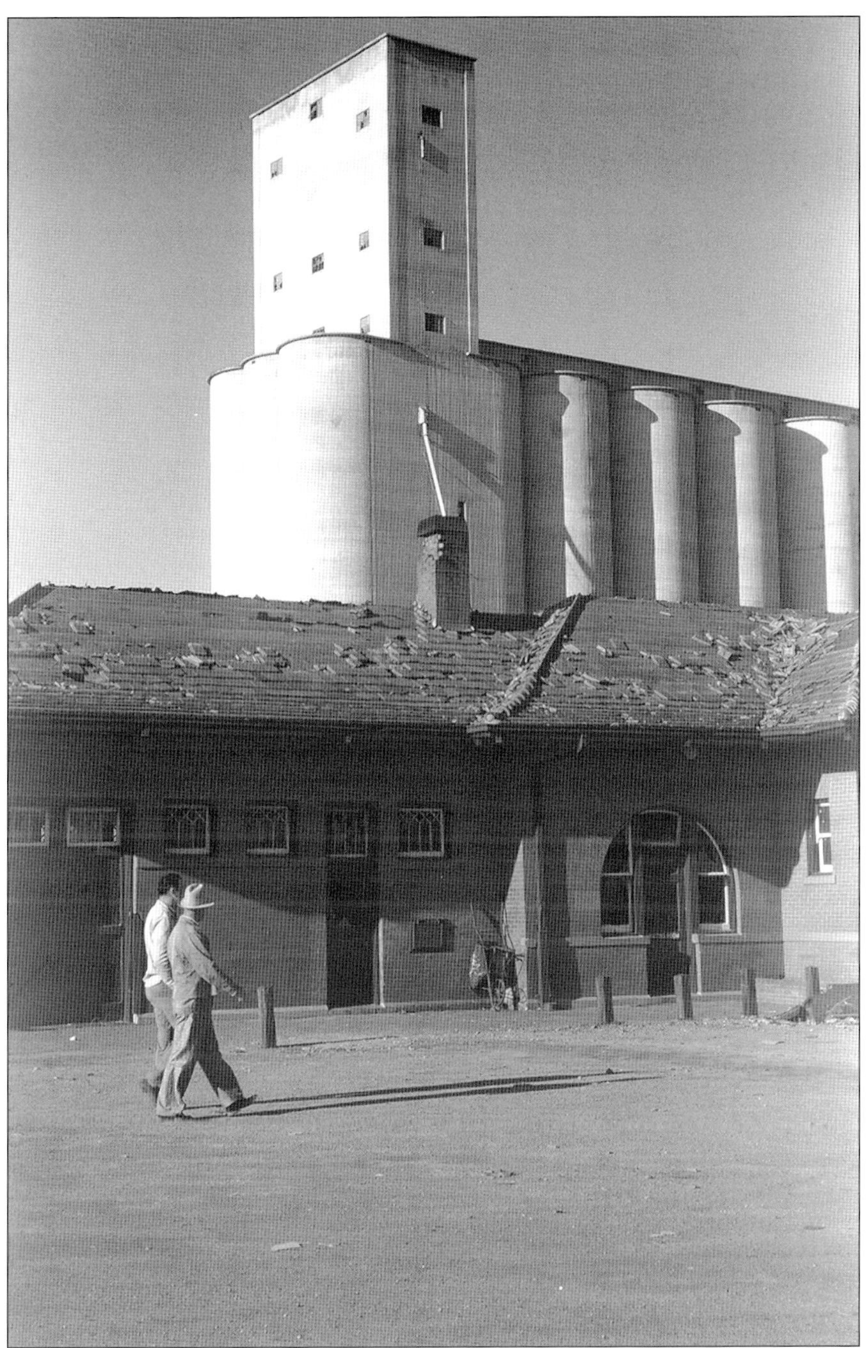

What is not seen in this photograph is most significant. The Santa Fe (AT&SF) Railway passenger terminal appears to have only minor roof damage compared with that of the Katy Terminal several blocks away. What is not seen is the freight warehouse that would have been just to the left of this photograph. It was completely smashed by the tornadic winds. It is possible that the Fisher Grain complex offered some protection to the depot from the high winds as opposed to the freight warehouse, which was more exposed. The remarkable thing in this image is that the entire elevator complex was relatively undamaged—just some broken windows in the headhouse.

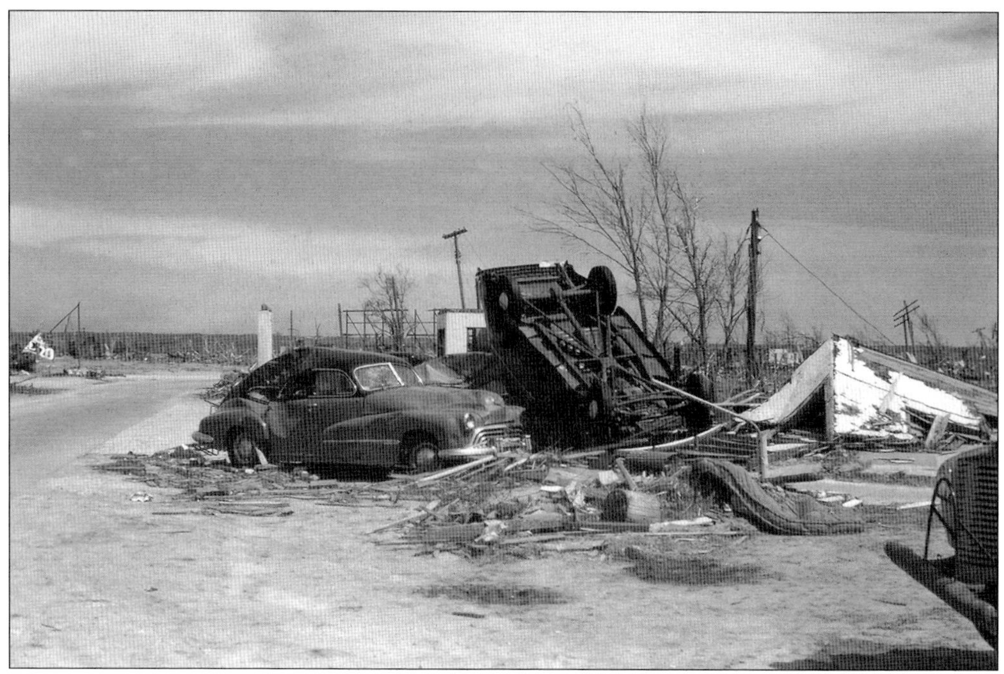

Three automobiles are shown piled atop of one another. This was a common sight around town: smashed vehicles randomly dropped in a different location from where they were originally parked. Note the other common thing seen around the city: someone's mattress picked up by the winds and dropped somewhere else. This location appears to have been the Oasis Steak House.

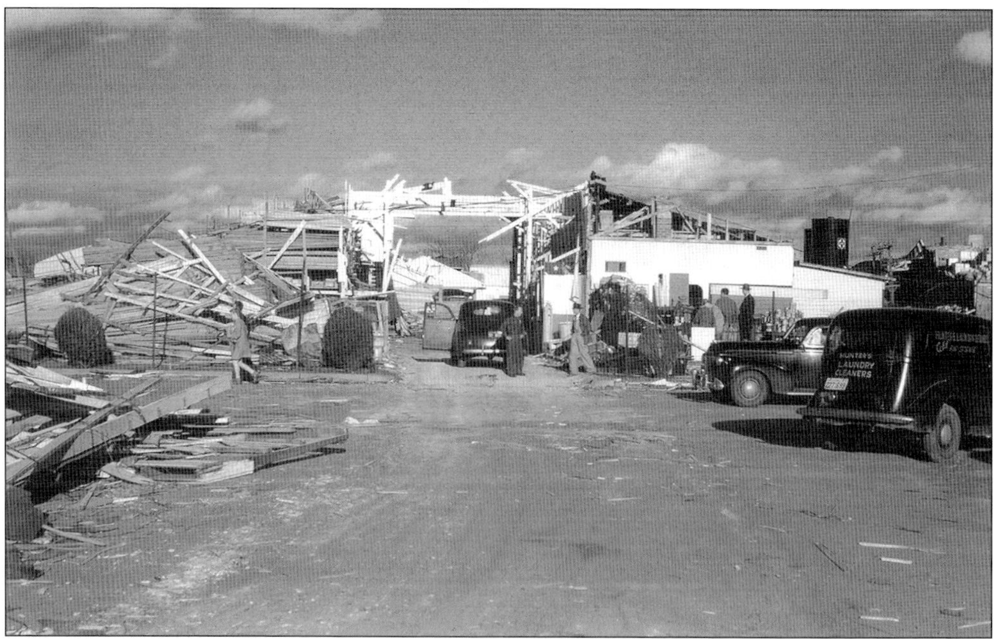

It's just another business day at the Osborne-Peebles Lumber Company as people gather to purchase lumber and whatever other supplies were needed to repair or rebuild. Note the delivery vehicle for Hunter's Laundry & Cleaners, which was located catty-corner to the lumber yard. Also viewable in this photograph is the Santa Fe storage tank to the southeast.

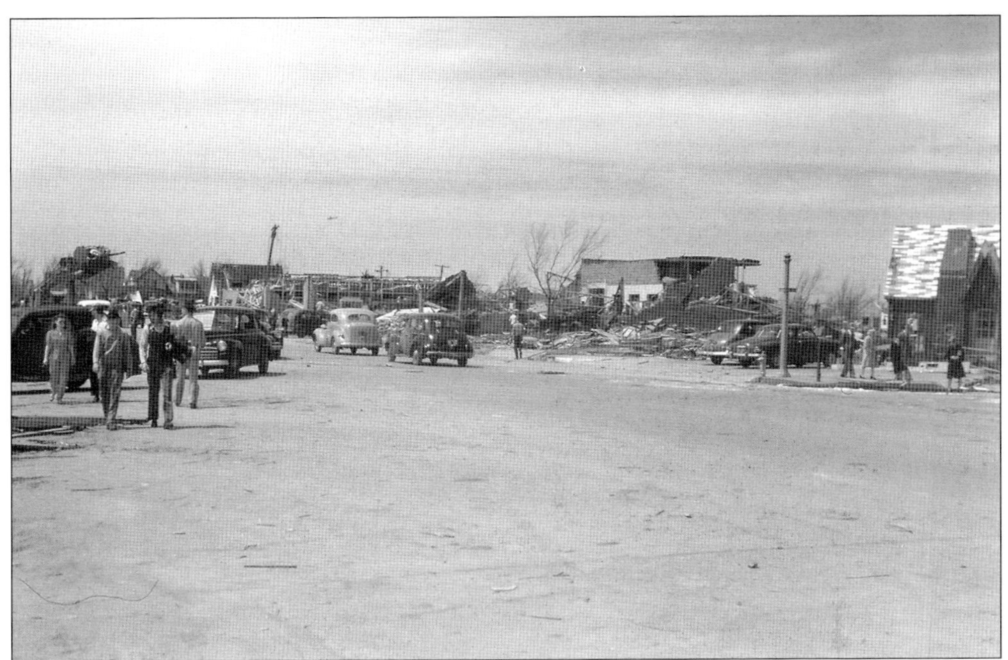

This street scene shows the intersection of Main and Eleventh Streets looking to the northwest. Johnson Lumber Company is in the background. In the foreground on the right side of the photograph is the gas station building that currently serves as the headquarters for the Woodward Main Street organization. Note the seemingly large numbers of people just walking along the street.

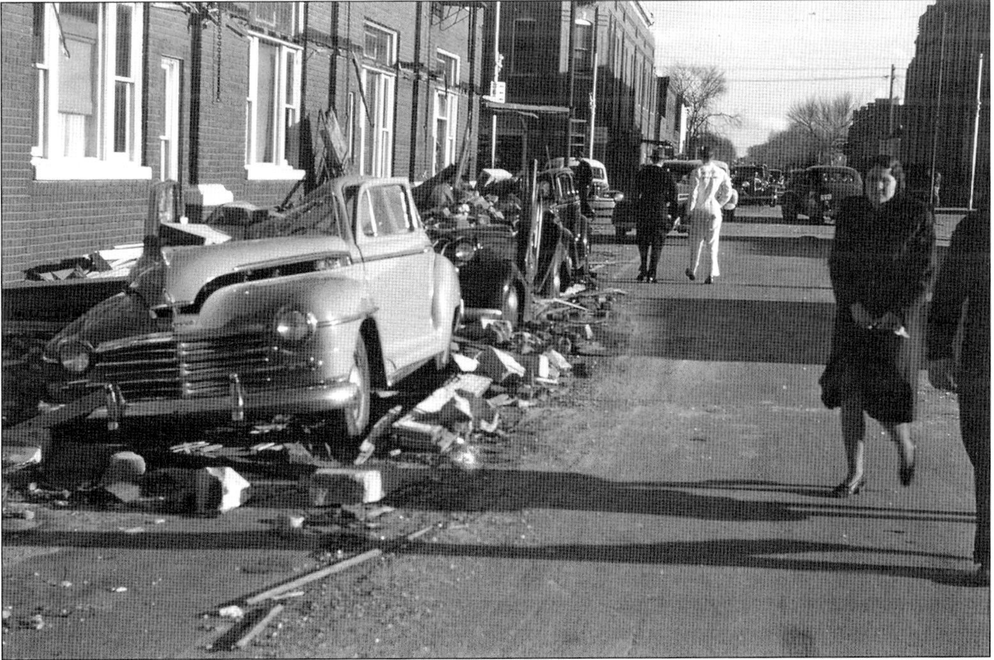

This photograph was taken on the west side of the Baker Hotel on Eighth Street looking south. It shows two vehicles smashed by bricks and blocks from the roofline of the hotel. Again, there seems to be a large amount of foot and vehicle traffic moving around town, probably sightseers.

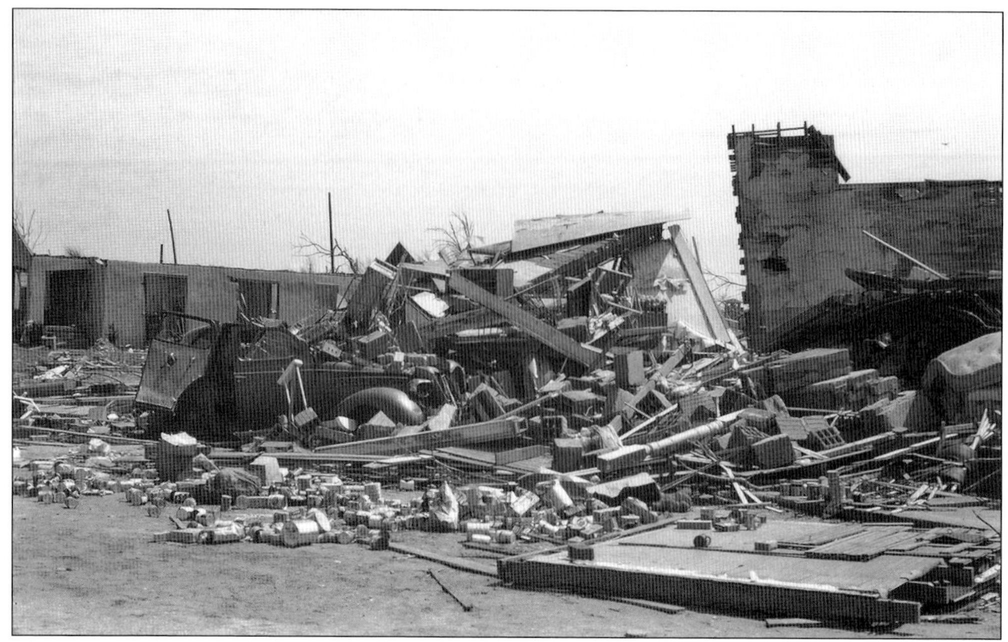

This image shows an automobile buried beneath the rubble of the Vogel Grocery building. Debris and canned goods litter the ground surrounding the vehicle. The tornado ended the Vogel family's run with this store, though by the early 1950s, they were managing another grocery store along Main Street.

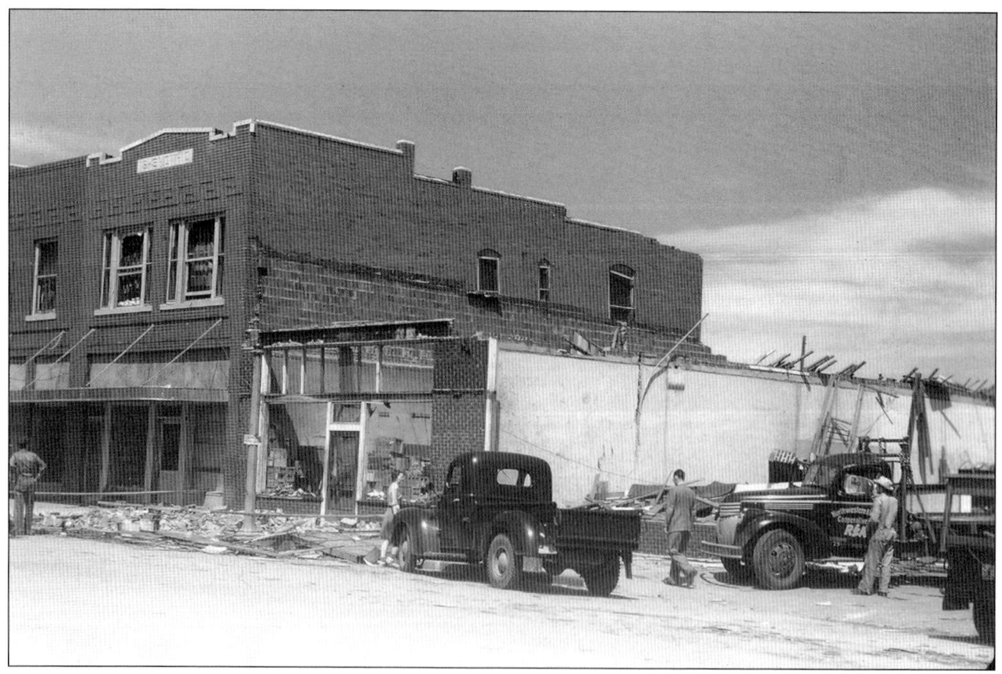

Damage to the Northwestern Electric Cooperative building, located in the 700 block of Main Street, was significant. Snow Hardware is located just to the west was owned and run by Ed "Pop" Snow, a well-known fixture in Woodward. He was the longtime fire chief, saloon owner, business owner, and entrepreneur.

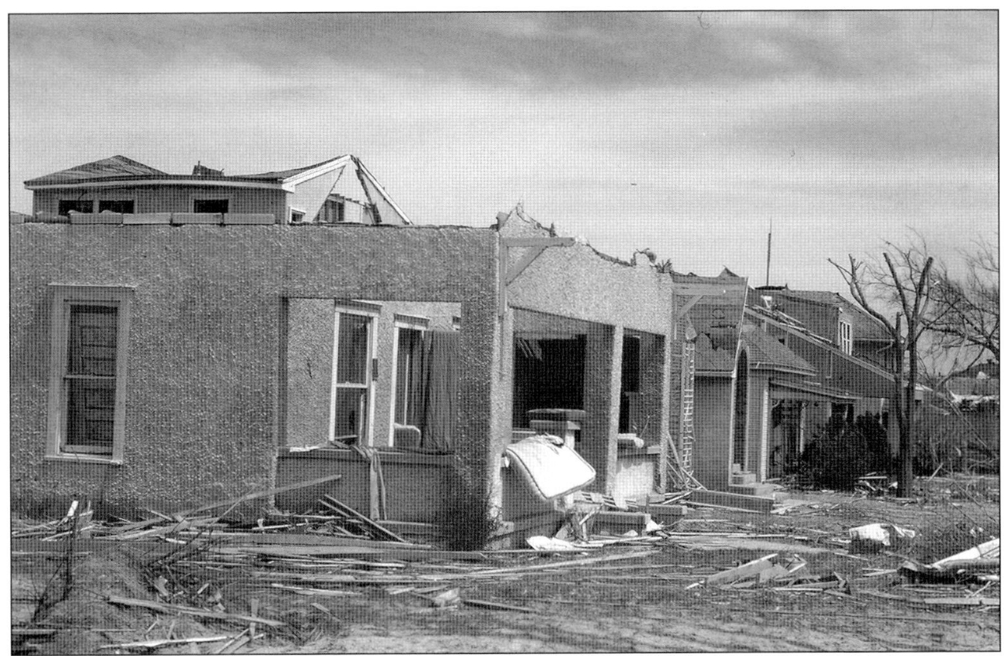

These are shots of two houses in the 1300 block of Texas Avenue that stood side by side. Although the above photograph shows the roof of the house on the corner of Fourteenth Street and Texas Avenue completely blown off, the structure itself, other than broken glass, appears structurally sound. People who lived through the 1947 Woodward tornado have commented that in blocks of houses that were destroyed often only the stucco houses remained. Also, note in the image above that houses farther down the street appear to have comparatively less damage. Seen below (next door) is the home of H.B. Heaton torn up, but the basic structure remains intact. This home was rebuilt following the tornado and remains today. The home above is gone, and there is now a self-storage building on the site.

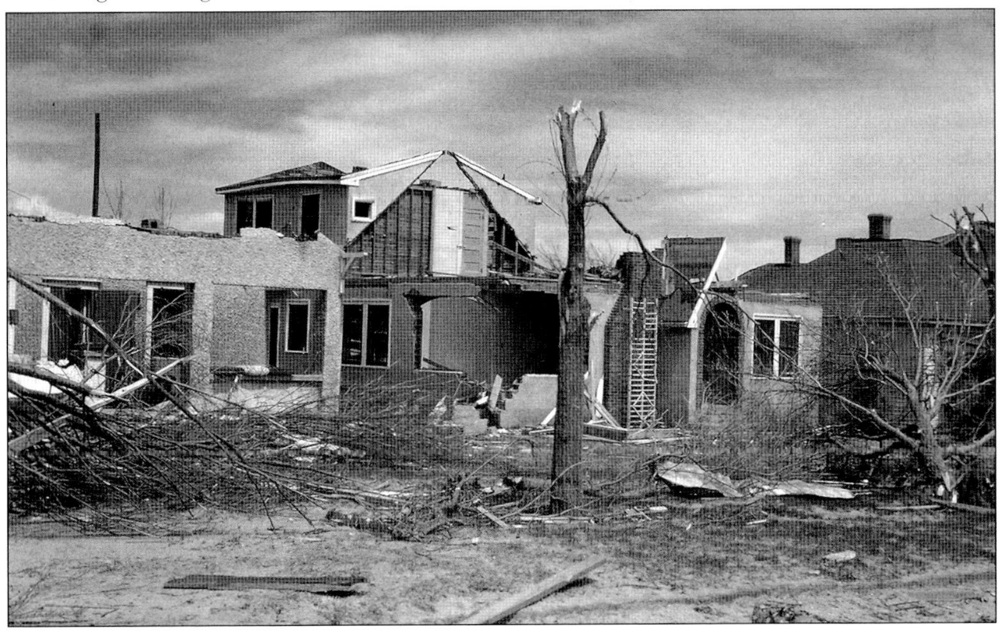

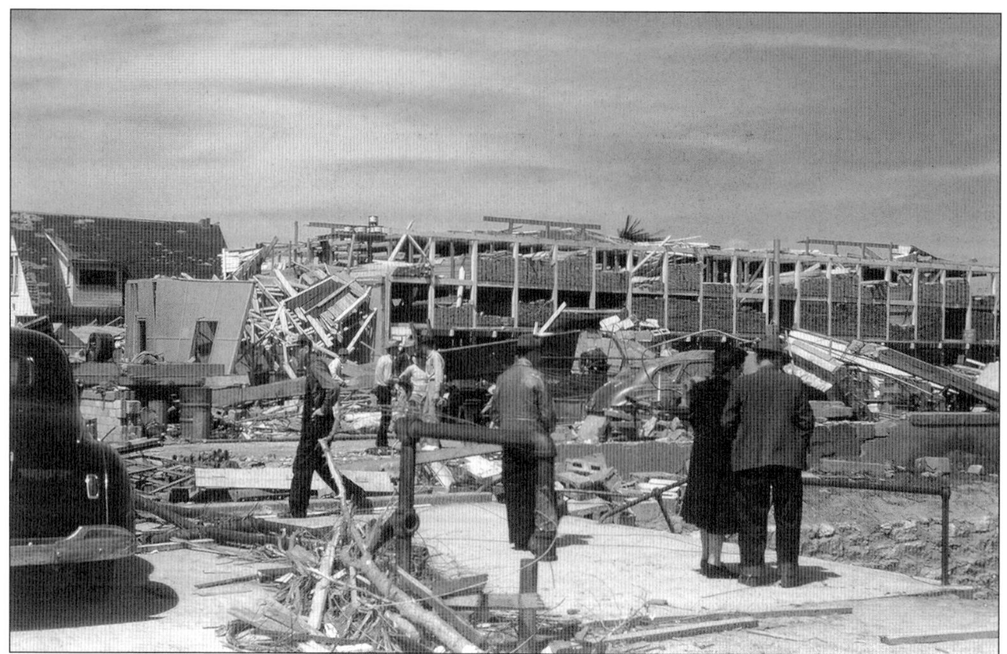

A shot along Main Street just to the west of the Katy Railroad tracks shows Johnson Lumber Company in the background. The people on the bridge over the storm drainage ditch staring down into the ditch are most likely observing a vehicle (out of camera view) that somehow landed there. Note that the pipe guardrail across the bridge has been torn apart.

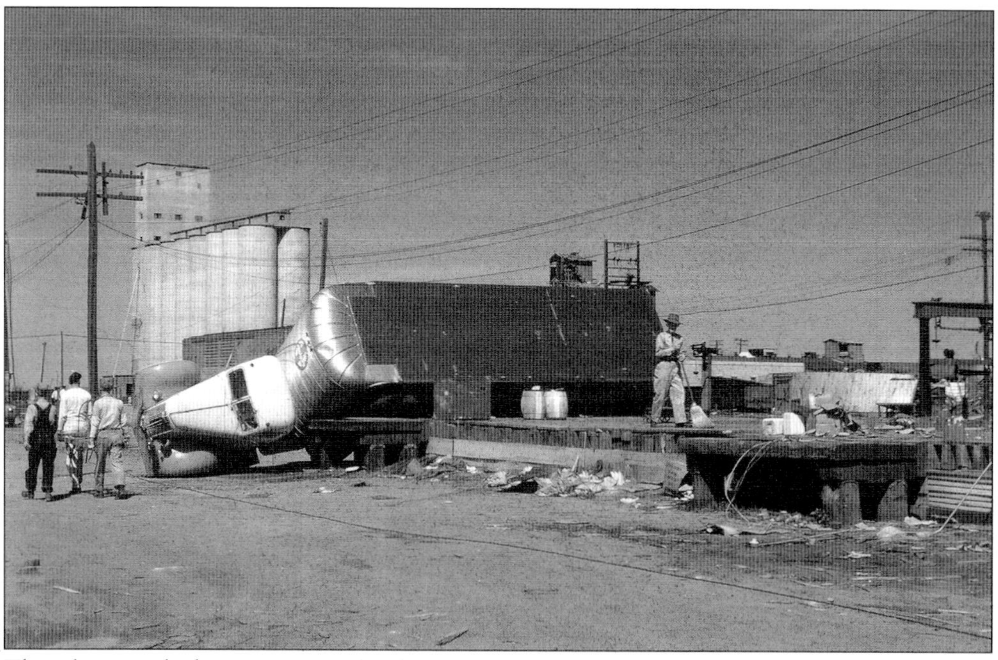

This photograph shows a man with a broom attempting to sweep off debris from a platform or loading dock somewhere along the railroad tracks just to the east of the Fisher Grain elevator. That is a Santa Fe Railway tractor-trailer toppled over. The peak in the background (standing above the trailer) with most of its tin torn off was an elevator and feed mill.

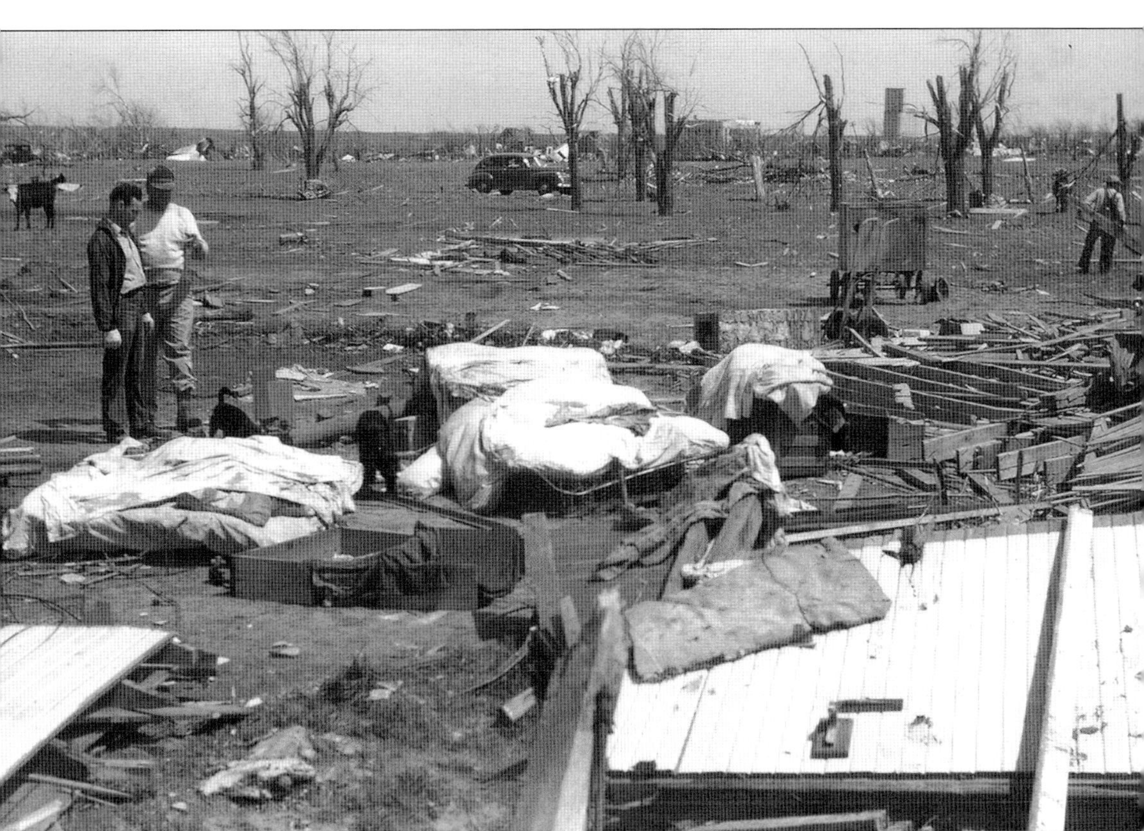

The scene in this photograph was the west end of town in what was known as the Highland Park section. The ground for hundreds of yards around is all but barren, with only debris scattered. The two men in the foreground appear to be discussing the wreckage of one home that does not show much left except for some bedding and part of a fence. Two cattle can be seen in the background, one on the left (white face) and one on the right (standing amid the trees). Bovines were a common sight in many of the photographs taken in this area of town. Their pasture fences had been blown down in the storm, and they wandered until their owners were able to reclaim them. As always, the Woodward County Courthouse and the Fisher Grain elevator complex stand as silent witnesses watching over a desolate landscape.

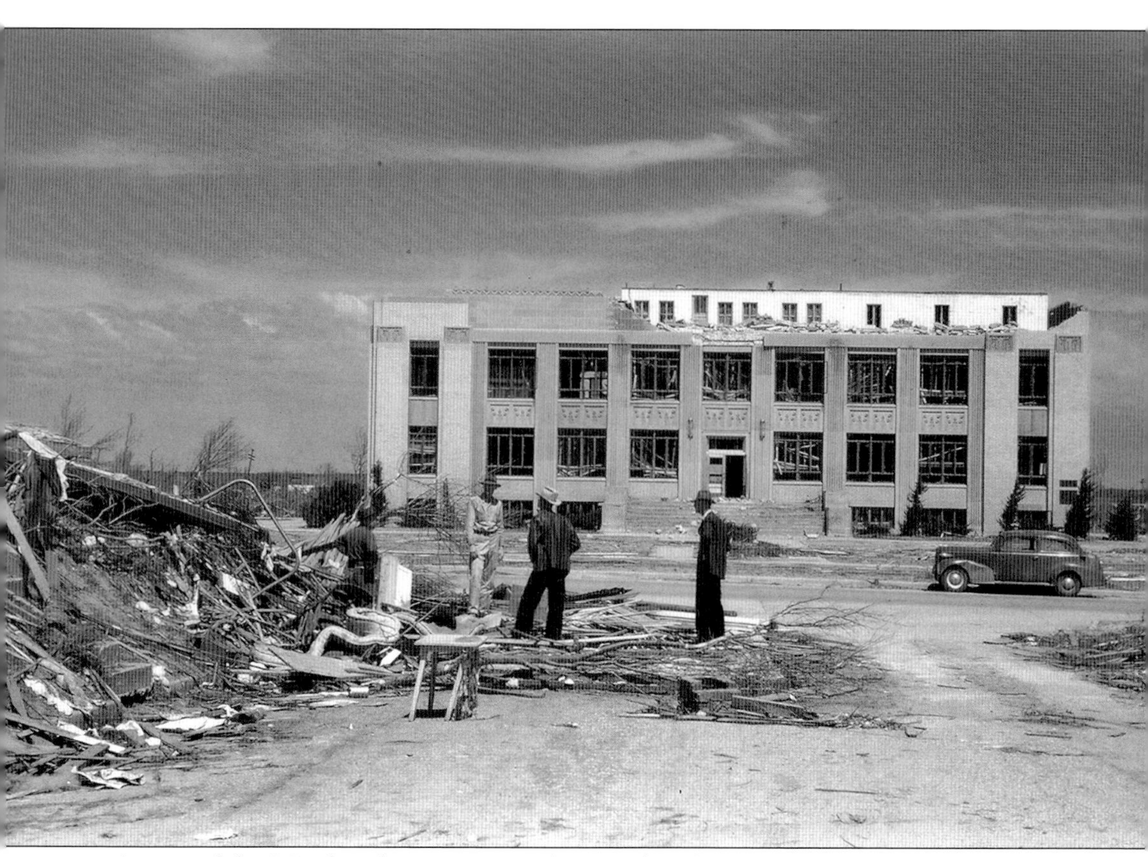

A view of the Woodward County Courthouse taken from Hillcrest Drive looks north. The damage to the courthouse building is very apparent from this angle, with much of the upper edifice damaged or missing. It appears that nearly every bit of glass is broken out. This image was captured after cleanup had begun. Main Street appears to be clear of debris, and even the courthouse lawn has been partially cleared.

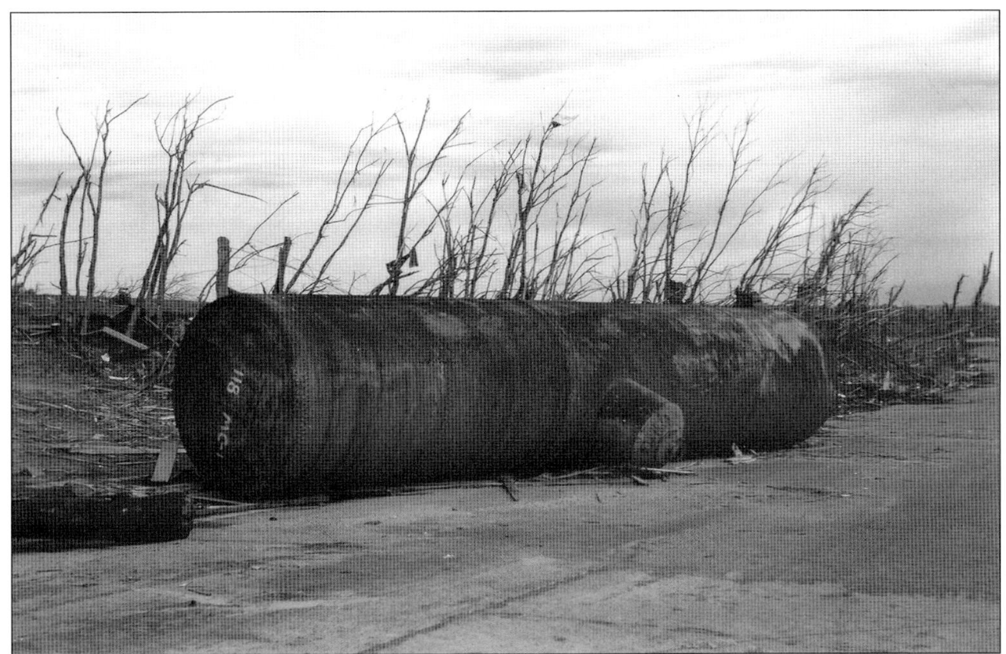

This photograph shows a railroad tanker car, without its undercarriage, that was blown into the street near the City Power Plant. The original City Power Plant was located near the Atchison, Topeka & Santa Fe (AT&SF) Railway lines, so it is possible that the tornadic winds picked this up and deposited it into the street. That is 30 tons of steel (empty).

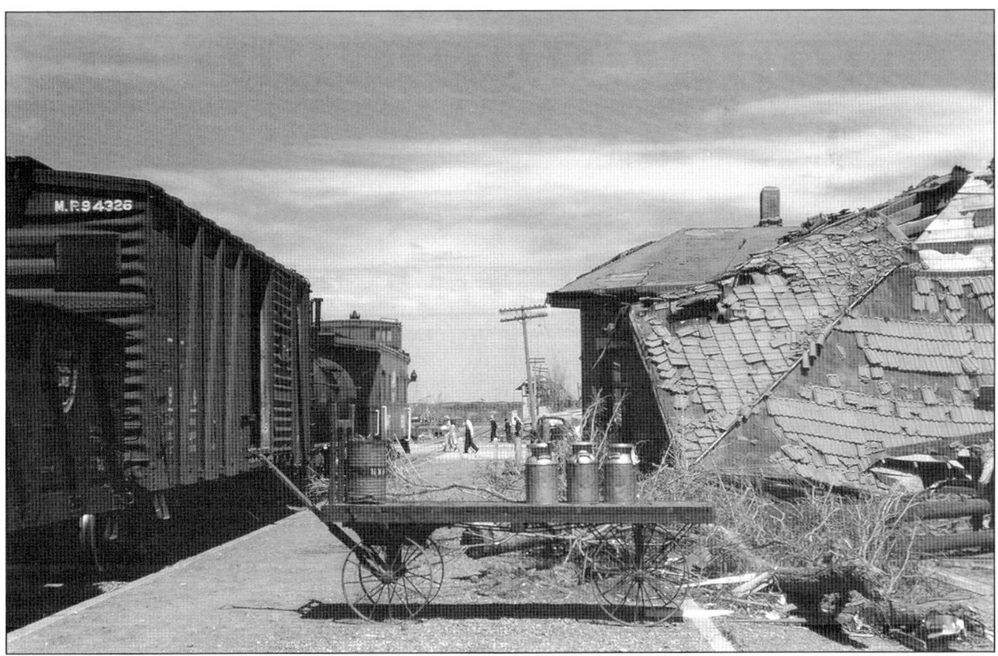

This photograph was taken on the west side of the Katy Railroad depot while a train was stopped there. It shows a close-up view of the collapsed south end of the depot. Note the switching tower to the north behind a utility pole.

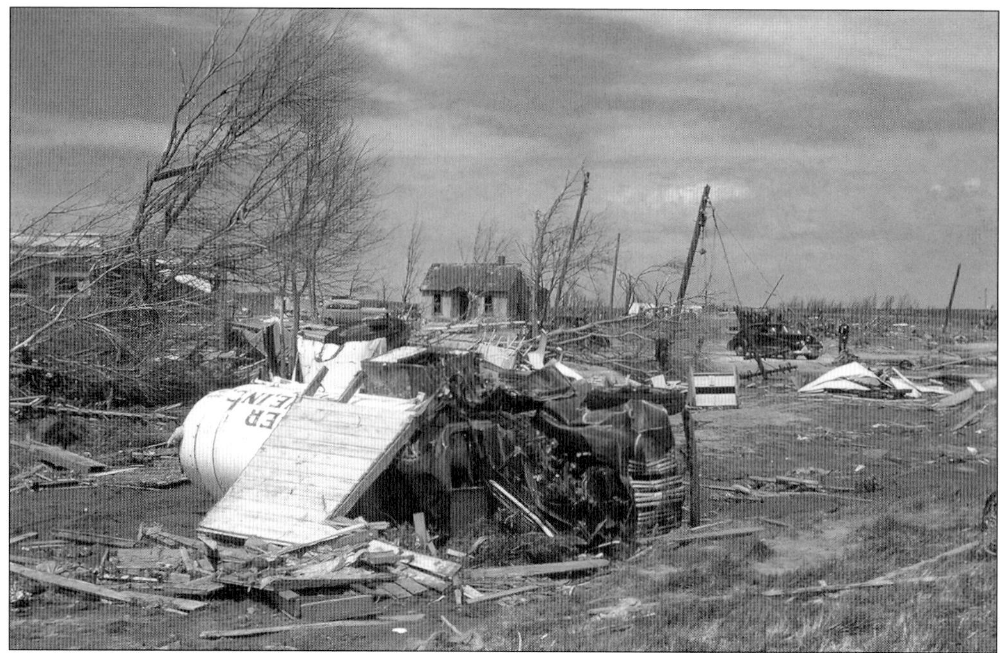

This photograph was taken in an unidentified section of town that shows a tank truck, possibly either a water truck or septic pumper, turned on its side. There is a section of someone's wall blown up against it. Note the police officer standing in the road in the background, probably wanting to know what the photographer is doing out there.

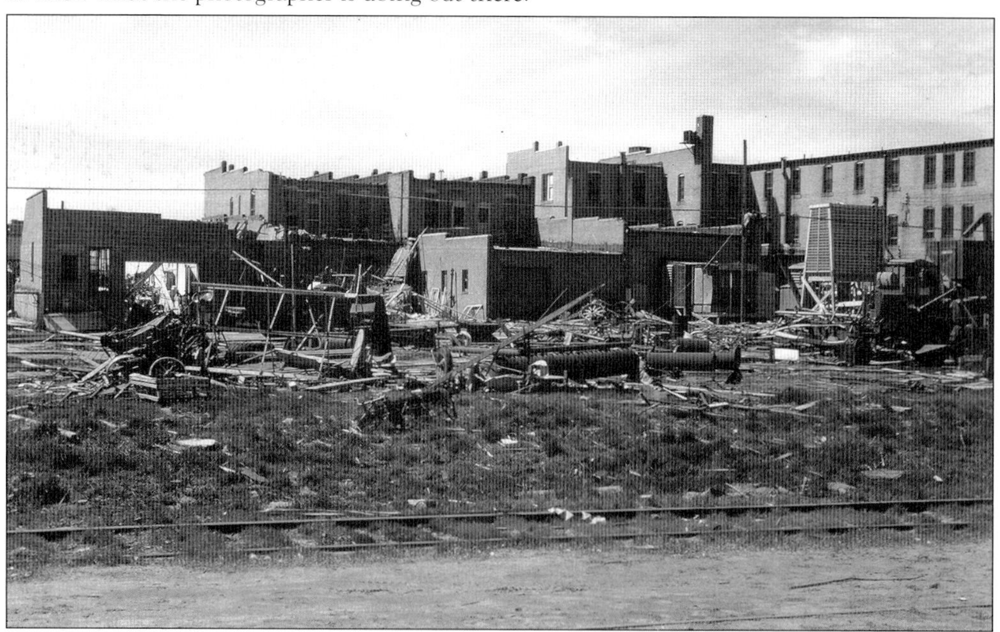

The view in this image is of the backs of a block of buildings most likely located along Main Street. Two sets of railroad tracks are viewable in the foreground. Farm implements or pieces of farm implements are scattered throughout the debris. This was probably the 600 or 700 block of Main Street. There were implement dealers on both blocks. Note the man working aloft on the utility pole on the right side of the photograph.

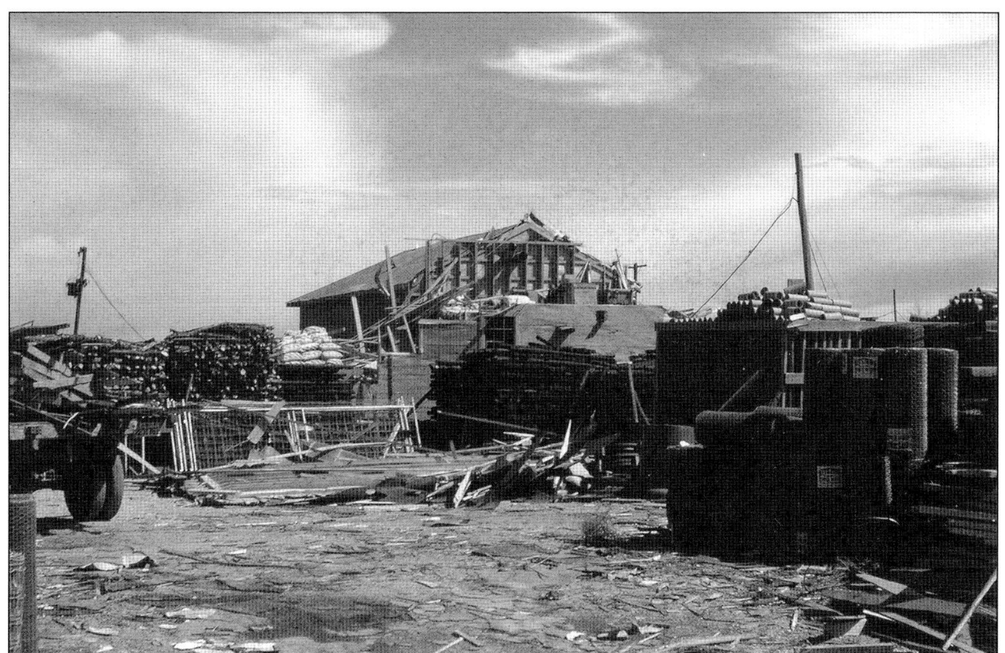

Seen here is an unidentified farm supply or hardware store yard. Stacks of fence posts, rolls of fencing, and the bin of tile drains give it away. It is hard to put a location on this photograph, but it is believed to be somewhere in the north end of the city. It appears that a cleanup of the yard is already underway.

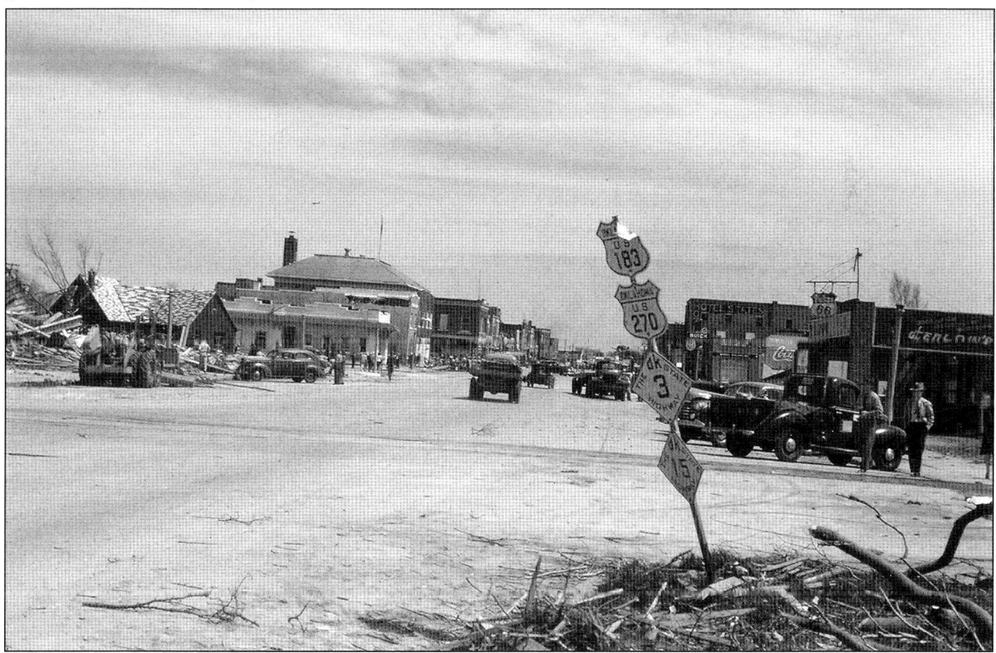

This image shows a view to the east along Main Street from just beyond the Katy Railroad tracks. The businesses along the street include the States Hotel, the US Post Office (former Federal Building), the King Hotel, Phillips 66 Service Garage, and signage for US Highways 183 and 270 and State Highways 3 and 15.

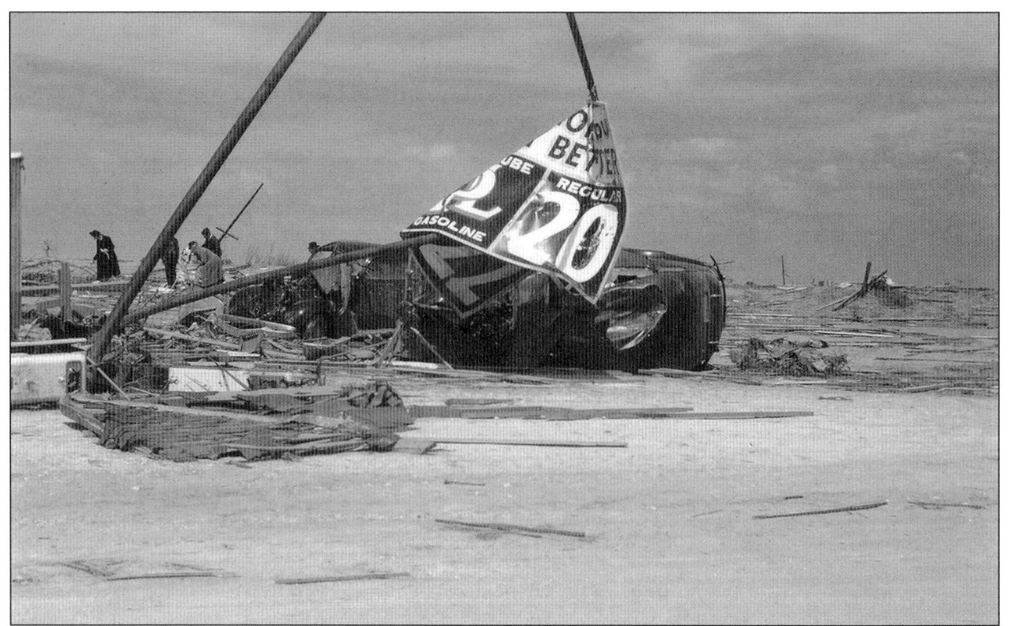

In this photograph of an unidentified area in Woodward, probably the west end, people can be seen in the background quite possibly picking through the remains of their home. Two tornado-blown and wrecked cars are in the center of the photograph. There is also a mangled gas station sign advertising 20¢ regular and 22¢ premium gas prices.

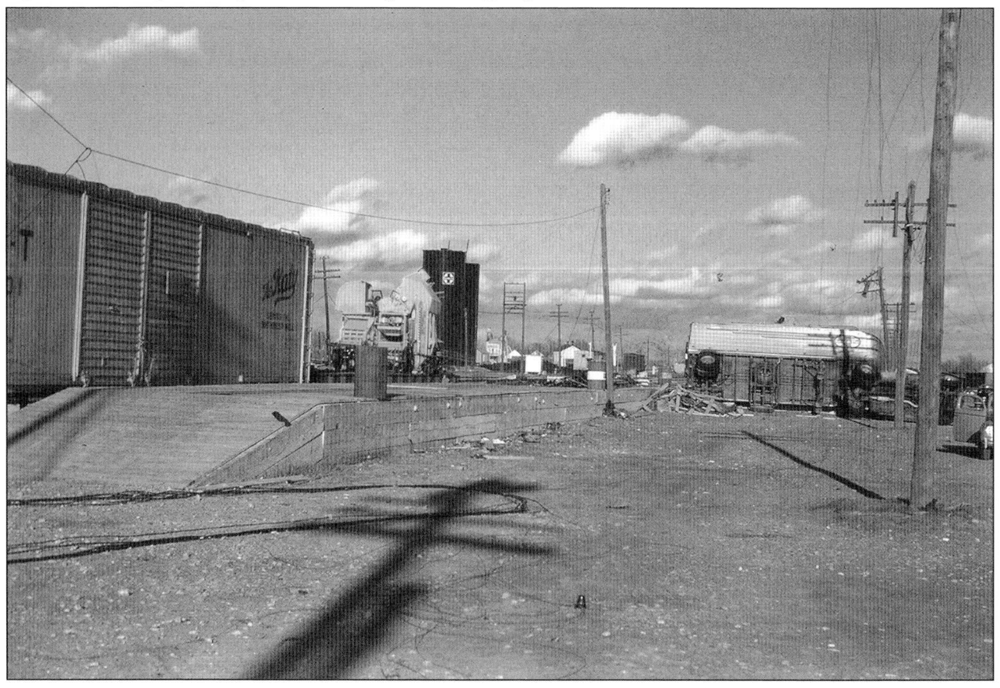

This scene was photographed somewhere east of the Santa Fe Railway depot. The overturned Santa Fe Railway tractor-trailer seen in other photographs is to the rear. The Santa Fe storage tanks are viewable. There is a Katy Railroad boxcar parked along the loading dock. Bundles of utility lines litter the ground.

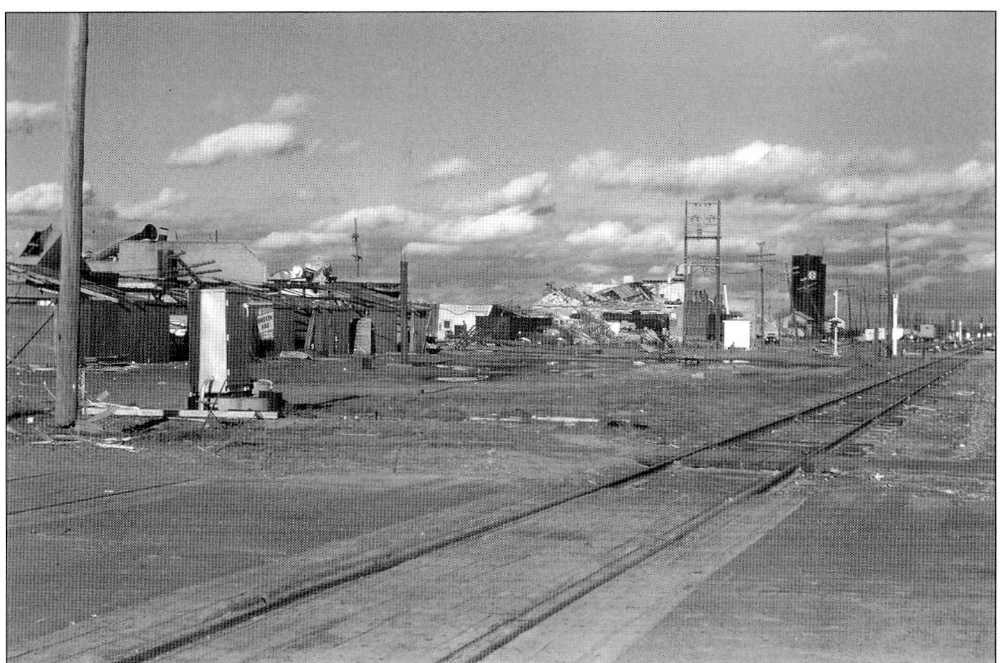

This image shows the destruction of businesses that were located along the AT&SF Railway. The two Santa Fe storage tanks are visible. To the left of the tanks, there appears to be a warehouse of some sort with its goods exposed.

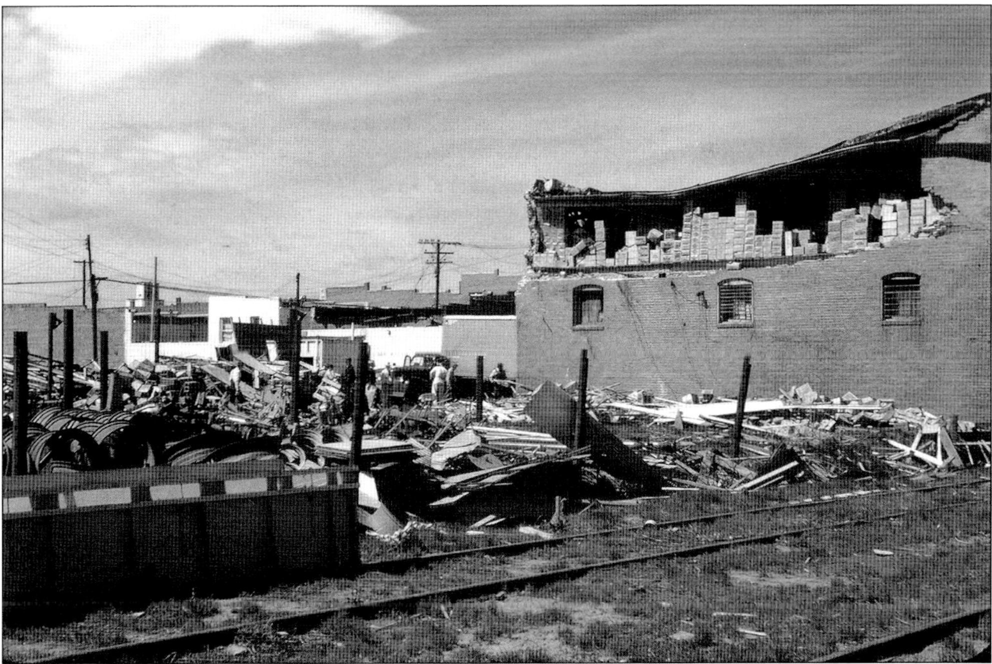

Another view shows a business or warehouse building located next to the Santa Fe Railway. One wall of the building has collapsed, exposing its contents. Some of the boxes have spilled onto the ground. There appears to be a crew at the back of the building conducting a salvage operation. Large metal rims can be seen among the debris spread across the area next to the building.

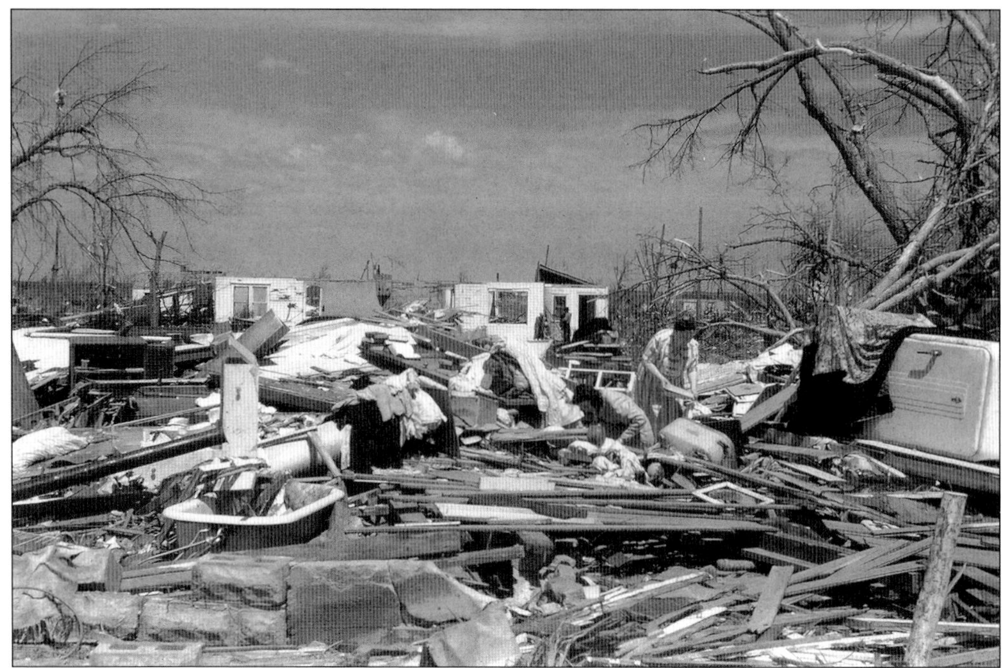

This image shows two women rummaging through the wreckage of a home, searching for anything they can salvage. Piles of clothing and quilts are laid out around them as they search. There is a refrigerator on its side to the right. Note the iron bathtub in the foreground. In several of the photographs taken of damaged homes, there are bathtubs standing undamaged.

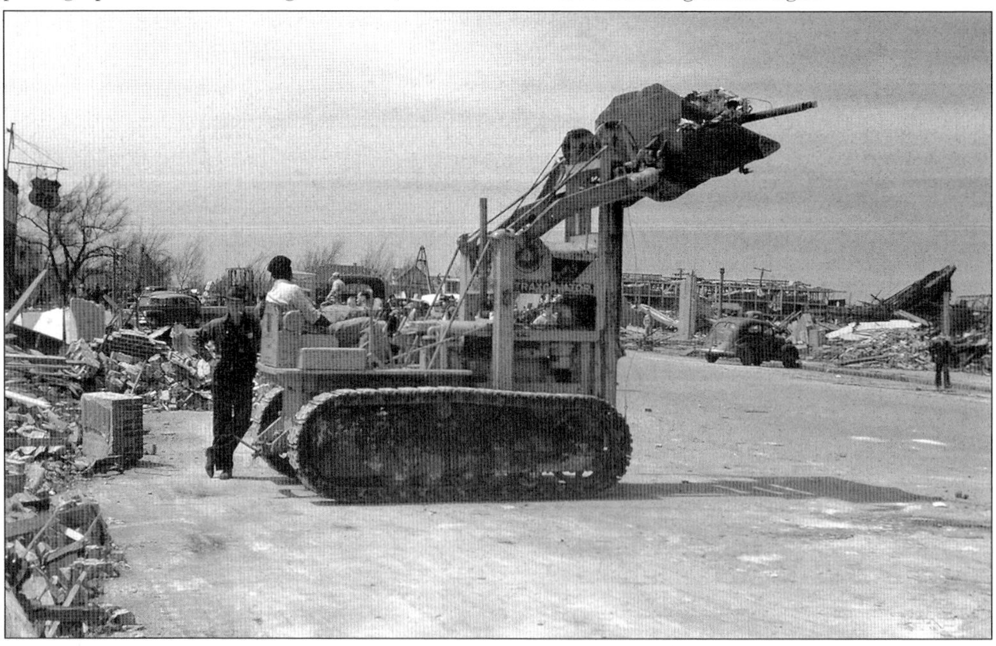

This photograph was taken on the south side of Main Street looking west near the intersection with Eleventh Street. Men doing cleanup with a bulldozer with a front-end loader appear to be taking a break while waiting for a dump truck. Debris and rubbish picked up during the cleanup were trucked to a site southwest of town to be dumped.

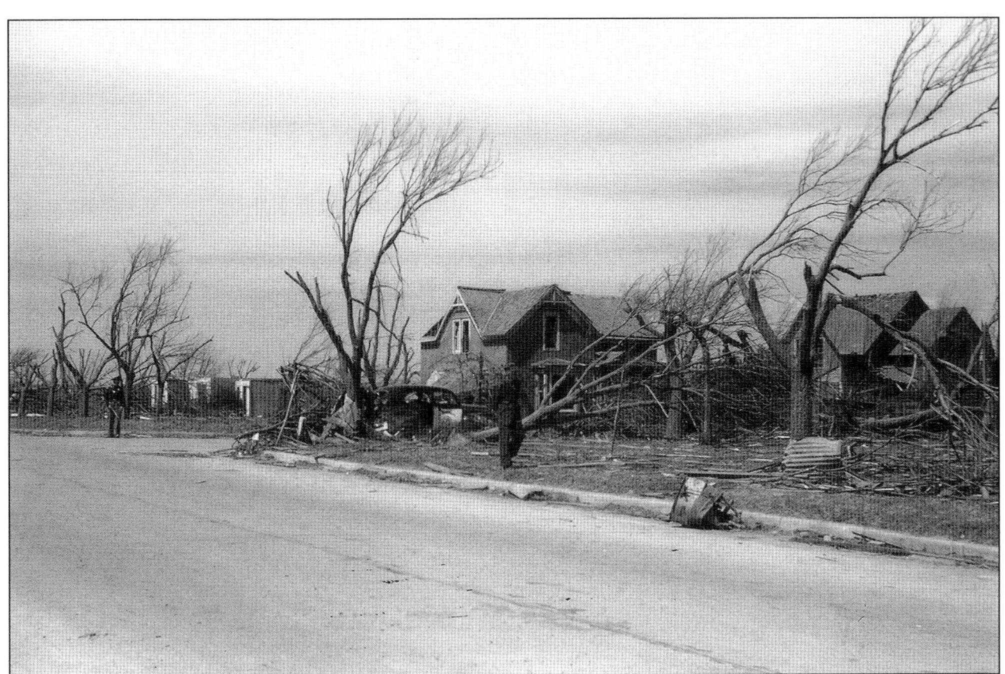

This photograph shows two homes with some damage in an unidentified area of Woodward. A large number of trees appears to be down across the street from the homes. A Woodward police officer stands on one corner of the intersection, and his police car is parked across the street. There is also a man walking along the street.

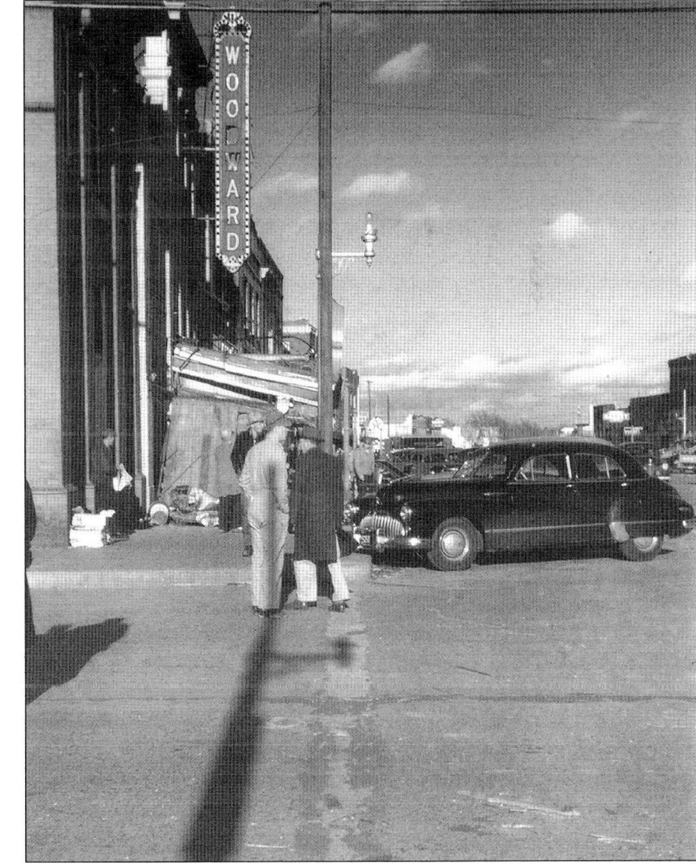

This street scene from the northwest corner of Ninth and Main Streets looks east along Main Street. The damaged front of the Woodward Theatre is clearly visible and is apparently blocked, as people are stepping out into the street in front of the theater to walk around. In the distance, in possibly the 600 block, a Texaco gas station sign is visible.

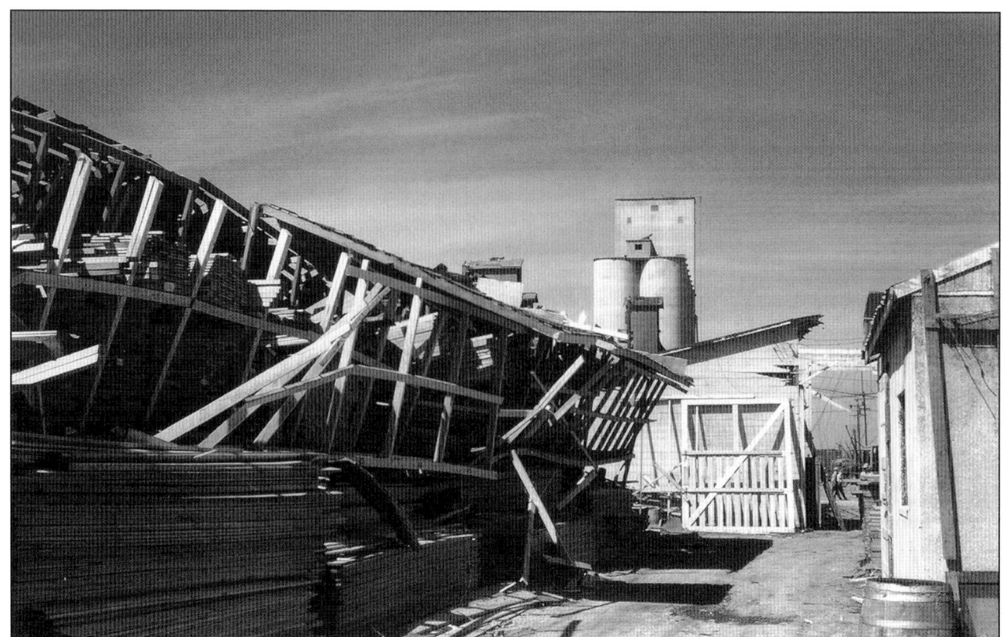

This photograph was taken well inside the Osborne-Peebles Lumber Company yard looking west. The stacks of lumber stock are visible on the left side of the image. Above the stacks is the damaged roof of the feed mill. The Fisher Grain elevator complex is the dominant feature in this picture.

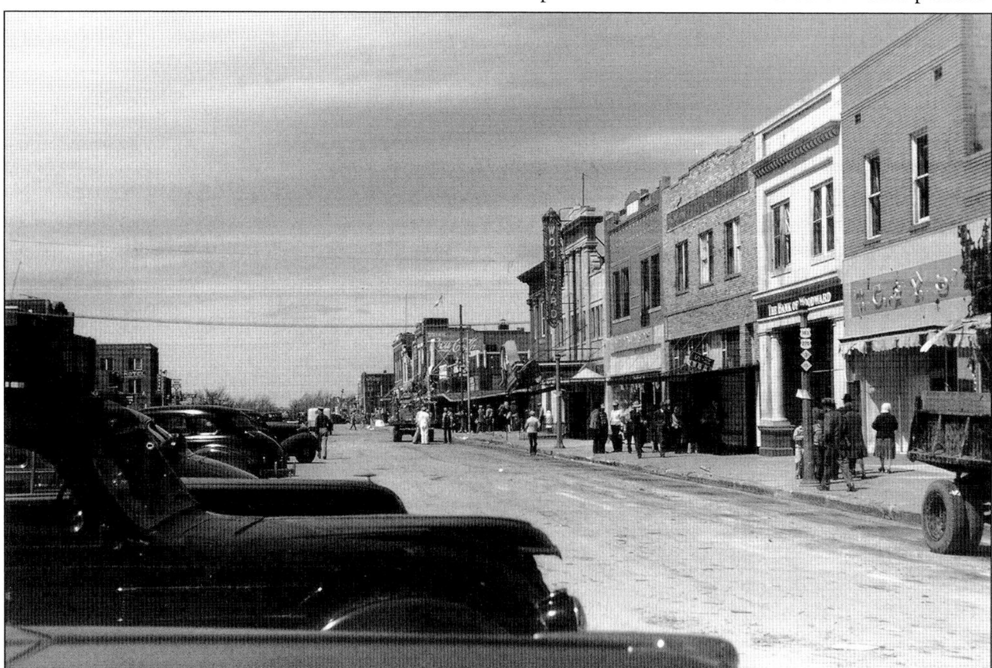

This photograph shows the 800 block of Main Street (south side) looking west after the cleanup. Visible in the photograph are businesses including the TG&Y store (present-day Longshots Bar & Grill), the Bank of Woodward (present-day H&R Block), the Woodward Theatre, and farther down, the King Hotel (on the right) and the States Hotel (on the left). A group of people stands in front of the café, possibly waiting for it to open.

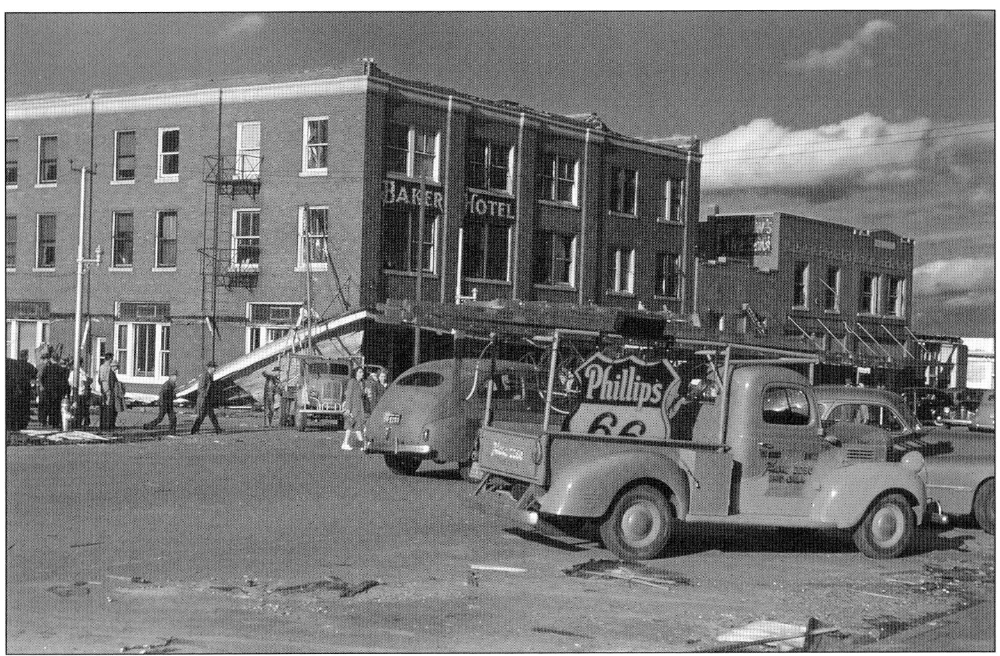

Work has begun on the severely damaged front awning of the Baker Hotel on the corner of Eighth and Main Streets. The orange-and-blue pickup and crane truck belong to a sign company in Enid that was probably brought in to help with the cleanup and repairs. To the right of the hotel is the building that housed the Terry Theatre (the present-day city chambers building). The building to the right of the Terry Theatre is the Snow Building. Both the Terry building and the Snow Building remain standing and in use today. The image below also shows a Mistletoe Express truck backed up to the Baker Hotel. It may have been used to help haul away debris.

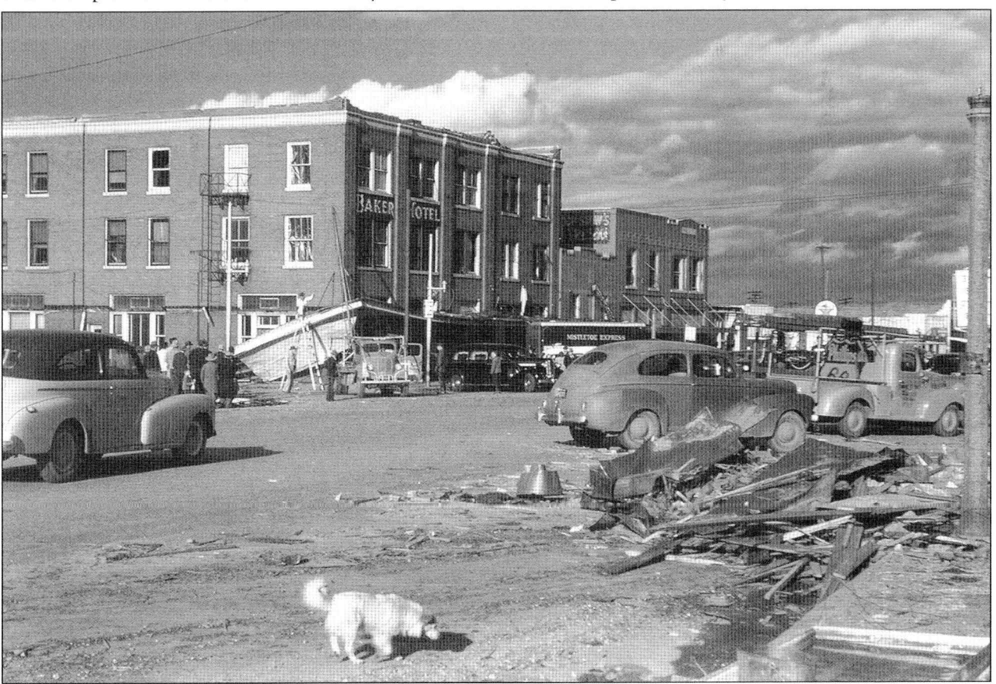

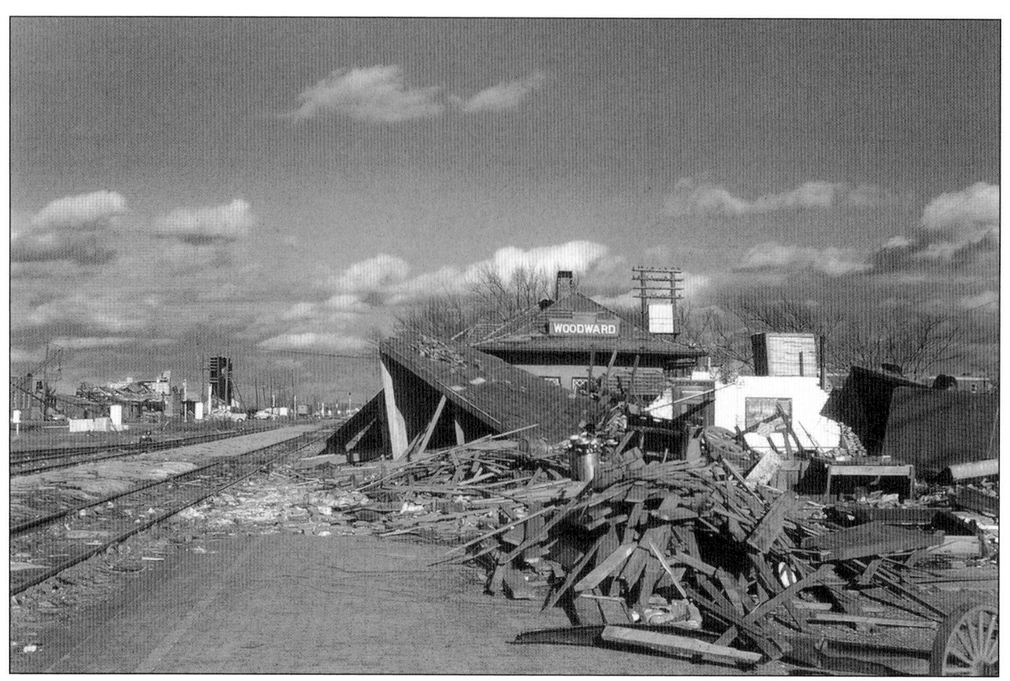

This photograph looks to the east and shows a close-up view of the west end of the Santa Fe depot, where the freight building collapsed. Much of the debris remains stacked on the platform awaiting trucks for transport to a dump site. Obviously, the priority for railroad personnel was clearing the tracks to allow the trains to move on schedule.

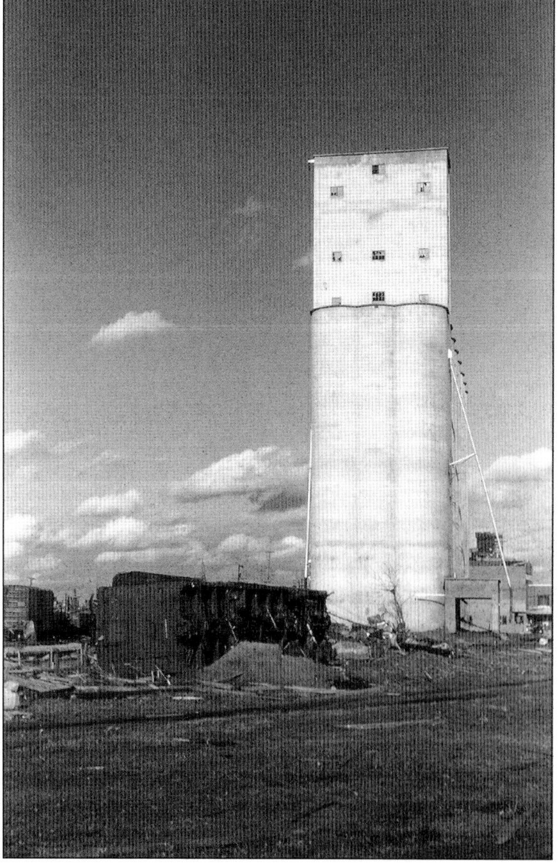

This photograph, looking east, provides a view of the Fisher Grain elevator complex. There is a railroad boxcar on its side in the foreground, probably blown off the track (out of the frame to the right). As this image shows, the windows in the elevator headhouse were blown out in the storm—the only real damage done to the structure.

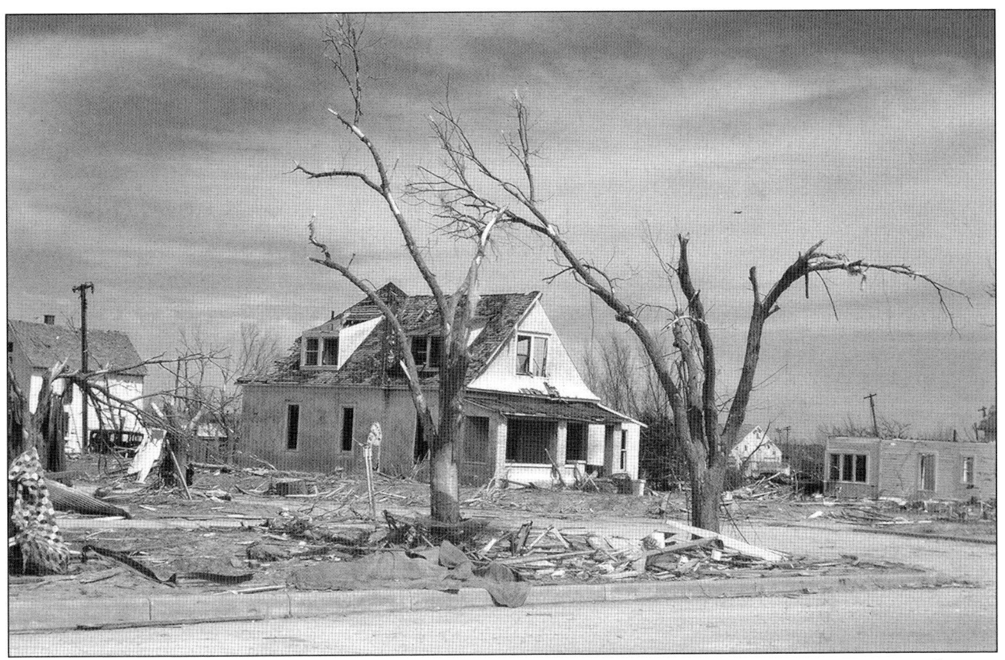

The home in this image, believed to be located just to the east of the Woodward County Courthouse, shows considerable damage to the roof. In fact, the entire east side of the roof appears to be missing. There is considerable damage to trees around the home as well. The camera's point of view is to the northeast.

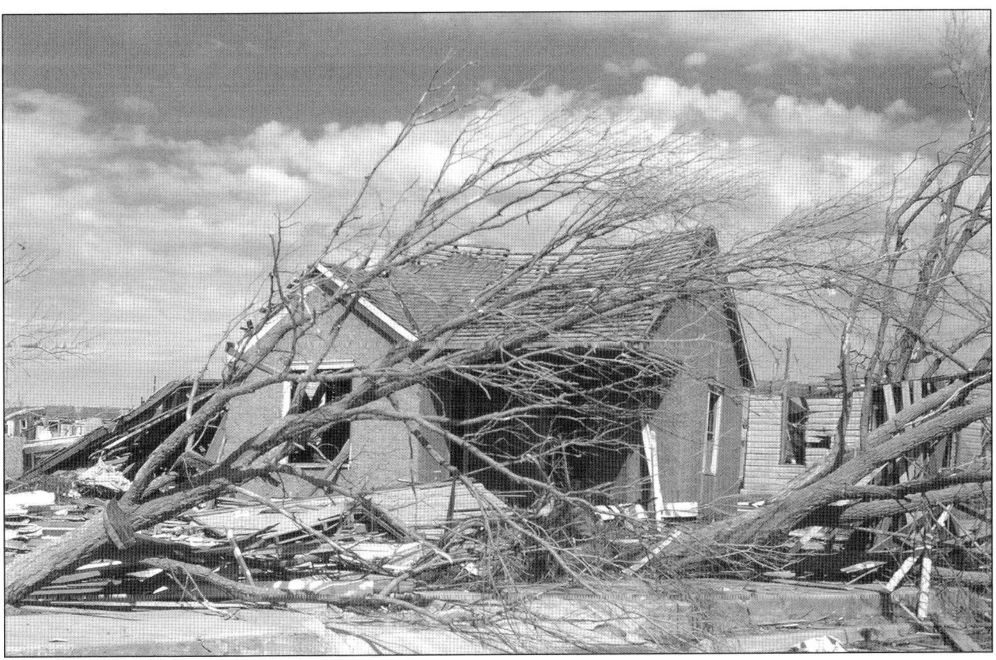

This home, in an unidentified location, appears to have been blown completely off its foundation and in danger of collapsing. The stucco exterior seems to have held together, but the tornadic winds were too much to hold the structure on its foundation. It would appear that this particular block was hard hit, given the amount of downed trees and other debris.

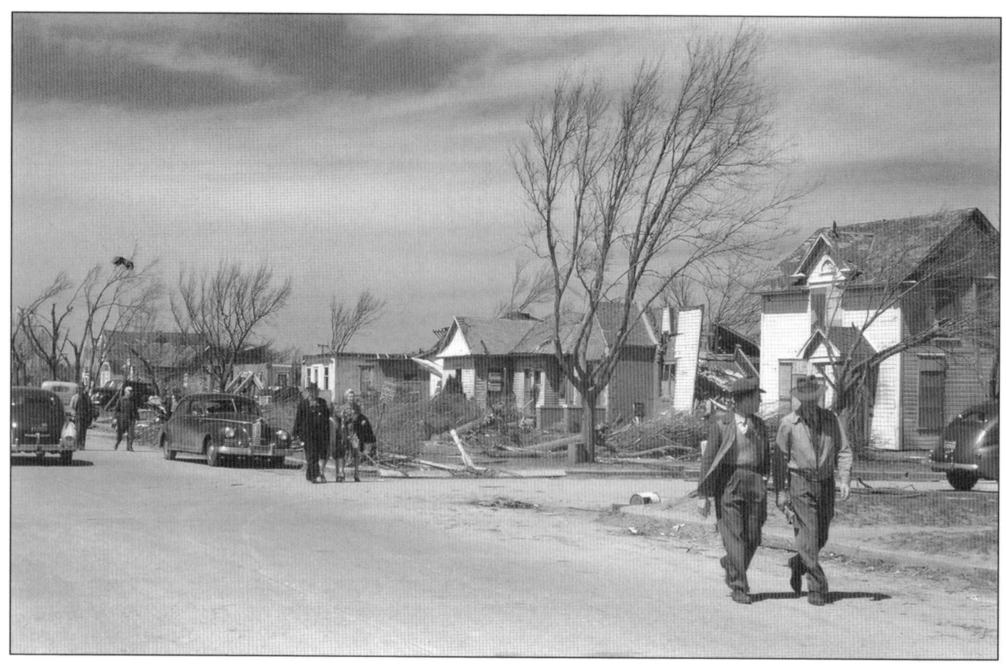

A stream of sightseers moves west along Main Street, viewing for themselves the destruction of the storm. The remains of St. Peter's Catholic Church are seen on the other side of the white house on the right side of the photograph. It would be nearly 13 years later before parishioners moved into their new church on the corner of Oklahoma Avenue and Twenty-First Street.

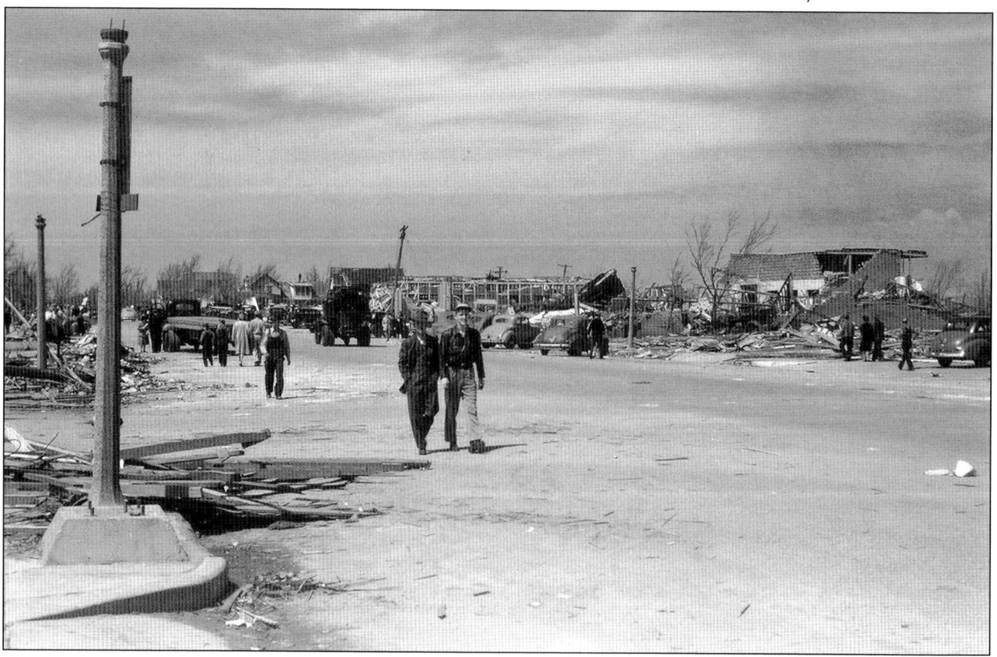

This photograph shows a view of Main Street looking to the west from Eleventh Street. The sightseers are out in force in this image, with pedestrians moving along both sides of the street. The Johnson Lumber Company yard is visible in the background. Although there is still debris along the edges of the street, the roadway itself appears to have been cleared.

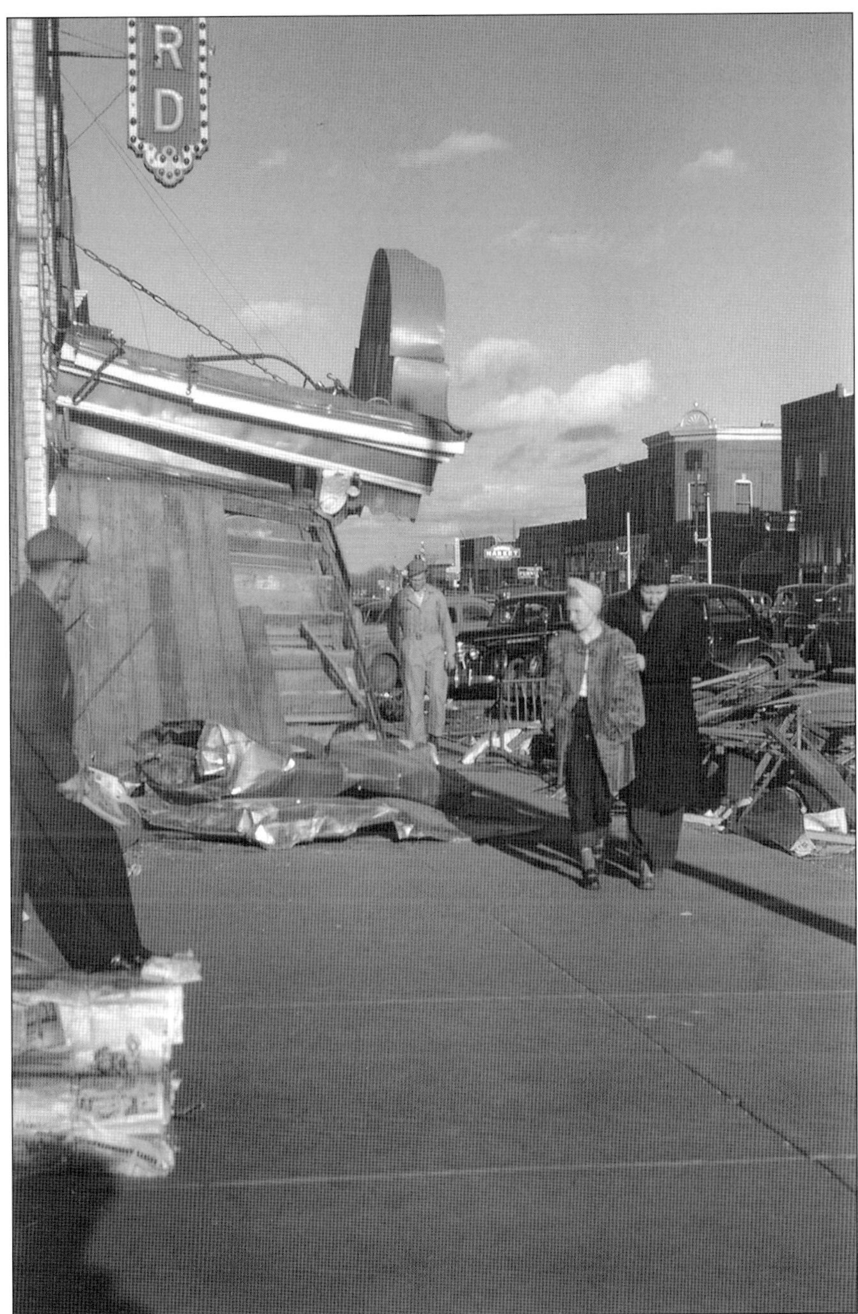

This image provides a close-up view of the front of the Woodward Theatre before the obstructions were cleared out of the way. The view looks toward the east. Pedestrians on the sidewalk were forced to step out onto the street in order to keep moving. A newspaper seller works the corner of Ninth and Main Streets. The Terry brothers would rebuild the marquee and signage outside their theater, adding neon lighting that became an iconic landmark in downtown Woodward. The movie house closed in the late 1970s. In the early 1980s, the building underwent a major renovation and reopened as the Woodward Arts Theatre. It remains in operation today as a live arts venue.

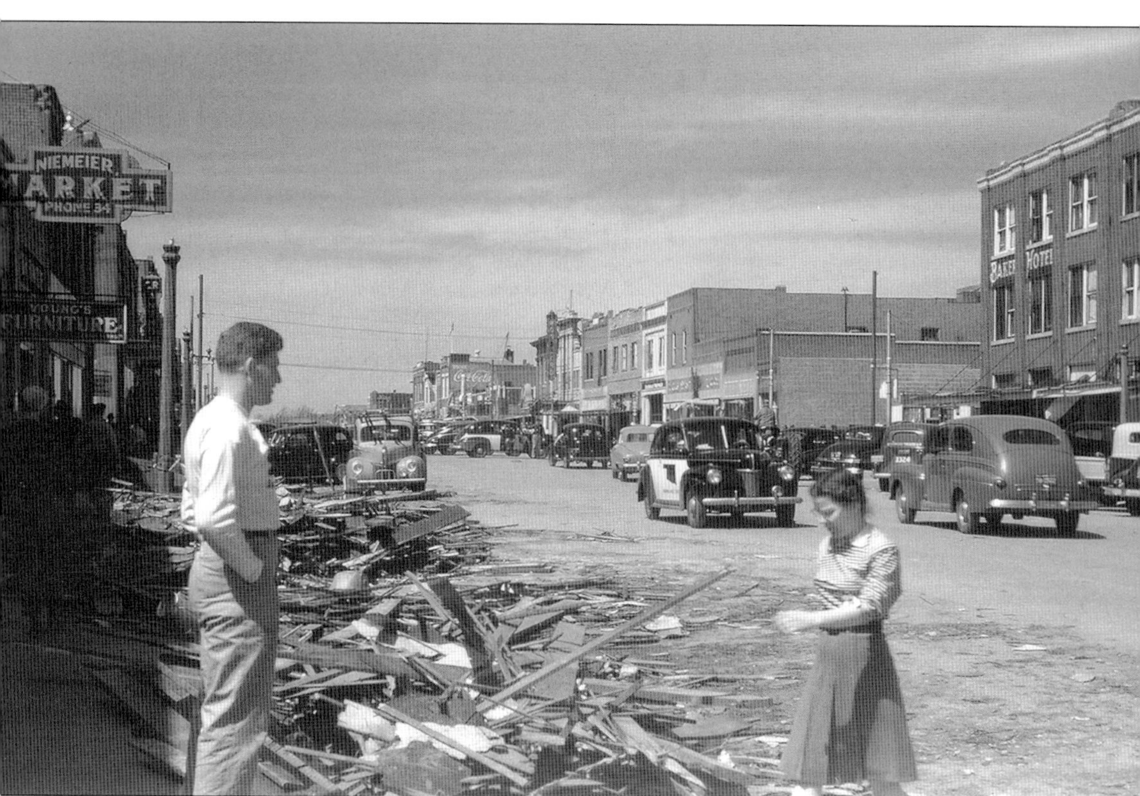

This image was taken in the 700 block of Main Street looking to the west. Business signs that are shown include the Niemeier Market and Young's Furniture. Across the street, the Baker Hotel is viewable, its front awning having been repaired. Beyond, in the 800 block, the very top of C.R. Anthony's store sign is visible on the south side of Main Street. On the north side of Main Street are the TG&Y store, the Bank of Woodward, and the Woodward Theatre, with a now unobstructed sidewalk in front. There is an Oklahoma Highway Patrol car at the intersection of Eighth and Main Streets, with two troopers directing traffic through the intersection. Another highway patrol car is moving down the 700 block going east.

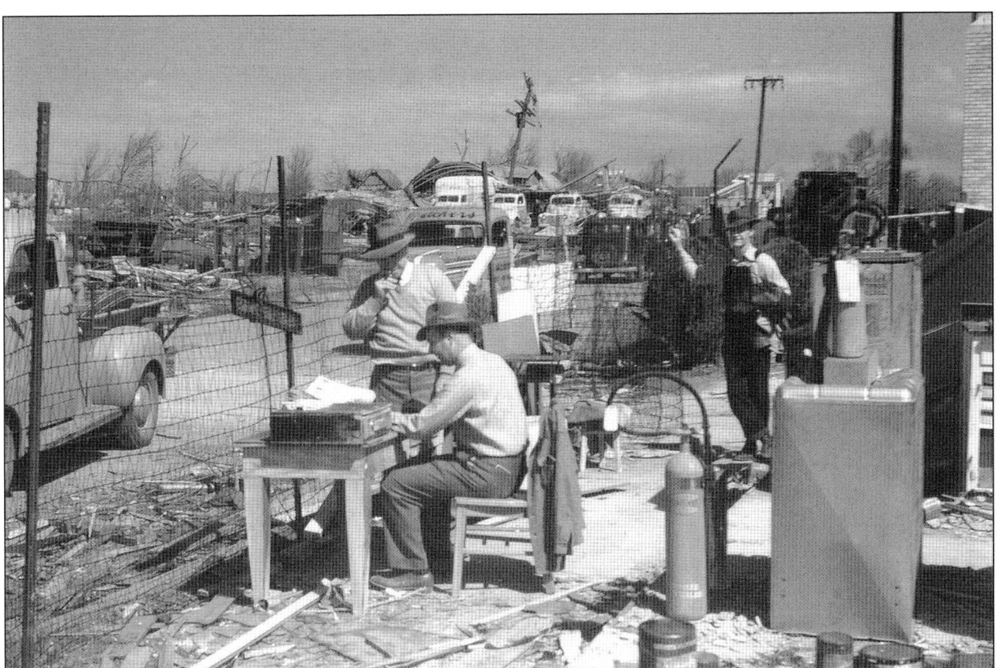

Following the 1947 Woodward tornado, lumber was a valuable resource. Many of the city's lumber yards suffered major damage. Still, miraculously, much of the lumber stored on the sites survived with minimal damage. The photograph shows a man working with a customer at the entrance gate to one such lumber yard, Osborne-Peebles Lumber on Eighth Street.

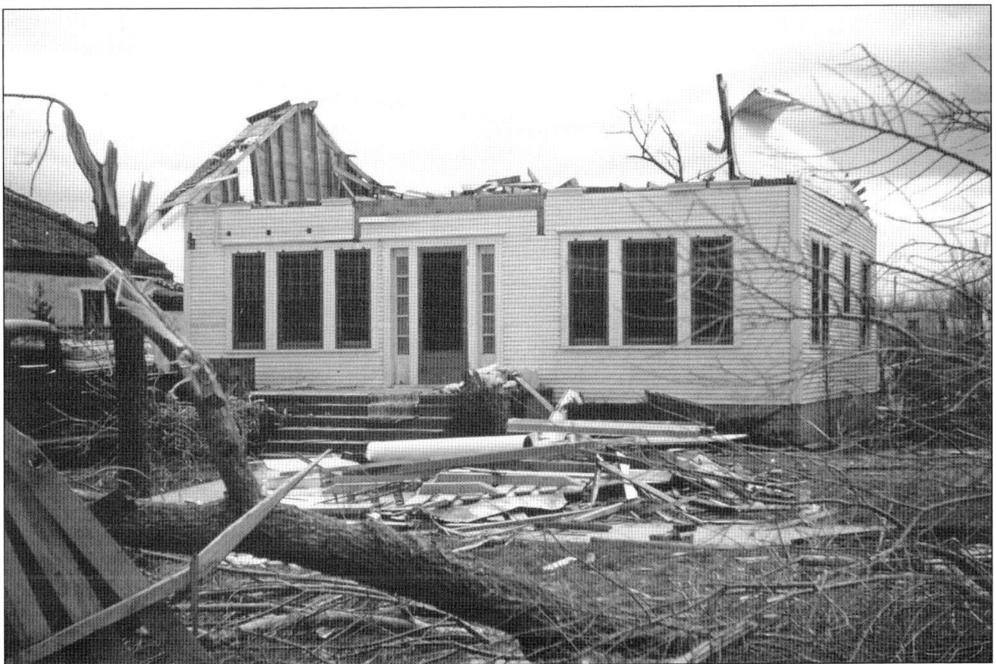

This home, belonging to L.O. Street, was in the 1300 block of Main Street. The entire roof has been torn off the structure, but help is apparently at hand. The pickup truck backed up to the left side of the house appears to have lumber stacked in the bed.

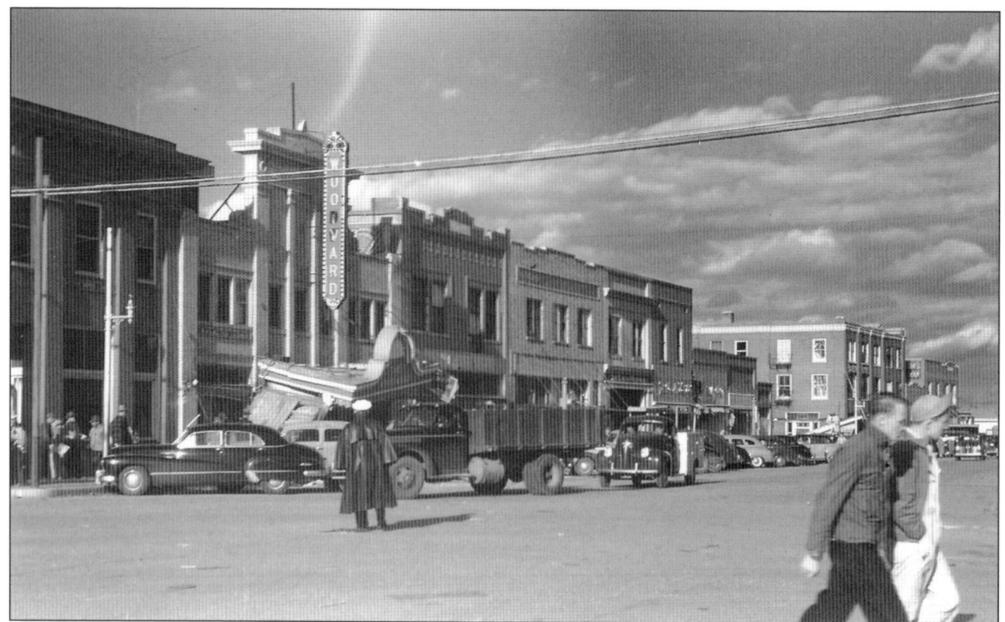

This photograph shows a cleanup effort underway in the 800 block of Main Street. The view is to the northeast from the intersection of Ninth and Main Streets. There is a Woodward police officer standing in the intersection to direct traffic. Down the block, the Baker Hotel appears to be covering some of the broken windows in the upper floors with some sort of reflective covering.

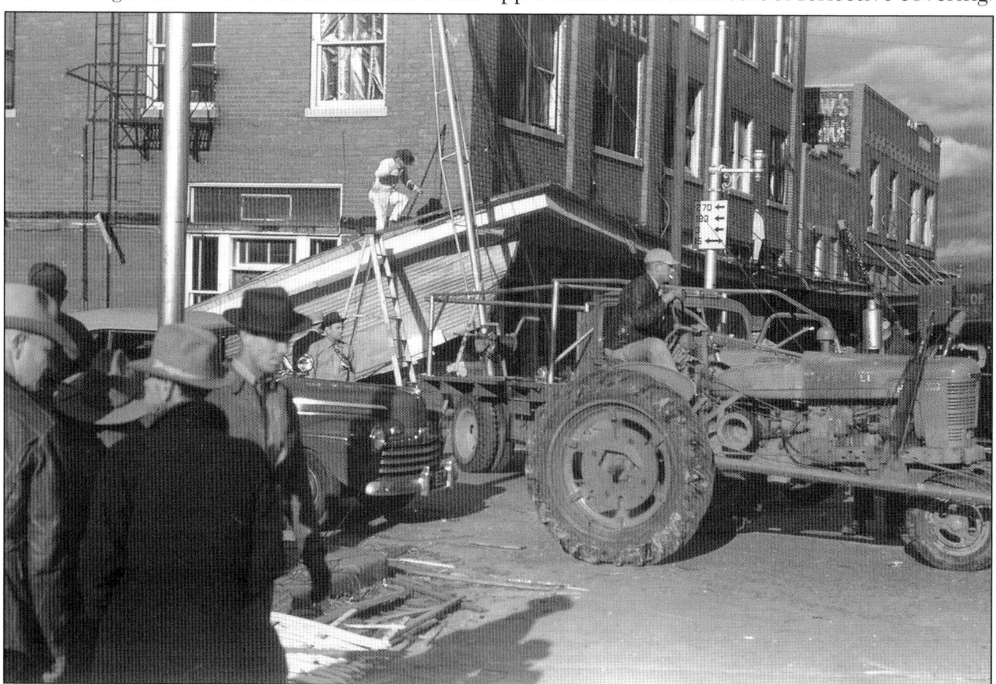

There is a great deal of activity near the southwest corner of the Baker Hotel at Eighth and Main Streets. A man with a crane truck is attempting repairs on the sagging awning in front of the hotel. Another man is attempting to drive a tractor with a plow blade through the intersection. There is a car close behind the tractor trying to get through the intersection as well.

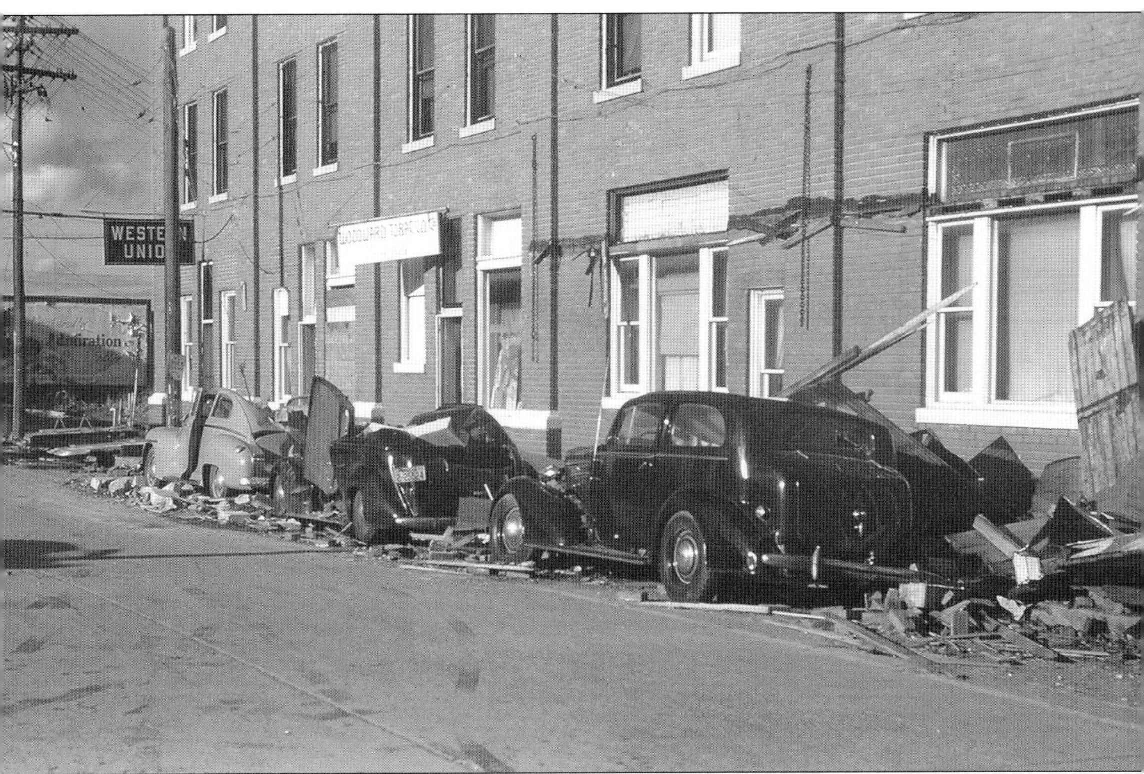

This image was taken not long after the tornado struck Woodward and shows the entire length of the west side of the Baker Hotel from the intersection of Eighth and Main Streets. Three vehicles whose owners had the misfortune of parking along the street on the night of the tornado are total wrecks. The Western Union office on the northwest corner of the hotel building is visible. Also, the Woodward Tobacco Company is visible. Despite the damage to the upper floors of the Baker Hotel, the structure remained intact and was used as a triage center for patients following the tornado. The building remained in this location until the 1960s, when it was demolished to make way for a new Bank of Woodward building. The site is currently Woodward City Hall.

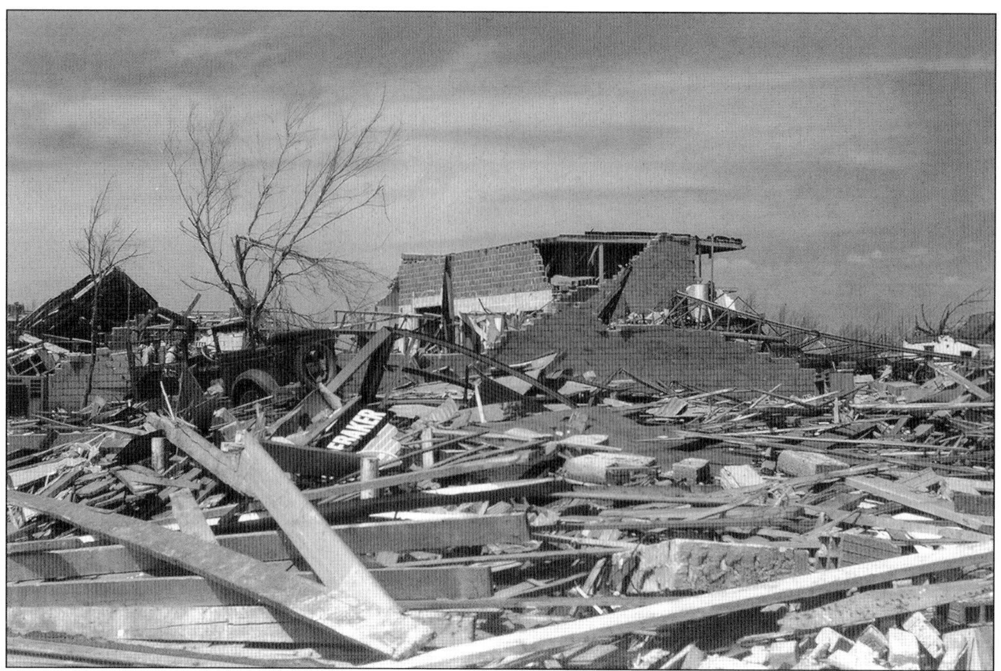

The location where this picture was taken is unclear, but there is a Studebaker sign (it may have blown in the wind) showing in the rubble. The Studebaker automobile dealership known as the Belew Garage Studebaker Agency was located along Main Street just west across the Katy Railroad tracks and to the east of Johnson Lumber Company.

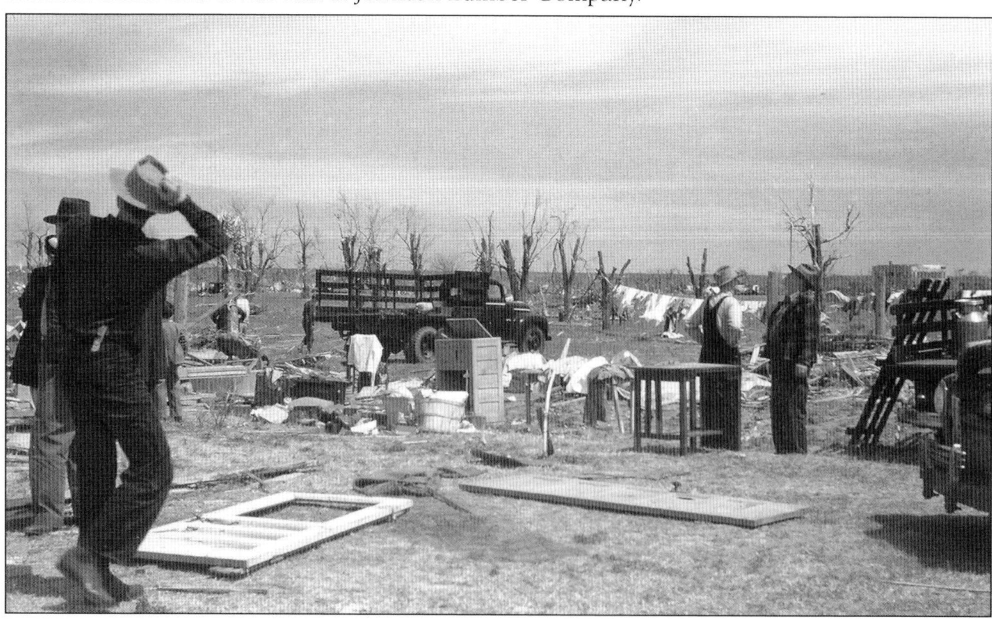

This photograph was likely taken in the Highland Park section of Woodward. The area received the worst of the storm in terms of the tornadic winds, leaving nothing much left standing. Several people are gathered in the area and appear to be searching for personal belongings. A few of the individuals are looking up, probably at a passing airplane. Clothes are hanging on the line on the right side of the image.

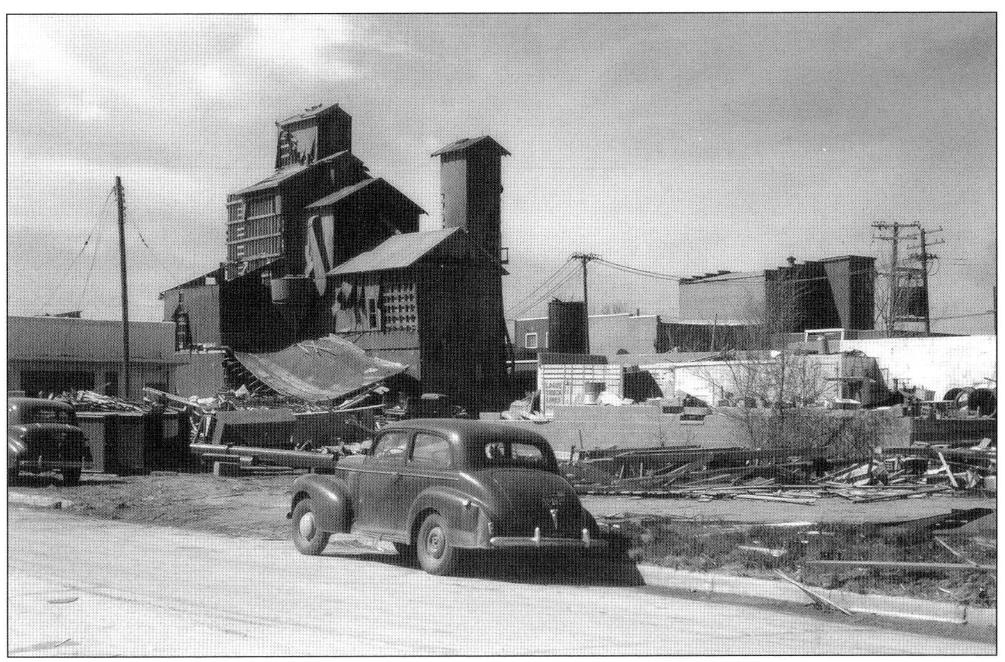

This photograph shows a view to the northwest from near Eighth Street and Santa Fe Avenue. The imposing structure in the center is a badly damaged granary, possibly a feed mill. The northeast corner of Henry Hunter's Laundry and Cleaners (the white building) can be seen in front of the mill.

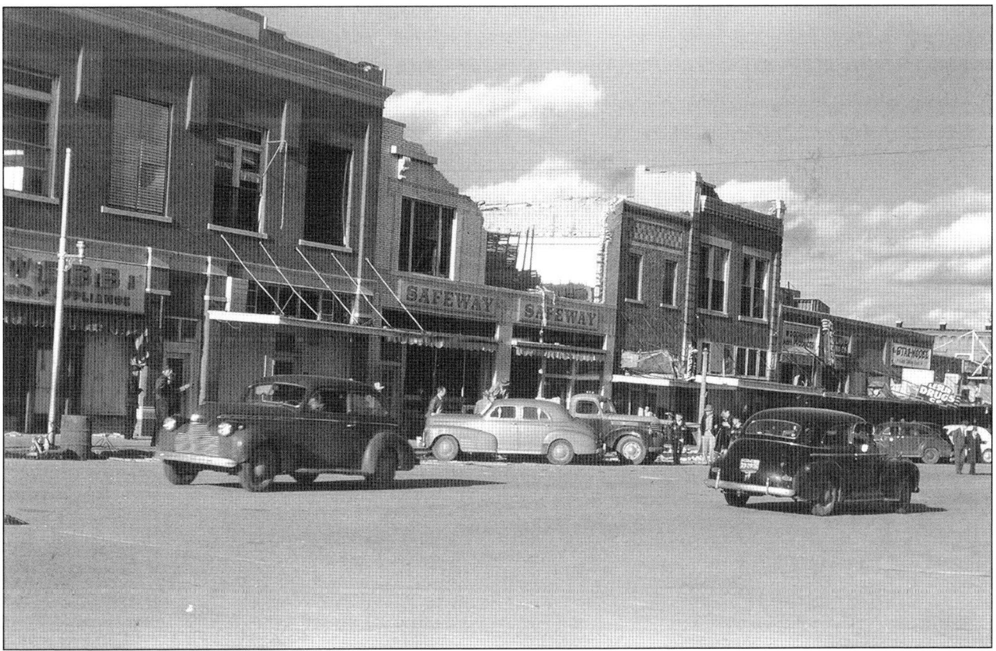

This image was taken of the 900 block of Main Street (north side) looking to the northeast. Besides countless residential and commercial buildings being destroyed in those four minutes on April 9, 1947, thousands of birds were reported to be dead on the ground. It was more than a month before birds were once again heard singing.

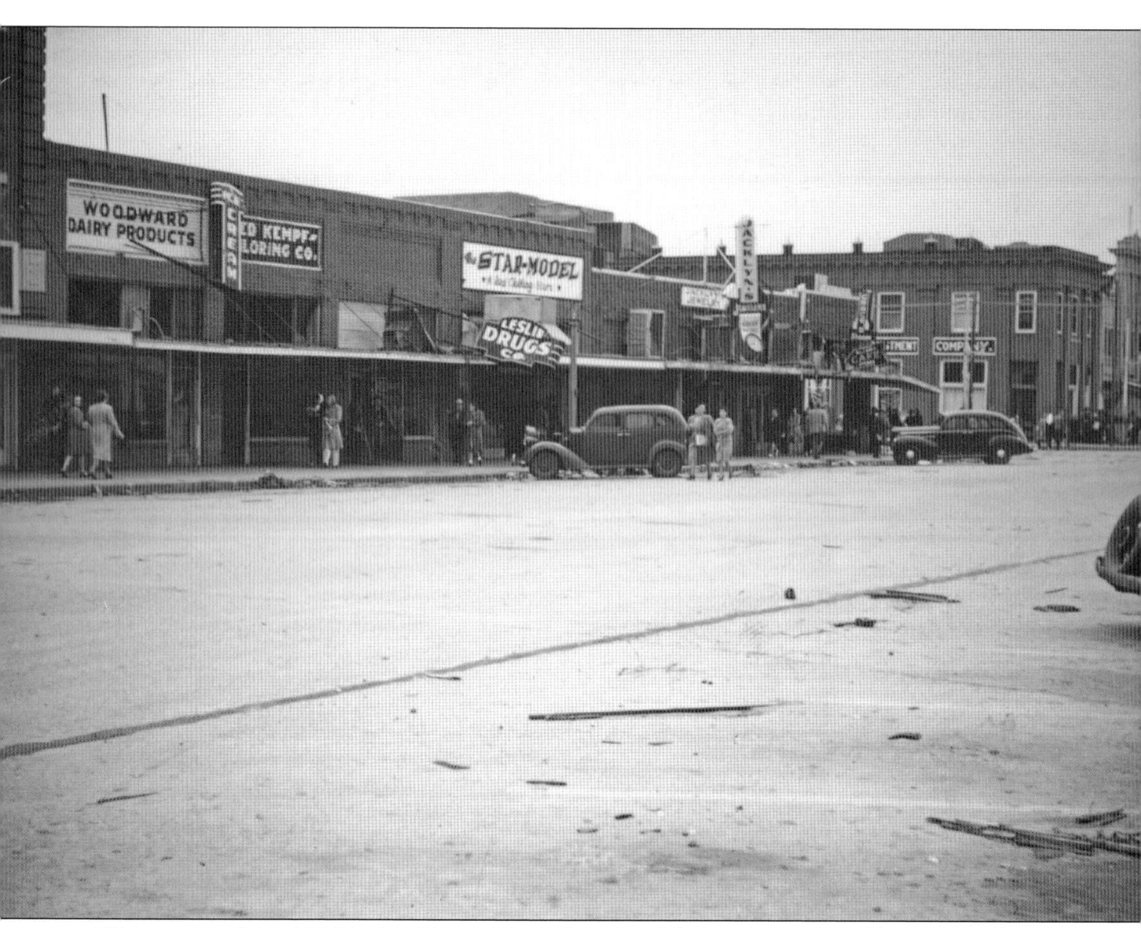

This image of the 900 block of Main Street (north side) shows people walking around to view damage the day after the tornado. Businesses include Woodward Dairy Products (now All Things Special), Fred Kempf Tailoring and Clothing Co. (now Fix-A-Screen), Leslie Drug Co. (now Trend Hair Lounge), the Star-Model (now Persimmon Creek), Devine's (now Baby Persimmon), Jacklyn's Jewelry (now Cowboy Driving Academy), the Polly Anna Café, and Grace's Shoppe (now the Annex). Other than damage to signage and an awning at the far end of the block, these businesses appear to be relatively unscathed by the storm.

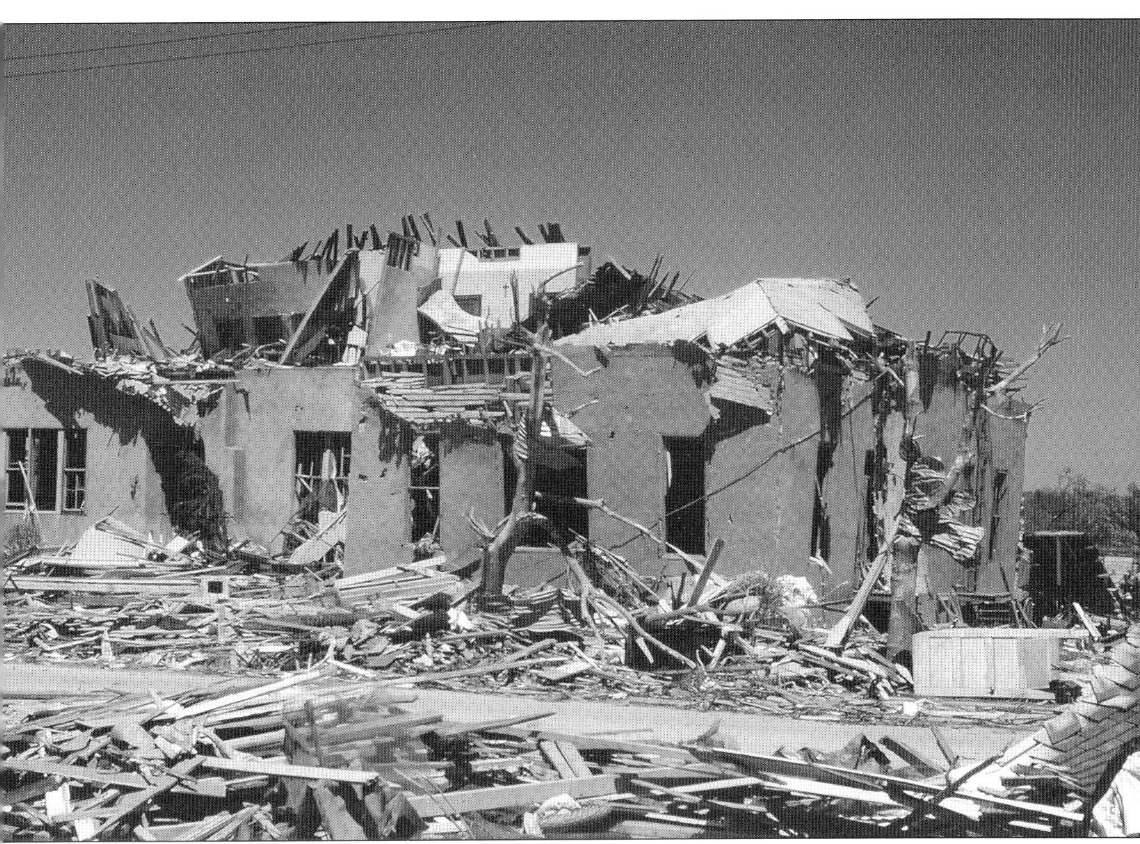

It is difficult to believe that destruction such as occurred with this home took only four minutes, but that was all it took for the 1947 Woodward tornado to wreak havoc in people's lives. This home, in an unidentified location of the city, appears to be a testament to the theory that stucco homes are able to withstand the force of what was believed to be an F-5 tornado. All the windows on the lower level are gone. The debris field surrounding the home is deep. The stucco walls appear to have been punctured by boards turned into unguided missiles. The entire upper level is all but completely gone. The one thing that stands out in this photograph is that despite all that destruction and debris, on the upper level in what is most likely a bedroom, a cross still hangs in place on a wall.

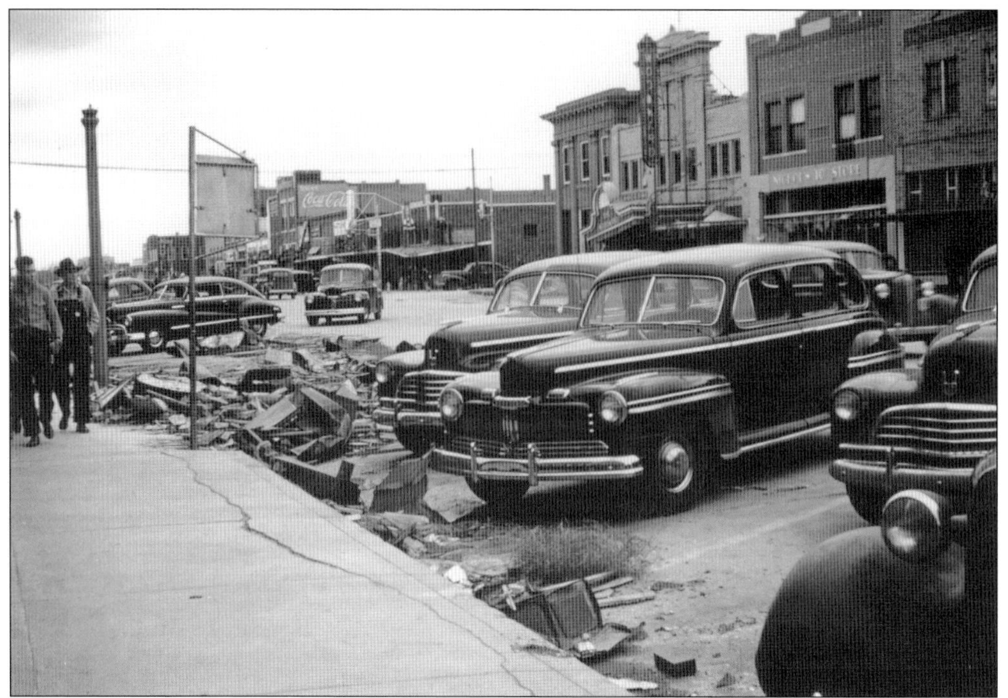

This is another view of Main Street looking toward the northwest from the middle of the 800 block. Other than the obvious damage to the Woodward Theatre's marquee, the buildings in this section of downtown appear relatively undamaged. The buildings seen within this photograph are still in use today. This image was most likely taken in the immediate aftermath of the storm. Note the debris that remains along the curb.

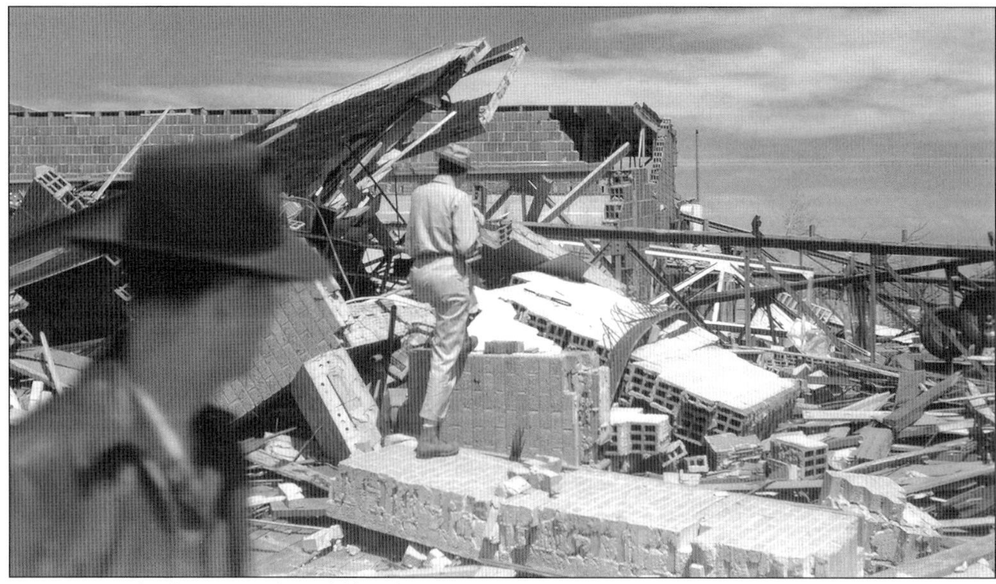

A man stands observing the rubble of an unidentified commercial building. Given the exposed beams in the positions they are, the authors believe this was either Ferguson Ford or the Ticer Equipment building on Main Street. The photograph was taken the day after the tornado by Dr. Clayton Young of Alva.

Five

Tornado Town

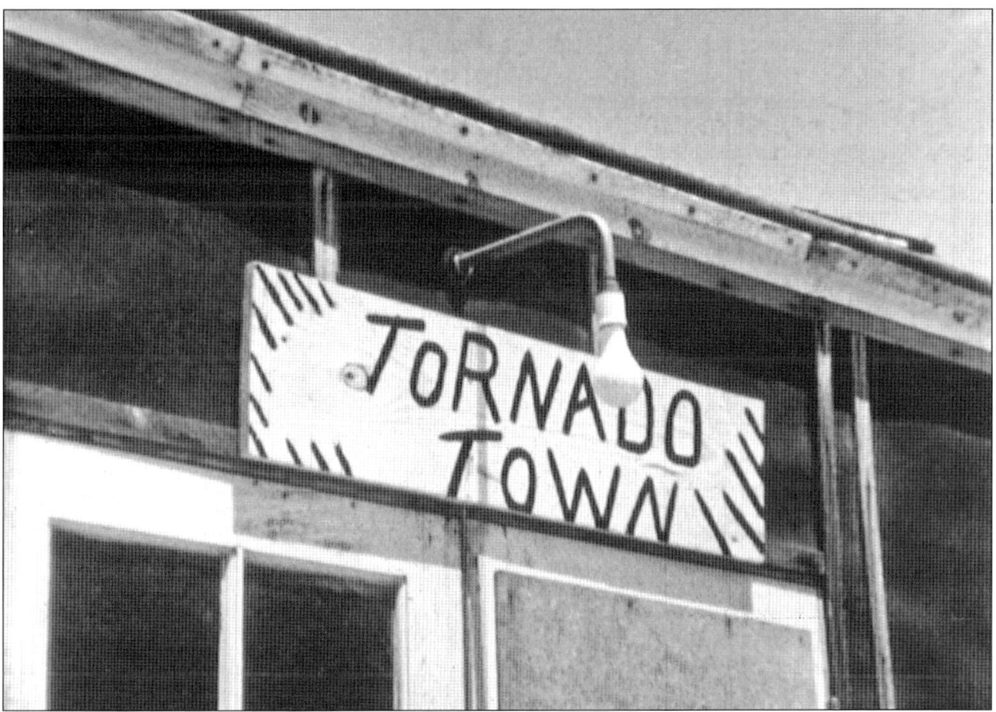

The establishment of Tornado Town on the site of a former Army air base west of Woodward is one of the least told stories involving the 1947 tornado. With more than 100 blocks of Woodward obliterated in the storm, there were scores of homeless people and families needing shelter until homes could be rebuilt or repaired. While many took refuge with friends or relatives with adequate space, others simply had no place to go.

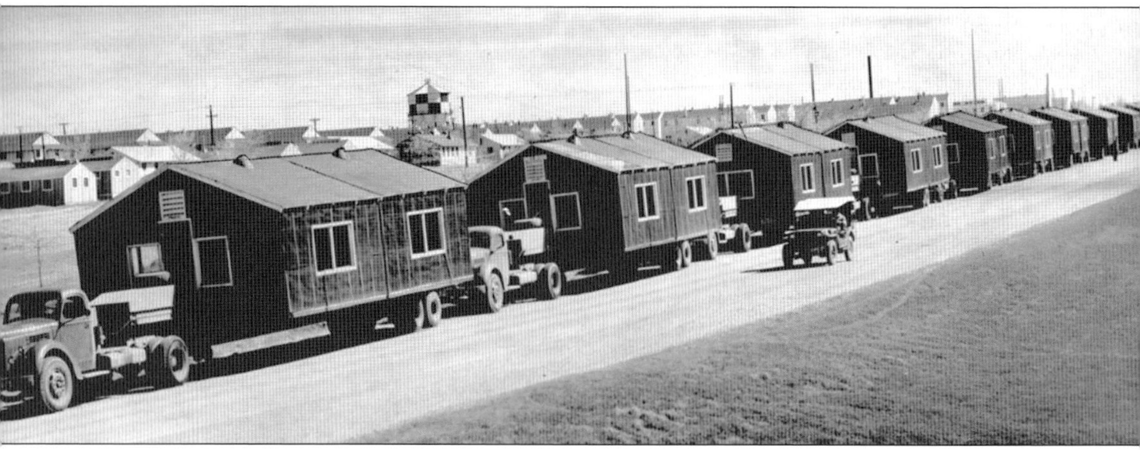

Many of the Army's structures on the base remained on the site and required only minimal rehabilitation to make them livable. The Red Cross hired carpenters to come in and partition off the former barracks buildings into family apartments. The Army brought in additional prefab structures to ensure adequate housing for those in need. (Courtesy of Oklahoma Historical Society.)

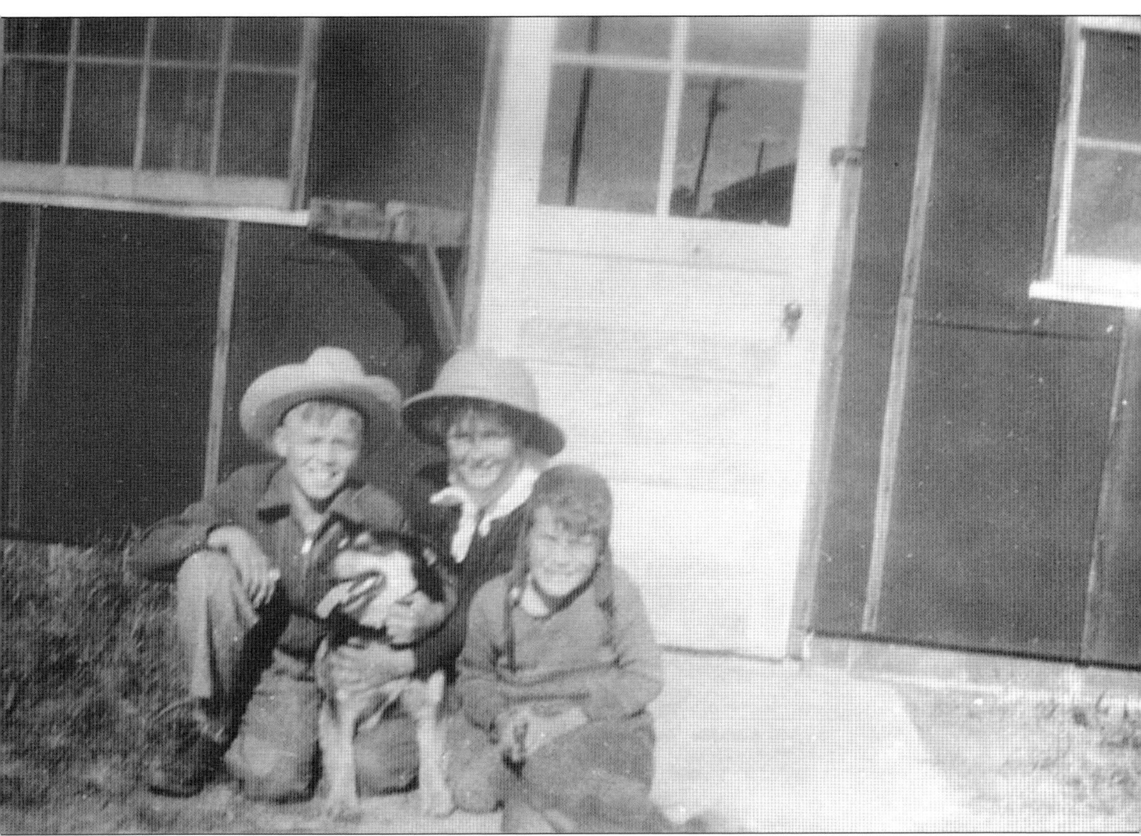

This image, captured by an unknown photographer, was donated by Gaynor MacLaren. His parents and two brothers lived at Tornado Town while their home in Woodward was being rebuilt. One of Gaynor's brothers, Duane MacLaren, is the middle boy in this photograph. The other two were identified only as "Donnie" (left) and "Larry" (right). The picture was taken in front of one of the prefab structures brought in by the Army.

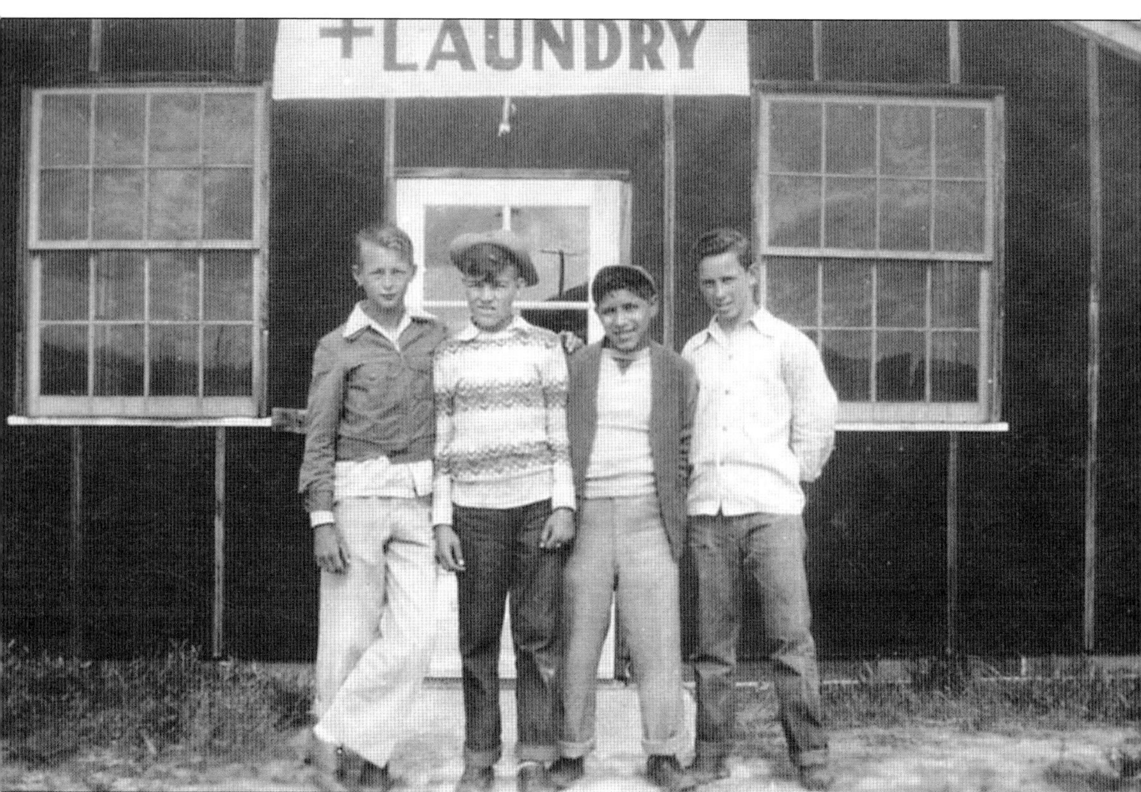

This photograph was taken in front of the Tornado Town laundry facility and shows four boys posing for a group shot. Only two of the boys are identified: Bobby Chalmers is on the far right, and next to him (second from the right) is Robert "Spud" Partido. The laundry appears to have been set up in one of the prefab Army structures moved onto the site. According to news reports of the day, the Red Cross bought three new washing machines for the facility, which, given that there were some 300 residents of Tornado Town, probably meant that they were in constant use. Many of the residents at the former Army air base remained until suitable shelter became available in town. For many, this meant a stay of more than one year.

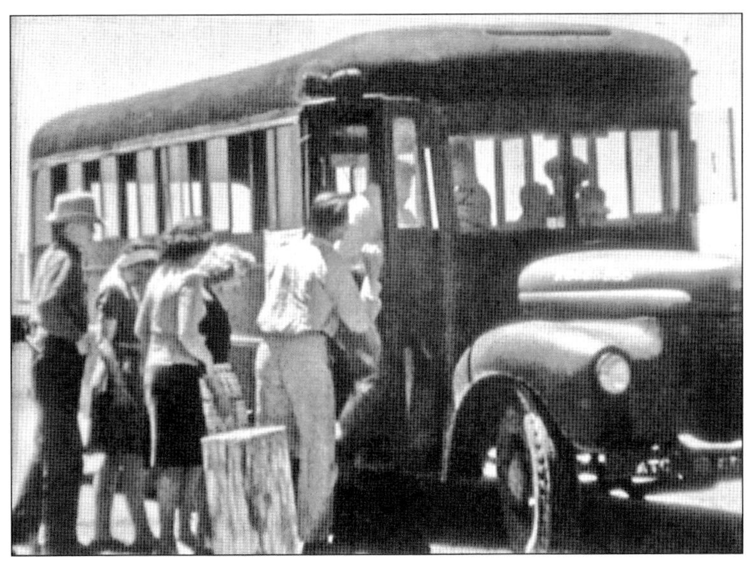

This photograph shows a War Assets Administration bus obtained by the Red Cross to ferry those residents without other transportation who still had jobs in Woodward to and from town. The bus also carried teachers back and forth from Woodward to ensure the children living on the site would not fall behind. (Courtesy of the Oklahoma Historical Society.)

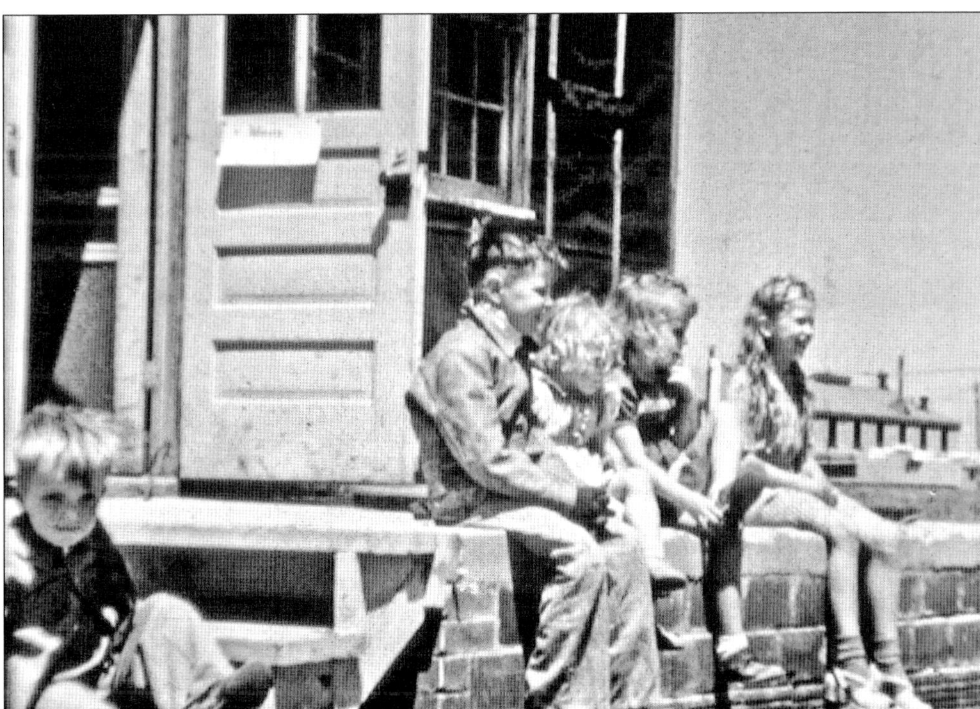

Keeping children at Tornado Town entertained and, by extension, out of trouble was an early consideration that the Red Cross and the local Girl Scouts Council solved. A recreation room for children was constructed in one of the buildings, and the Girl Scouts Council soon established a library. An overall children's recreation program was planned and administered by Edith Hawkins, the district Girl Scouts supervisor. (Courtesy of the Oklahoma Historical Society.)

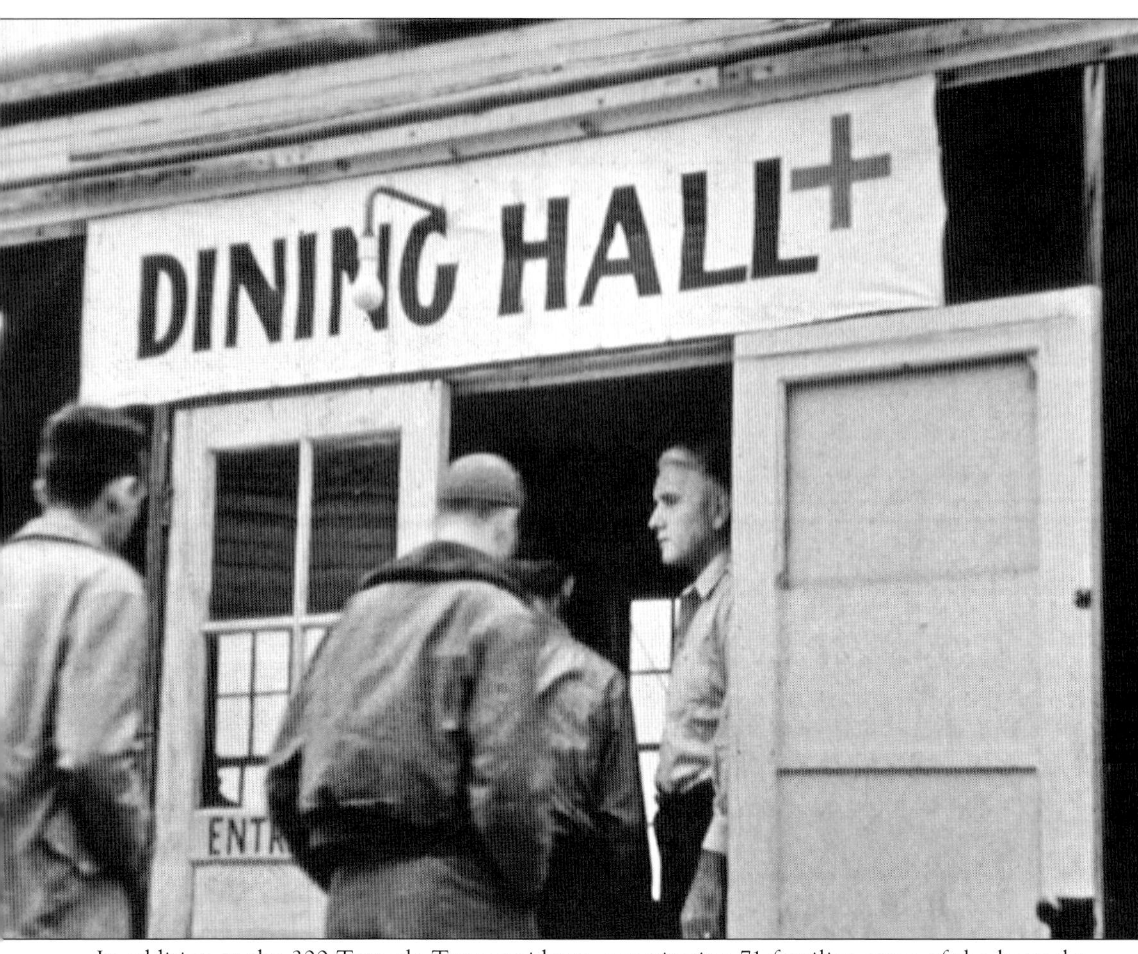

In addition to the 300 Tornado Town residents, constituting 71 families, some of the barracks at Tornado Town were set aside for use by outside contract laborers brought in to help with the rebuilding process. The contractors were charged $3 per week for their lodging, the proceeds of which went to city maintenance funds. In addition to lodging and meals for residents, the Red Cross also provided the medical services of a full-time doctor and nurse, who provided care 24 hours a day. Security was provided by a team of three paid residents working eight-hour shifts at the front gate to ensure only those who belonged in Tornado Town entered the site. Also, the Red Cross sought to ensure everyone at Tornado Town received help in rebuilding their home and making a new start. An eight-person advisory board of Woodward citizens was set up to review applications for housing financing. By the fall of 1947, there were only a reported 48 families remaining on the former military base. (Courtesy of the Oklahoma Historical Society.)

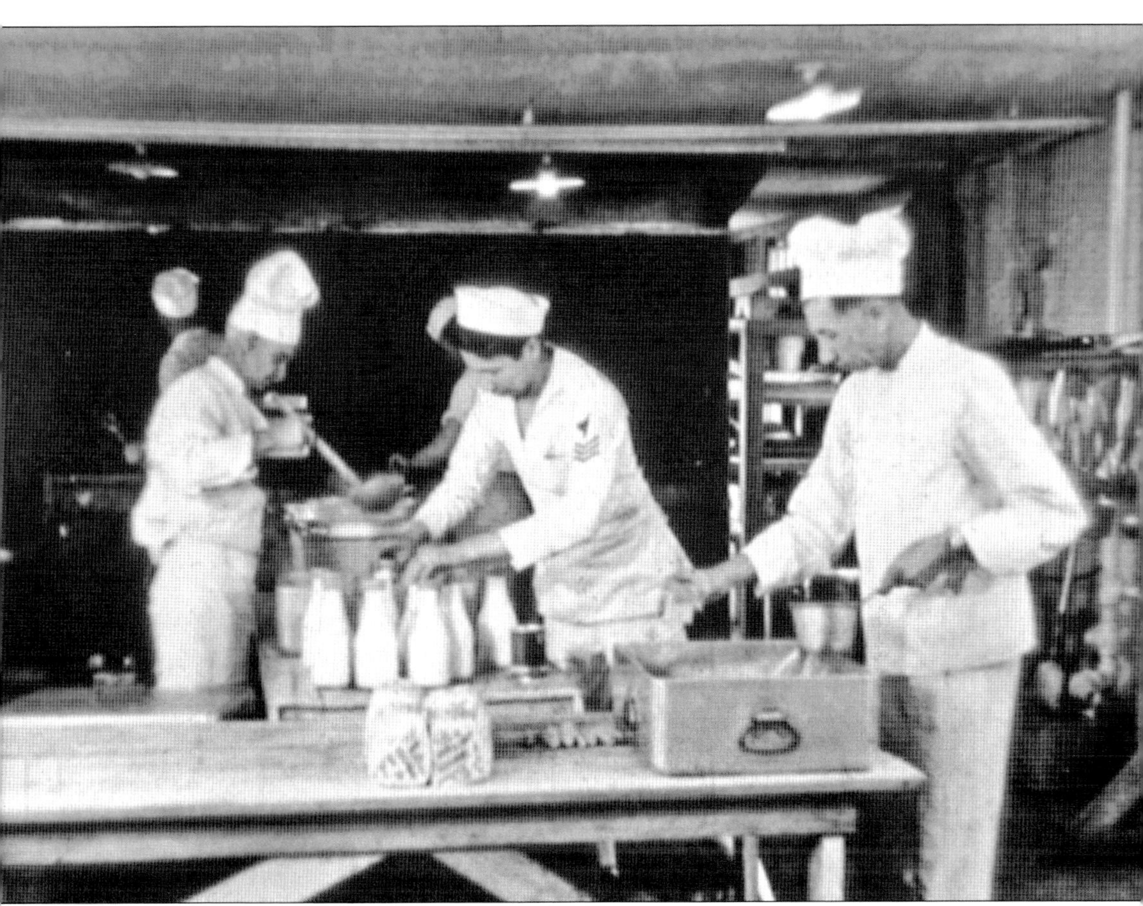

The former officers' club of the Army air base was converted to a mess hall for use by the residents. The Red Cross hired a chef from a hotel in Oklahoma City and several cooks and many more kitchen staff to serve three meals to residents and laborers for an average of 1,500 meals daily. In one extreme 10-day surge early in the crisis, the Red Cross reported 46,000 meals were served. (Courtesy of the Oklahoma Historical Society.)

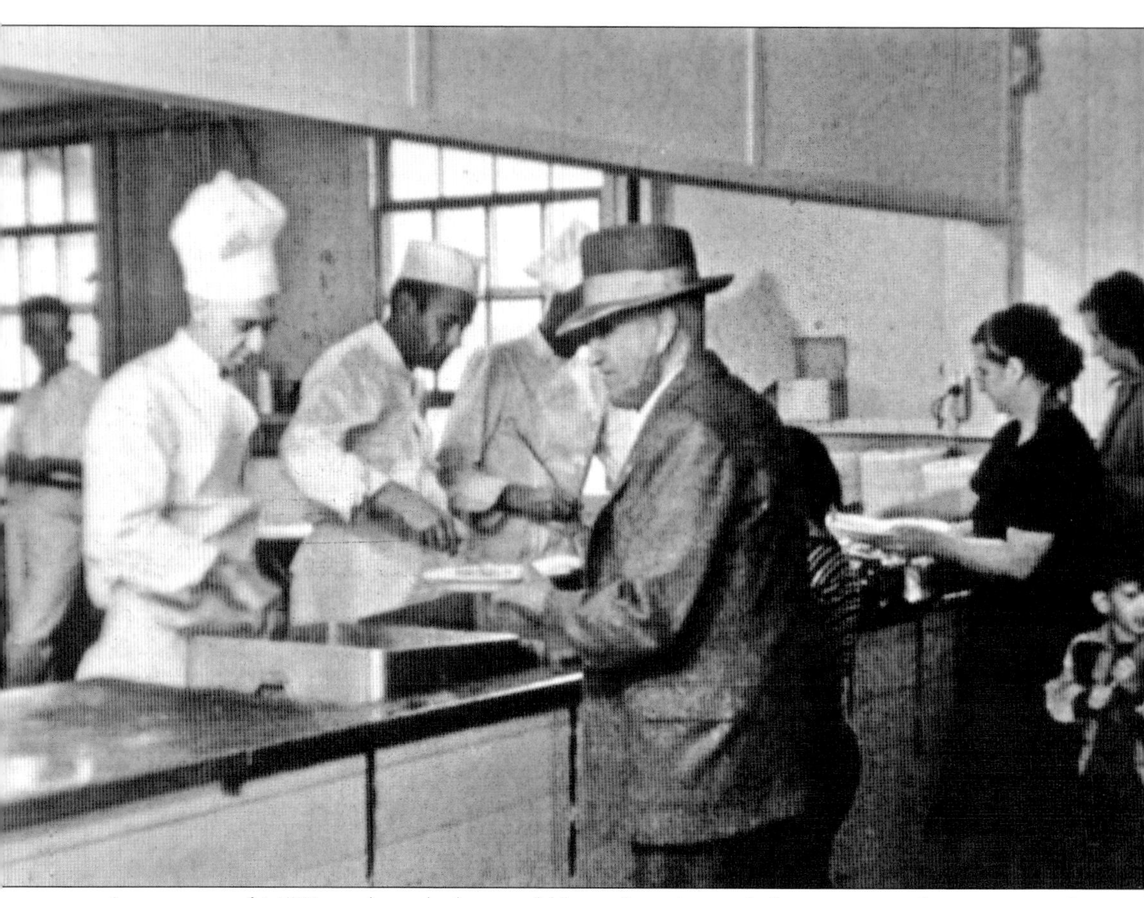

An average of 1,500 meals each day would be a daunting task for anyone and a strain on the resources of any organization. Regardless, the Red Cross, with its own dietitians helping to develop the menus, rose to the task and ensured that no one at Tornado Town went without the nutritious food they needed. (Courtesy of the Oklahoma Historical Society.)

Six

Epilogue

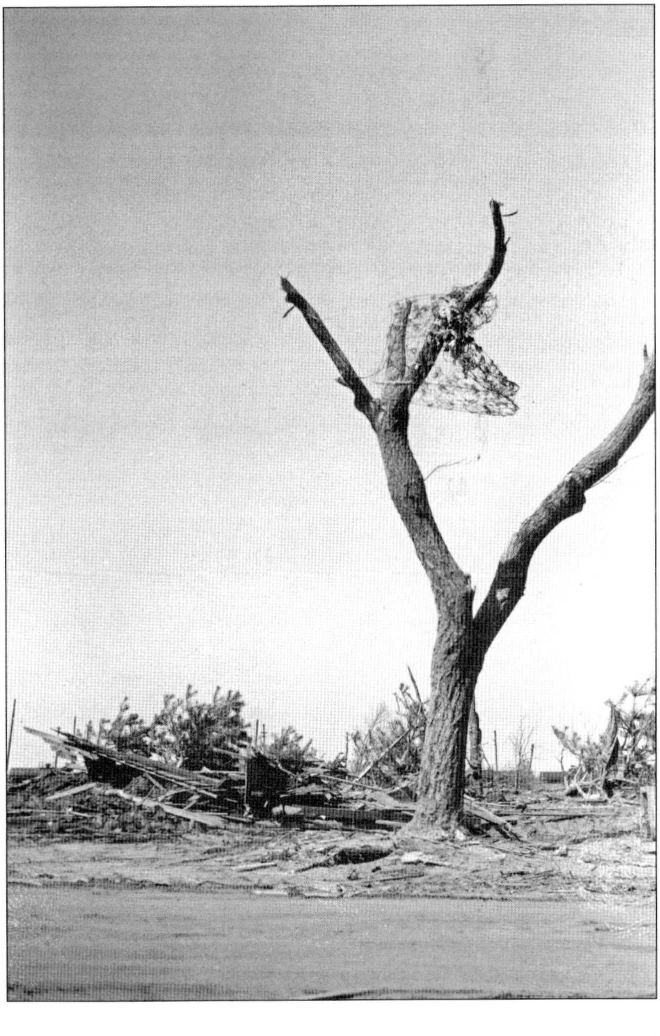

This photograph of a set of box springs wrapped in the upper trunk of a tree makes a fitting close to this visual record of one of the most horrific storms in the United States. This was a storm that haunted people's psyches for much of the 20th century. The authors thought it would be appropriate to list the names of the dead in the hope that if they are mentioned here, they will never be forgotten. Their graves are scattered throughout Elmwood Cemetery in Woodward. May they rest in peace.

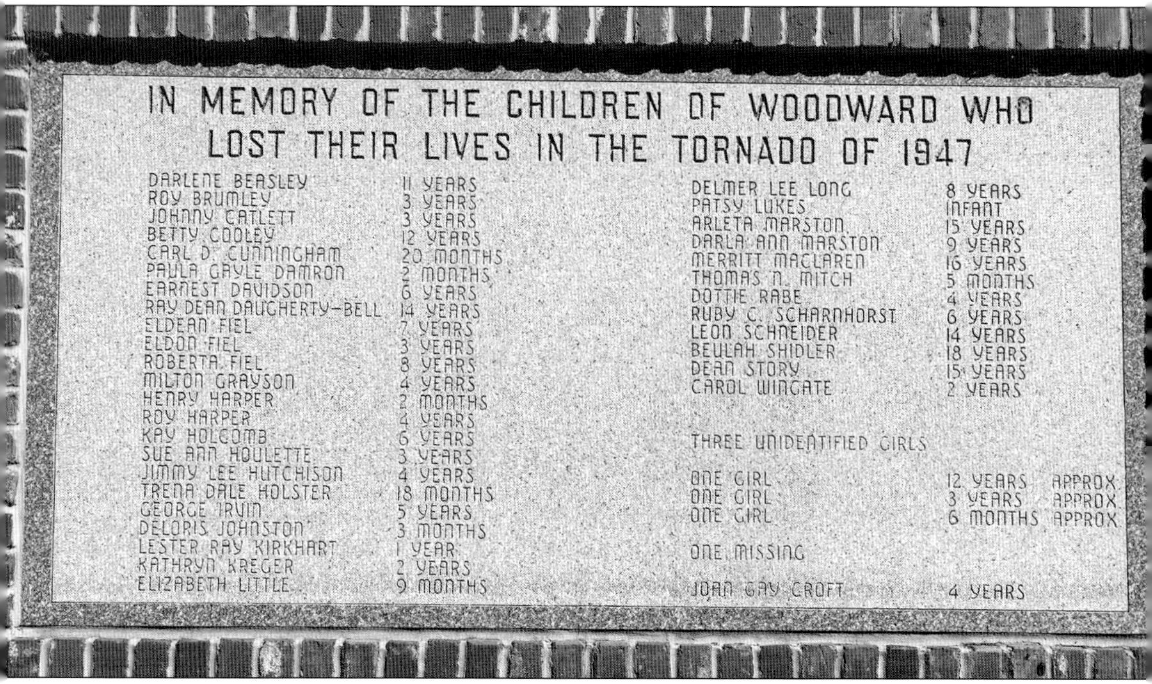

This photograph shows a memorial to the children who died in the 1947 Woodward tornado. It is embedded in a wall of the Woodward Middle School (South Campus). Those who passed in 1947 include: Alfred Atwell, Tom Baker, Hallie Ball, Darlene Beasley, James Behier, Roy Brumley, Johnny Catlett, Raymond Catlett, Sarah Catlett, Daniel Chance, Betty Cooley, Lorenzo Coombes, Mrs. A. Craft, Cleta Mae Croft, Ethel Crowl, William Crowl, Carl Cunningham Jr., Carl Cunningham Sr., Paula Damron, Fred Dart, Earnest Davidson, Lavina Davis, Roy Doughtery, Robert Duke, Lillie Durrill, Clyde Glass, Mrs. C.N. Good, Milton Grayson, Beryl Grimm, Irene Gusler, Ann Hagerman, John Hagerman, Henry Harper, Lou Harper, Monty Harper, Roy Harper, Mary Hawk, Cliff Hayes, Georgia Hingston, Treandale Holster, Sue Houlette, Jimmie Hutchinson, Olen Hutchinson, Flossie Irvin, George Irvin, Delores Johnston, Grover Jordan, Mary Eliza Kezer, and Georgia Kingston (continued on the next page).

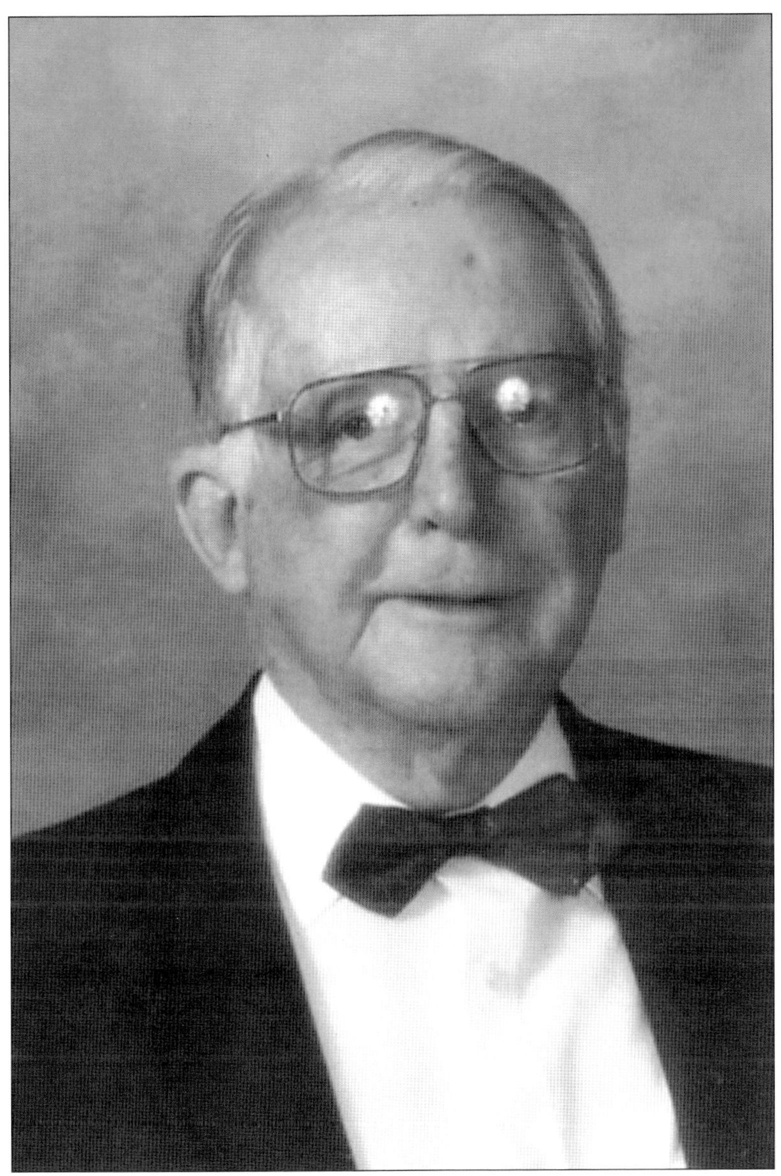

This photograph is of Franklin Stecher (1914–2010), a longtime funeral director in Woodward. Stecher served his community as a mortician for more than 60 years. When it came time to bury the victims of the 1947 Woodward tornado, several funerals were performed every day. He oversaw many of those. This page is dedicated to his memory. The list of victims of the 1947 Woodward tornado continues here: Louis Knight, Pauline Kollar, Catherine Kreger, Glendola Kreger, Muriel Lafon, Armanda Layer, Elizabeth Little, Delmer Long, George Lucas, Albert Lukes, Patsy Lukes, Eva Main, Arleta Marston, Darla Marston, Goldie Marston, Merritt McLeran, Thomas Mitch, Charles Morgan, Gloria Morrison, Fred Morrow, R.T. Myers, Flora Pierson, Earle Pollard, Pauline Pollard, Ruth Potter, Dottie Rabe, Bertha Reed, Peter Rieth, Albert N. Rosenbrook, Clarence E. Rosendale, Bessie Schamhorst, Ruby Schamhorst, Leon Schneider, Al Schutt, Beulah Mae Shidler, Everett Smith, Mrs. C.L. Sparks, Cora Steed, Dean Story, Erwin Walker, Laverne Warren, Arthur Warnner, Carol Wingat, Sam Wood, Girl (approximately 12 years old), Girl (approximately 3 years old), and Girl (approximately 6 months old).